Benner's Commentary on the Torah

Benner's Commentary on the Torah

~~~~~~~~~~~~~~~~~~~~~~~~~~~~~~~

Jeff A. Benner

Cover design by Jeff A. Benner

"Benner's Commentary on the Torah," by Jeff A. Benner. ISBN 978-1-951985-12-7.

Published 2020 by Virtualbookworm.com Publishing. P.O. Box 9949, College Station, TX 77842, US. ©2020 Jeff A. Benner. All rights reserved. Any part of this book may be copied for educational purposes only, without prior permission.

Contents

Benner's Commentary on the Torah

Benner's Commentary on the Torah

Benner's Commentary on the Torah

Benner's Commentary on the Torah

Verses

Genesis 1:2

> And the earth was <u>without form, and void</u>; and
> darkness was upon the face of the deep. And
> the Spirit of God moved upon the face of the
> waters. (Genesis 1:2, KJV)

The phrase תהו ובהו (*tohu v'vohu*), underlined in the verse
above, employs two different and common styles of Hebrew
poetry. The first is the use of similar sounding words together.
While the sentence, "The painter painted a painting with
paint," would be poor English, it is a perfect example of
Hebrew poetry. The second is the use of parallelisms where
multiple words are used to express one idea. The two words
tohu and *vohu* are not expressing two different states, but
rather, one state with two different words that have the same
basic meaning.

Genesis 1:10

Many will recognize *"miq'veh"* as the ritual immersion, similar
to baptism, as practiced in Judaism. However, unlike in
Christianity, the ritual of *miq'veh* is performed many times,
such as before the holy days. In Hebrew, this word is written
as מקוה (*miq'veh*) and appears in the Hebrew Bible, but not in
the same context:

> God called the dry land Earth, and the waters
> that were <u>gathered together</u> he called Seas.
> And God saw that it was good. (Genesis 1:10,
> RSV)

In this verse, the phrase "gathered together," is the Hebrew noun מקוה (*miq'veh*). Biblically, this word means "a pool or collection of water" and is also found in the following verse:

> And the LORD said to Moses, "Say to Aaron, `Take your rod and stretch out your hand over the waters of Egypt, over their rivers, their canals, and their ponds, and all their <u>pools</u> of water, that they may become blood; and there shall be blood throughout all the land of Egypt, both in vessels of wood and in vessels of stone.'" (Exodus 7:19, RSV)

While the word מקוה (*miq'veh*) means "pool" in Biblical Hebrew, the modern Hebrew word for a pool is בריכה (*beriykhah*), which comes from the verb ברך (*B.R.K*) meaning "to kneel," in the sense of kneeling down to a pool of water to get a drink.

Genesis 1:27

> "So God created man in his own image, in the image of God created he him; male and female created he them." (Genesis 1:27, KJV)

While the above is a common translation for this verse, it contains two words that when translated from a Hebraic perspective, illuminate the passage in a new light. The first word is ברא (*bara*), which in this verse cannot mean "create something from nothing," because the following verse would contradict this translation:

> And the LORD God formed man of the dust of the ground, and breathed into his nostrils the breath of life; and man became a living soul. (Genesis 2:7, KJV)

God did not create the man out of nothing; instead he formed him out of the ground. With our new understanding of the word, ברא he filled him with his image, which brings us to the next word.

In other passages, the word צלם (*tselem*), translated as "image" above, is also translated as "idol," which is an "image" of a god. A more Hebraic understanding of the word would be "shadow." An idol is meant to be a "shadow" of the original, a representation, just as a "shadow" is the image of the original. We can now read the above passage as:

> *"So God filled the man with his shadow, with the shadow of God he filled him; male and female he filled them."* (Genesis 1:27)

Man was formed from the dust of the ground, but unlike the other animals, man was shaped to be a shadow of God. All that God is, we were made to duplicate, just as a shadow duplicates the original. Genesis 2:7, quoted above, states that man was filled with God's breath. From an ancient Hebrew perspective, the breath is the character of the person; therefore, the shadow of God is the same as his character. God filled the man with his own breath, his own character.

Genesis 2:7

> *And the LORD God formed the man from the dust of the ground, and breathed into his nostrils the breath of life; and the man became a living soul.* (Genesis 2:7, KJV)

The Hebrew word for "fire" is אש (*esh*). Derived from this two-letter parent root is the three-letter child root איש (*iysh*) meaning "man." Not only do these two words share the same root word, but they are also related in meaning. To re-discover

3

this relationship between "fire" and "man", let's begin with the "creation" of fire from the ancient Hebrew perspective.

In ancient times, before the invention of lighters and matches, fire was made with a "bow drill" and tinder. Tinder is any fine organic material such as dried grass or inner bark fibers. The bow drill consisted of four parts: the fireboard, bow and string, rod, and handle. The fireboard was made of a flat board with a V-shaped cut at the edge of the board. The bow and string was constructed similar to an archer's bow. The rod was a round stick pointed at one end and rounded at the other. The handle was a flat round board. The fine tinder was compressed into a ball and laid on the ground.

The fireboard was placed on top of the tinder with the V-shape cut over the tinder. The string of the bow was wrapped once around the rod and the pointed end of the rod was set on the fireboard over the V-shaped cut. The handle was placed on top of the rod. One hand held the handle while the other hand moved the bow back and forth in a sawing motion. This action caused the rod to spin back and forth on the fireboard.

As the rod spun on the fireboard, fine wood dust was shaved off the rod and deposited in the V-shape cut on top of the tinder. The friction of the two wood pieces rubbing also created heat causing the dust to become very hot. After a short time working the fire drill, smoke would begin to rise from the heated dust. The fireboard was carefully removed, leaving the pile of smoldering dust on the tinder. The tinder was picked up and enclosed around the dust, and the fire maker blew on the dust, increasing the heat. The dust then ignited the tinder, creating fire.

In light of this ancient form of making a fire, let us now look at the passage in Genesis 2:7:

And the fire maker formed a man of dust on the tinder and he blew into the tinder the breath of life and the man became a living fire.

Genesis 2:18

And the LORD God said, It is not good that the man should be alone; I will make him an help meet for him. (Genesis 2:18, KJV)

While the KJV translates the Hebrew phrase כנגדו עזר (*ezer kenegedo*) as "help meet for him," other translations provide additional translations including; "a helper fit for him" (RSV), "a helper as his partner" (NRS), "a helper comparable to him" (NKJ), and "a helper as his counterpart" (YLT). What exactly does this Hebrew phrase mean?

The first word in the phrase, עזר (*ezer*), is simple and means "helper." The second word, כנגדו (*kenegedo*), is a little more complex. The base word is the word נגד (*neged*), which will be discussed shortly, with the prefix כ (*k*) meaning "like," and the suffix ו (*o*) meaning "of him" or "his."

The word נגד (*neged*) comes from the verbal root נגד (*N.G.D*) meaning "to be face-to-face." This verb is always used in the causative form where it is literally translated "to make to be face-to-face." It is always used to mean "to tell," in the sense of causing another to "come face-to-face" to tell them something.

The noun form נגד (*neged*) is often used for something that is face-to-face with something else. An example can be found in Genesis 21:16, where Hagar went and sat down "opposite" her son. Even though she and her son were a distance away, they were sitting "face-to-face."

5

Putting all of this together, the phrase עזר כנגדו (*ezer kenegedo*) literally means "a helper like his opposite." This could mean that Eve was to be his "other half," like him, but with the opposite attributes.

In Genesis 1:27 we read that *Elohiym* filled the Adam (a Hebrew word meaning "human") with his shadow, meaning he placed a representation of himself in the man. We also read in this verse that *Elohiym* filled them, male and female, meaning that he placed his attributes within each; his male attributes in the man and his female attributes in the woman. We do not normally think of *Elohiym* as having male and female attributes, but many Bible passages reflect this idea.

Genesis 2:23

In Genesis 2:23 the phrase "this is now" is an attempt at a translation of the Hebrew phrase "*zot hapa'am*." The word "*zot*" means "this," but the word *hapa'am* is a little more difficult. This is the word *pa'am*, with the prefix "*ha*" meaning "the." The word *pa'am* is literally a repetitive beat, like that of a drum. It can also mean a stroke of time or to repeat something, as seen in Genesis 33:3, "He himself went on before them, bowing himself to the ground seven times (*pa'am*)." Using this understanding of the word, Genesis 2:23 could be translated as, "*This time is bone from my bones.*" This translation implies that the previous times were not "*bone from my bones.*" Three verses prior to this it states, "*The man gave names to all cattle, and to the birds of the air, and to every beast of the field; but for the man there was not found a helper fit for him.*" In this context, we see that the "first times" were unsuccessful in finding a helper for Adam, but with Eve, this time it worked.

Genesis 3:15

Genesis 3:15 is a very interesting passage for many different reasons. Take a look at these three translations for this verse:

> And I will put enmity between thee and the woman, and between thy seed and her seed; <u>it</u> shall bruise thy head, and thou shalt bruise his heel. (KJV)

> And I will put enmity between thee and the woman, and between thy seed and her seed; <u>they</u> shall bruise thy head, and thou shalt bruise their heel. (JPS)

> And I will put enmity between thee and the woman, and between thy seed and her seed: <u>he</u> shall bruise thy head, and thou shalt bruise his heel. (ASV)

Notice that each version translates one pronoun in three different ways. The King James Version uses "it," the Jerusalem Publication Society uses "they," and the American Standard Version uses "he." In the Hebrew, the word that is found here is הוא (*hu*) and is the masculine singular pronoun "he." Other than this difference, all three say pretty much the same thing.

Now, let us examine the Hebrew behind the last part of the verse according to the ASV:

> "he shall bruise your head, and you shall bruise his heel"

The following is the Hebrew for this phrase:

הוא ישופך ראש ואתה תשופנו עקב
hu yeshuph'kha rosh v'atah teshuphenu eqev

Let's examine each of these words very carefully. The first word is the pronoun הוא (*hu*), meaning "he," which we previously discussed. The second word is ישופך (*yeshuph'kha*). This verb includes the letter *yud* (י) as a prefix and identifies the subject of the verb, which is the word הוא (*hu*), as masculine singular. The letter *yud* also identifies the verb as imperfect (similar to our future tense). Following the letter *yud* is the actual verb, which is שוף (*shuph*) and means "to fall upon another in an attack," or "to strike." Following the verb is the letter *kaph* (ך), which identifies the object of the verb as second person masculine singular (you). Thus, the entire verb ישופך means, "he will strike you." The third word is ראש (*rosh*), which is generally translated as "head." These first three words would literally be translated as "he will strike you head." As you can see, this really doesn't make a lot of sense and this is why the translators chose to translate this as, "he will strike your head." However, if this is what was meant by the author, it would have read, ראשך ישוף הוא (*hu yeshuph rosh'kha*). I will come back to this later.

The next word is ואתה (*v'atah*), which is the word אתה (*atah*), meaning "you," with the prefixed letter *vav* (ו), meaning "and." The next word is תשופנו (*teshuphenu*). This verb includes the letter *tav* (ת) as a prefix and identifies the subject of the verb, which is the previous word אתה (*atah*), as second person masculine singular (you). The letter *tav* also identifies the verb as imperfect (similar to our future tense). Following the letter *tav* is the actual verb, which is again the word שוף (*shuph*) meaning "to strike." Following the verb is the suffix נו (*nu*), which identifies the object of the verb as third person masculine singular (him). The entire verb תשופנו then means, "you will strike him." The next word is עקב (*eqev*), which is generally translated as "heel." Putting these three words together, we have the literal translation "and you will strike him heel," but again, this does not make sense, so the translators chose to ignore the grammar and translated it as, "you will strike his heel." If this is what was meant by the author, then it would have read, עקבו תשוף ואתה (*v'atah teshuph eqevo*).

Now let's put all of this together.

> *He will strike you head, and you will strike him heel.*

As the head is at the top of the body, the Hebrew word ראש (*rosh*-head) can mean "first." For instance, in 1 Chronicles 16:7, the King James Version, the American Standard Version and the Revised Standard Version translate this word as "first." Likewise, the heel is at the bottom of the body and the Hebrew word עקב (*eqev*-heel) can mean "last." For instance, in Genesis 49:19 the King James Version and Young's Literal Translation translate this word as "last." With this understanding, we can now translate this phrase as follows.

> *He will strike you first, and you will strike him last.*

Genesis 4:1

I have found this verse to be very perplexing. The first part of the verse is pretty straightforward and can literally be translated "and the man knew Eve his woman and she conceived and bore Cain, and she said…"

It is the next part of this verse where the translation gets a little tricky. The KJV translates it as, "I have gotten a man **from** the LORD." The RSV translates it as, "I have gotten a man **with the help of** the LORD." Now, let's take a look at the Hebrew and see what it says.

קניתי איש את יהוה

Let's look at each of these words individually:

- קָנִיתִי (*qaniytiy*): This is the verb קָנָה (*Q.N.H*) meaning "to purchase" or "to acquire." The conjugation *qaniytiy* means "I acquired."

- אִישׁ (*iysh*): This Hebrew word means "man" (both *iysh* and *adam* mean "man").

- אֶת (*et*): This may be the Hebrew word meaning "with" or it may be the Hebrew word that simply identifies the definite object of a verb.

- יהוה (*Yahweh*): This is the tetragrammaton that is sometimes transliterated as Jehovah, Yahweh, Yehovah, Yahu'ah, etc. It is the name of God.

Now we have two possible translations from the Hebrew.

> *"I have acquired a man with Yahweh"*

> *"I have acquired Yahweh, a man"*

I am sure you will agree that both possible translations are problematic. The translator's solution is to "fix" the text by adding words to the text and simply "remove" the problem, which, in my opinion, is a disservice to the reader who should be made aware of the problem.

There is one other possible solution. The Hebrew text could be written in error. This is not as uncommon as you may think, as the Hebrew text contain grammatical, spelling and contextual errors. Two thousand years ago, the Hebrew Bible was translated into Greek and was called the *Septuagint*. We do not know exactly what Hebrew text the *Septuagint* used for its translation, but we do know that it is different from the Hebrew text we use today. The Greek translation for this part of the verse reads as follows:

$$\textit{ἐκτησάμην ἄνϑρωπον διὰ τοῦ ϑεοῦ}$$

This translates as "I acquired a man **for** God."

So, which of the three, if any, is correct? Unfortunately, I cannot answer that, but now that you have the facts about this verse, you have what information is available to come to your own conclusions.

Genesis 4:1-2

The name Cain is derived from the word קִין (*qayin*), meaning "to acquire or possess something." This is why Eve (חוה *hhavah* in Hebrew) said, "I have gotten/acquired (*qanah*) a man" (Gen 4:1). The name Abel is derived from the word חבל (*hhevel*), meaning "to be empty" and is often translated "vain" or "vanity," in the sense of being empty of substance.

In Hebrew thought, one's name is reflective of one's character. For example, the word *shem*, most often translated as "name," but literally means "breath" or "character." The Hebraic meanings of the names of "Cain and Abel" are windows into their characters. Cain is a "possessor," one who has substance, while Abel is "empty" of substance.

Another interesting fact about these two that is often overlooked is that Cain and Abel are the first twins. In normal Hebraic accounting of multiple births, the conception, then birth, of each child is mentioned such as in Genesis 29:32,33:

> And Leah <u>conceived</u> and <u>bore</u> a son... She <u>conceived</u> again and <u>bore</u> a son...

But notice how it is worded in Genesis 4:1,2:

> She <u>conceived</u> and <u>bore</u> Cain... And again, she <u>bore</u> his brother Abel.

There is only one conception, but two births. The Hebrew word for "again" is "*asaph*" meaning "to add" something. In this case the birthing of Abel was added to the birthing of Cain. Cain and Abel were not just brothers, they were twins.

Genesis 4:7

> *If thou doest well, shalt thou not be accepted?*
> *and if thou doest not well, <u>sin</u> lieth at the door.*
> *And unto thee shall be <u>his</u> desire, and thou*
> *shalt rule over <u>him</u>.* (Genesis 4:7, KJV)

In this verse, God is speaking to Cain and most people interpret the "his" and "him" to be "sin." However, this is not possible, as the Hebrew word "sin," which is הטאת (*hhatat*), is a feminine noun. The words "his" and "him" must be referring to someone or something of masculine gender. The only masculine gender noun in this verse is "door," but this does not make any sense within the context. Therefore, it must be another masculine noun found in a nearby verse.

A verse that will help with the interpretation of this verse is Genesis 3:16:

> *Unto the woman he said, I will greatly multiply*
> *thy sorrow and thy conception; in sorrow thou*
> *shalt bring forth children; <u>and thy desire shall</u>*
> *<u>be to thy husband, and he shall rule over thee.</u>*
> (Genesis 3:16, KJV)

Compare this verse with Genesis 4:7:

> *If thou doest well, shalt thou not be accepted?*
> *and if thou doest not well, sin lieth at the door.*
> *<u>And unto thee shall be his desire, and thou</u>*
> *<u>shalt rule over him</u>.* (Genesis 4:7, KJV)

A literal rendering of the underlined portions of these two verses from the Hebrew is as follows:

> *and to* your man *is* your *desire and* he *will rule in* you. (Genesis 3:16)

> *and to* you *is* his *desire and* you *will rule in* him. (Genesis 4:7)

With the exception of the pronouns, these two passages are identical. Because Genesis 3:16 refers to Adam and Eve, it makes sense that Genesis 4:7 refers to Cain and Abel.

Genesis 4:26

What does it mean to "call upon the name of YHWH?" The Hebrew word translated as "call" is the verb קרא (*Q.R.A*), which can mean "to call," but this same word can also mean "to meet." The Hebrew word שם (*shem*) often means "name," but it can also mean "character." Therefore, this phrase could also be translated as "meet with the character of YHWH."

> *O give thanks unto the LORD; call upon his name: make known his deeds among the people.* (Psalm 105:1, KJV)

In this passage, the phrase "call upon his name" is a poetical parallel with "make known his deeds." When we meet with the "character" of YHWH, we are meeting his "deeds" and by making these deeds known to others, we are literally causing them to "meet the character of YHWH."

13

Genesis 9:22-25

> *And Ham, the father of Canaan, saw the nakedness of his father, and told his two brethren without. And Shem and Japheth took a garment, and laid it upon both their shoulders, and went backward, and covered the nakedness of their father; and their faces were backward, and they saw not their father's nakedness. And Noah awoke from his wine, and knew what his younger son had done unto him. And he said, Cursed be Canaan; a servant of servants shall he be unto his brethren.* (Genesis 9:22-25, KJV)

I have always had two problems with this passage. First, why is it wrong for a son to see his father naked? Secondly, why was Canaan, the son of Ham, cursed for this act? It was not until I stumbled across the following passage that everything made sense:

> *You shall not uncover the nakedness of your father, which is the nakedness of your mother; she is your mother, you shall not uncover her nakedness.* (Leviticus 18:7, RSV)

"Uncovering the nakedness of your father" is a Hebrew idiom meaning to have a sexual union with your mother. Ham did not see his father's nakedness; instead, he had a sexual union with his mother and, evidently, the product of that union was his son, Canaan. Hence, his being cursed.

Genesis 11:1

> *And the whole earth was of one language, and of <u>one speech</u>.* (Genesis 11:1, KJV)

Why are the plural words דברים אחדים (*devariym ehhadim*) in Genesis 11:1 translated as a singular "one speech?" The first thing that we have to recognize is the types of words in this phrase. The word דברים (*devarim*) is the plural form of דבר (*davar*) meaning a "word." The plural form, דברים (*devariym*), therefore, means "words." The second word is אחדים (*ehhadim*), the plural form of אחד (*ehhad*), which is frequently translated as "one." What we must also recognize though, is that אחדים (*ehhadiym*) is an adjective, a word that modifies the preceding noun: דברים (*devariym*). In Hebrew, every adjective must match the number (singular or plural) of the noun it modifies. So grammatically, if דברים (*devariym*) is plural, the word אחד (*ehhad*) must also be plural: אחדים (*ehhadiym*). The word אחד (*ehhad*) does not always mean "one," but also "unified." So now we can translate דברים אחדים (*devariym ehhadim*) as "unified words," which is a way of describing "a common language" or speech. Therefore, "one speech" is a fair translation of this Hebrew phrase.

Genesis 14:22

> *And Abram said to the king of Sodom, I have lift up mine hand unto the LORD, the most high God, the <u>possessor of heaven and earth</u>,* (Genesis 14:22, KJV)

The phrase קנה שמים וארץ (*qoneh shamayim va'arets*) is usually translated as "possessor (or maker) of heaven and earth." The Hebrew verb קנה (*qoneh*) comes from the parent root קן (*qeyn*), meaning *"nest."* The verb קנה (*qoneh*) literally means "building a nest," and with this understanding placed within the verse, the phrase means "*Elohiym*" has gathered all the materials together to build a nest: a home for us, his children.

Genesis 15:13

> *Then the LORD said to Abram, "Know of a surety that your descendants will be sojourners in a land that is not theirs, and will be slaves there, and they will be oppressed for four hundred years;* Genesis 15:13 (RSV)

From this passage, it would appear that the nation of Israel served at least 400 years in captivity in Egypt. The lineage of Levi, as recorded in Exodus 6 and 1 Chronicles 6, indicates only three generations between Levi and Moses (Levi-Kohath-Amram-Moses). If the slavery began shortly after Ya'aqov (Jacob), his children and his grandchildren entered Egypt (70 in all), the maximum amount of time that this lineage could have existed in slavery is approximately 350 years. This assumes that Kohath was at least an infant and part of the 70 entering Egypt; that Amram was born to Kohath in the year of his death; and that Moses was born in the year of Amram's death plus the 80 years of Moses' life before the exodus.

There are two possible ways of interpreting this passage. The first is to assume that persons are missing from the lineage, though there is no indication of this anywhere in the text. The second possibility is to interpret this passage with the four hundred years being between Abraham and the exodus, as Rabbinic Judaism, as well as Rabbi Shaul (Paul) of the New Testament, interprets it:

Now the promises were made to Abraham and to his offspring. It does not say, "And to offsprings," referring to many; but, referring to one, "And to your offspring," which is Christ. This is what I mean: the law, which came four hundred and thirty years afterward, does not annul a covenant previously ratified by God, so as to make the promise void. Galatians 3:16, 17 (RSV)

In this passage, Shaul is comparing the giving of the Law to the promises given to Abraham, which he identifies as 430 years. With this interpretation, Genesis 15:13 is interpreted to mean that Abraham's seed will live in a strange land. Since Ishmael was born in a strange land (Canaan), the years would begin with the birth of Abraham's first seed. His descendants would also serve as slaves in a land not their own (Egypt).

Abram was 86 years old at the birth of Ishmael, his first seed to be born in a strange land. Abram was 100 years old at the birth of Yits'hhaq (Isaac). Fourteen years between births. Yits'hhaq was 60 when he bore Esau and Jacob. Assuming that each generation began at the father's age of 60, there are 300 years between the birth of Isaac and the birth of Moses. Moses lived 80 years before the exodus. Adding the 14 years between the birth of Ishmael and Isaac, we have 396 years between the birth of Ishmael and the exodus. This is a very close approximation to the prophecy of Genesis 15:13.

This interpretation does have three problems. The first is that Paul says 430 years, while the actual prophecy states 400 years. This is fairly easy to resolve by simply saying that one or both of these numbers are approximated. Paul takes the number 430 from a passage in the Tenakh though, which brings us to the second problem:

The time that the people of Israel dwelt in Egypt was four hundred and thirty years. And at the end of four hundred and thirty years, on that very day, all the hosts of the LORD went out from the land of Egypt. Exodus 12:40, 41 (RSV)

This text indicates that Israel dwelt in Egypt for 430 years, bringing us back to the problem of the lineage. This problem may be solved easily with the following observation: The text translated as "four hundred and thirty years" is "*sheloshiym* (thirty) *shana* (year) *v'arbah* (and four) *me'ot* (hundred) *shanah* (year)." It is possible that the original Hebrew was written as "*sheloshiym* (thirty) *shana* (year) *v'me'ot* (and hundred) *shanah* (year)." This alternate reading would be translated as "one hundred and thirty years" placing the time of bondage shortly after Jacob's entrance into the land of Egypt.

Now there arose a new king over Egypt, who did not know Joseph. Exodus 1:8 (RSV)

It has been assumed that this passage takes place after the death of Joseph (Exodus 1:6), but the Hebrew text often demonstrates that stories are not written chronologically. It is possible that this is the reign of the Hyksos who conquered Egypt that may have happened while Joseph was still alive and they "did not know Joseph."

A later scribe, attempting to reconcile Exodus 12:41 with Genesis 15:13, inserted the word "*arbah*," hence the translation of "four hundred and thirty years." This may also explain the reason for the two different numbers given for the "slavery" of the nation of Israel in Egypt.

The third problem is the number of male descendants of Jacob that came out of Egypt:

And the people of Israel journeyed from Rameses to Succoth, about six hundred thousand men on foot, besides women and children. Exodus 12:37 (RSV)

According to this passage, 600,000 male descendants of Jacob left Egypt. If each man was married and had an average of five children, it would bring the entire population of Israel to 6,000,000. This is not including the mixed multitude that came out with them (Exodus 12:38) or the flocks and herds that they brought out. This large number of people creates a few problems: The first is the size of this "army" (Exodus 12:41): "hosts" meaning "army." Also, in Exodus 12:37 the men are called "*gevoriym,*" or warriors, compared to the size of Pharaoh's army of 600 chariots (Exodus 14:7), which brought fear to the Israelites. How could 600 chariots be considered a threat to 600,000 warriors of Israel? Equally puzzling is the fear the Israelites felt at entering the Promised Land, where each city probably contained no more than 5,000 warriors compared to their 600,000.

Another problem is the simple logistics of supplying food and water, and of moving such a large number of men. According to the quartermaster general of the army, it would take 1,500 tons of food, 4,000 tons of wood as fuel and 11,000,000 gallons of water each day to supply the basic needs of such a group.

A third problem is the location of the latrine:

You shall have a place outside the camp and you shall go out to it; and you shall have a stick with your weapons; and when you sit down outside, you shall dig a hole with it, and turn back and cover up your excrement. Deuteronomy 23:12,13 (RSV)

A camp of this size would be approximately five by five square miles, assuming only 1,000 square feet per family. Someone located in the center of the camp would require a hike of 2.5 miles to use the restroom.

Yet another problem is the estimated population of the nation of Israel compared to the estimated population of Egypt at that time. It is estimated that the whole population of Egypt at the time of the Exodus was between two and five million. According to the population estimates of Israel, the people of Israel would outnumber the population of Egypt.

Another issue was the large number of people not being possible, given the number of generations available from Levi to the Exodus. The average number of children born to the descendants of Jacob is three to five. If we assume that each of the twelve children of Jacob had five children, and the generation of Kohath, Amram, and Moses had five children each, the maximum number of people (men, women and children) descended from Jacob at the time of the Exodus would be approximately 7500.

The Hebrew text of Exodus 12:41: "about six hundred thousand men on foot, besides women and children" reads "k'shesh me'ot eleph rag'liy hagebariym l'vad mitaph." This could also be translated as "about six hundred chiefs (eleph) on foot are the warriors apart from the children." We now have a group of warriors that would find the 600 chariots of Pharaoh a formidable army. If we also assume that each chief (head of the family) included a wife and five children, we have 6,000 people, correlating the previous calculation of descendants from Levi to the Exodus.

Changing the translation of the word "eleph" to chiefs will also fit the census records of numbers:

The number of the tribe of Reuben was forty-six thousand five hundred. Numbers 1:21 (RSV)

The Hebrew of this passage could also be translated as: "The number for the tribe of Reuben is six and forty (forty-six) chiefs and five hundred." With this alternate translation, we have 46 chiefs and 500 family members. When we apply this method to the remainder of the tribes, we come to a total number of 598 chiefs and 5,550 others (The standard translation of the complete census is 603,550; if the three is changed to a five, a possible error, we have 605,550, very close to the 598-- two short of 600) chiefs and 5,550 people. Note that the *Septuagint* (LXX) does have a change of five to a four, so the error is not out of the realm of possibility).

In summary, it appears that the slavery of the Israelites in Egypt lasted 130 years, and approximately 7,000 individuals traveled to Mt. Sinai.

Genesis 17:1

And when Abram was ninety nine years old and the LORD appeared to Abram, and he said to him, I am <u>El Shaddai</u>, walk before me, and be perfect. Genesis 17:1

The Hebrew word אל (*el*) means "mighty one" as can be seen in the following passage:

I have therefore delivered him into the hand of the <u>mighty one</u> of the heathen; (Ezekiel 31:11, KJV)

Most Bible translations translate the word שדי (*Shaddai*) as "Almighty." Many times, a translator will not translate a Hebrew word literally because the literal meaning would mean nothing to the Western mind and in some cases would actually be offensive to the Western reader. Such is the case with the word *Shaddai*. The use of the word "Almighty" by the translator is his attempt to translate the text in a manner that will make sense to the Western reader, as well as to retain some of the meaning of the original Hebrew word.

The root for this word is שד (*shad*), which in its original pictographic script appeared as ▽ᴖ. The ᴖ (*sh*) is a picture of the two front teeth and has the meaning "sharp" or "press" (as from chewing) as well as "two." The ▽ (*d*) is a picture of a tent door meaning to "hang" or "dangle," as the fabric or skin of the door hangs or dangles down from the top of the tent.

The combined meanings of these two letters would be "two danglers." The goat was a very common animal within the herds of the Hebrews. It produces milk within the udder that goat kids extract by squeezing and sucking on the "two" teats "dangling" below the udder. The function of these teats is to provide all the necessary nourishment for the kids, as they would die without it. The Hebrew word *shaddai* also has the meaning of a "teat." Just as the goat provides nourishment to its kids through the milk, God nourishes his children through his milk and provides all the necessities of life. This imagery can be observed in the following passage:

> *"And I will come down to snatch him [Israel] from the hand of the Egyptians and to bring him up from that land to a functional and wide land to a land <u>flowing with milk</u> and honey."*
> *Exodus 3:8*

The word *shaddai*, meaning "teats," is often coupled with the word *el*, meaning mighty one, creating the phrase *el shaddai*, literally meaning the "mighty teat." Hence, we can see the translator's reluctance to literally translate this phrase in this manner, and instead uses the more "sanitized" "God Almighty."

Genesis 18

> *And Jehovah appeared unto him by the oaks of Mamre, as he sat in the tent door in the heat of the day.* (Genesis 18:1, ASV)

The word "appeared" in this passage is a translation of the *niphil* form of the verb ראה (*R.A.H*) and literally means "was seen," and because YHWH can be "seen," he evidently had a physical form. The text does not specifically state by whom YHWH was seen, but by context, we can conclude it was Abraham:

> *And he lifted up his eyes and looked, and, lo, three men stood over against him: and when he saw them, he ran to meet them from the tent door, and bowed himself to the earth.* (Genesis 18:2, ASV)

Abraham saw "three men." At this point we can only speculate that YHWH was one of the three men, but the important thing here is that they are identified as "men." It should also be noted that Abraham "bowed" toward them. The Hebrew word behind "bowed" is שחה (*shahhah*), which literally means "to prostrate oneself before another." This is the very same verb often translated as "worship." In verses 3 through 9 Abraham had a meal prepared for these men and they asked him where his wife was:

> *And he said, I will certainly return unto thee when the season cometh round; and, lo, Sarah thy wife shall have a son. And Sarah heard in*

the tent door, which was behind him. (Genesis 18:10, ASV)

One of the men informed Abraham that he would have a son, something that neither Abraham nor Sarah knew, telling us that these men had extraordinary power to be able to foretell the future. In verses 11 and 12 Sarah overheard the conversation and Sarah laughed:

> *And Jehovah said unto Abraham, Wherefore did Sarah laugh, saying, Shall I of a surety bear a child, who am old?* (Genesis 18:13, ASV)

In the context of this passage, one of the three men is speaking to Abraham about his son, and then in this verse it states that YHWH is speaking to Abraham. Again, it is still speculation that YHWH was one of the three men, but it looks more and more like it is.

Verses 14 and 15 continue with a dialogue between YHWH and Sarah:

> *And the men rose up from thence, and looked toward Sodom: and Abraham went with them to bring them on the way.* (Genesis 18:16, ASV)

This verse says, "the men" rose up to leave, but it does not say specifically how many:

> *And Jehovah said, Shall I hide from Abraham that which I do.* (Genesis 18:17, ASV)

YHWH is now speaking to "the men." Verses 18 through 20 continue the dialogue between YHWH and the men:

> *I will go down now, and see whether they have done altogether according to the cry of it, which is come unto me; and if not, I will know.* (Genesis 18:21, ASV)

YHWH states that he is going to go to Sodom to check things out.

> *And the men turned from thence, and went toward Sodom: but Abraham stood yet before Jehovah.* (Genesis 18:22, ASV)

This passage does not specifically state how many of the men left for Sodom. Either it was all three, and YHWH, who remained with Abraham, was not a part of three; or else YHWH was a part of the three and only two left for Sodom. Verses 23 through 32 continue with a dialogue between YHWH and Abraham about the number of righteous men in Sodom.

> *And Jehovah went his way, as soon as he had left off communing with Abraham: and Abraham returned unto his place.* (Genesis 18:33, ASV)

At this point YHWH goes on his way and Abraham returns home.

> *And the two angels came to Sodom at even; and Lot sat in the gate of Sodom: and Lot saw them, and rose up to meet them; and he bowed himself with his face to the earth.* (Genesis 19:1, ASV)

While this translation uses "angel," the Hebrew word is *malakhiym* meaning "messengers." Based on the context, we can conclude that these "messengers," who arrived at Sodom, were the very same "men" that left Abraham heading for Sodom, but notice that there are only two. This confirms that the third one was YHWH, who remained behind with Abraham. Also note that just as Abraham bowed down (worshiped) to the men when they arrived, so did Lot. Verses 2 through 10 detail the events of the two men coming to Lot's house and the incident with the men of the city:

> And they smote the men that were at the door of the house with blindness, both small and great, so that they wearied themselves to find the door. (Genesis 19:11, ASV)

Again, we see that these "men" were not ordinary men, as we see that they had extraordinary power to strike the men of the city with blindness. In verses 12 through 23 the men/messengers explained to Lot what was about to happen and they worked out their escape plan.

> Then Jehovah rained upon Sodom and upon Gomorrah brimstone and fire from Jehovah out of heaven. (Genesis 19:24, ASV)

Back in verse 18:33, YHWH left Abraham to go to Sodom, and it appears from this verse that YHWH had arrived. But what is more interesting is that YHWH, who appeared to be standing before Sodom and Gomorrah, was raining down brimstone and fire from YHWH who is in the sky. Verses 25 through 28 narrate Lot's escape from Sodom:

> And it came to pass, when God destroyed the cities of the Plain, that God remembered Abraham, and sent Lot out of the midst of the overthrow, when he overthrew the cities in which Lot dwelt. (Genesis 19:29, ASV)

According to this verse *Elohim* sent Lot out from the city, but it was not YHWH who sent Lot out. It was the other two messengers, who were identified as *Elohiym* (plural, as in the two men/messengers).

Genesis 20:17

> *So Abraham prayed unto God: and God healed Abimelech, and his wife, and his maidservants; and they <u>bare</u> children. (Genesis 20:17, KJV)*

The Hebrew word behind the word "bare" is the verb ילד (*Y.L.D*), which literally means "to bring forth." Translators added the word "children," which does not exist in the Hebrew text and because of this insertion of this word; the reader assumes Abimelech's punishment was that his women could not "bear children." However, there is another interpretation of this verse.

First note that God healed not only the women, but Abimelech as well, as it states in the verse above, "and God healed Abimelech..."

Prior to this, God came to Abimelech in a dream by night, and said to him:

> *Behold, thou art but a dead man, for the woman which thou hast taken; for she is a man's wife. (Genesis 20:3, KJV)*

Here God tells Abimelech that because of his sin he is a dead man, and evidently, the punishment is something that causes death, possibly an illness, but definitely not the inability to bear children. Now, let's look at verse 17 again, but this time with a literal translation from the Hebrew text:

> *And Abraham interceded to Elohiym and Elohiym healed Abimelech and his woman and his maid servants and they brought forth.*

It is my opinion that they were constipated.

Genesis 22:14

> *And Abraham called the name of that place Jehovahjireh: as it is said to this day, In the mount of the LORD it shall be seen.* (Genesis 22:14, KJV)

In this verse, the word יראה appears twice. In the Masoretic Hebrew text, dots and dashes called *nikkudot* (singular-*nikkud*) were added above and below the Hebrew letters to represent the vowel sounds. The first time this word appears in this verse, where the KJV has transliterated it as *jireh*, it is written as יִרְאֶה (*yir'eh*) and means "he sees." The second time it appears in this verse, where the KJV has translated it as "it shall be seen," it is written as יֵרָאֶה (*ye'ra'eh*) and means "he appears." To explain the difference in meaning for the word יראה, we need to understand the different verb forms. The verb יִרְאֶה (*yir'eh*) is the *qal* (simple) form and identifies the subject of the verb, which is YHWH (Jehovah), as third person, masculine, singular and the tense of the verb as imperfect that would be translated as "he sees" ("he" being YHWH). The verb יֵרָאֶה (*ye'ra'eh*) is the *niphil* (passive) form and also identifies the subject of the verb as third person, masculine, singular and the tense of the verb as imperfect and would be translated as "he was seen," but means "he appeared." However, remember that in the original text the vowel pointings did not exist, so we are relying on centuries of tradition for these verb forms being the *qal* and *niphil* forms. While the verb in question literally means "to see," some translators have interpreted this to mean "to provide," in the sense of "seeing" a need and filling it.

Genesis 24:67

> *And Isaac brought her into his mother Sarah's tent, and took Rebekah, and she became his wife; and he loved her: and Isaac was comforted after his mother's death.* (Genesis 24:67, KJV)

I had always assumed, based on this verse, that Abraham and Sarah each had their own tent. However, while researching the modern-day Bedouins of the Near East, whose culture and lifestyle is very similar to the Hebrews of Abraham's day, I found that the family tent belonged to the mother, not the father. This is also supported by the following passage:

> *And he drank of the wine, and was drunken; and he was uncovered within his tent.* (Genesis 9:21, KJV)

> *And he removed from thence unto a mountain on the east of Bethel, and pitched his tent, having Bethel on the west, and Hai on the east: and there he builded an altar unto the LORD, and called upon the name of the LORD.* (Genesis 12:8, KJV)

> *And he went on his journeys from the south even to Bethel, unto the place where his tent had been at the beginning, between Bethel and Hai;* (Genesis 13:3, KJV)

> *And Israel journeyed, and spread his tent beyond the tower of Edar.* (Genesis 35:21, KJV)

In each of these verses is the phrase "his tent." The Hebrew word for "tent" is אוהל (ohel) and "his tent" would be אוהלו (ohelo), but that does not appear in each of these verses. Instead, it is אוהלה (ohelah), which means "her tent."

Genesis 25:27

I begin this study with a comparison of two people, Jacob and Job:

> And the boys grew: and Esau was a cunning hunter, a man of the field; and Jacob was a _plain_ man, dwelling in tents. (Genesis 25:27, KJV)

> There was a man in the land of Uz, whose name was Job; and that man was _perfect_ and upright. (Job 1:1, KJV)

From these two verses, we could conclude that Jacob was plain, just an ordinary person, nothing special, but Job, on the other hand, was rather extraordinary, as he was "perfect." What you might find interesting is that the word "perfect" in Job 1:1 is a translation of the Hebrew word תם (tam), but so is the word "plain" in Genesis 25:27. So, why wasn't Jacob considered "perfect" by the translators just as they did with Job? This is another case of translators relying on the _Greek Septuagint_ for their translation rather than on the Hebrew text itself. The Greek used the word _amemptos_, meaning "blameless," for Job and the word _haplous_, meaning "simple," for Jacob.

The word תם (tam) can be best defined as "mature in thought and action" and is the parent root of the verb תמם (tamam) meaning "to be whole, finished or completed." From this verb comes another noun with similar meaning: תמים (*tamiym*):

> Thou shalt be perfect (tamiym) with the LORD thy God. (Deuteronomy 18:13, KJV)

Can anyone be perfect? From a Greek perspective, no, because everyone has his faults, but in Hebraic thought, there is no concept of "perfect." A better translation of the verse above is: "you will be complete (*tamiym*) with YHWH your *Elohiym*."

Genesis 26:8

> They said, "We see plainly that the Lord has been with you. So we said, let there be a sworn pact between us, between you and us, and let us *make a covenant* with you." (Genesis 26:28, ESV)

We will begin this study with the Hebrew word for a "covenant," which is ברית (*b'riyt*). This noun is derived from the verb ברה (*B.R.H*), which means "to select the best:"

> He stood and shouted to the ranks of Israel, "Why have you come out to draw up for battle? Am I not a Philistine, and are you not servants of Saul? *Choose* a man for yourselves, and let him come down to me." (1 Samuel 17:8, ESV)

In this passage, the Hebrew verb ברה is used for the choosing of the best man to fight Goliath. This word can also mean "to eat," in the sense of selecting, such as we see in the following verse:

> *So Amnon lay down and pretended to be ill. And when the king came to see him, Amnon said to the king, "Please let my sister Tamar come and make a couple of cakes in my sight, that I may <u>eat</u> from her hand." (2 Samuel 13:6, ESV)*

The Hebrew language is a root-oriented language, meaning that every Hebrew word is derived from a root word and that root word is the foundation of other Hebrew words. Each word derived from one root will be closely related in meaning to all the other words derived from the same root. In the case of the word ברית (*b'riyt*) we found that it was derived from the root verb ברה (*B.R.H*), but also derived from this verbal root are the nouns ברות (*barut*) meaning "choice meat" and בריה (*bir'yah*) meaning "fattened." Livestock that will be slaughtered are fed special grains to make them fat, thereby making the meat of the fattened livestock the choicest.

So how is fattened choice meat related to the word for "covenant?" The phrase "make a covenant," such as we saw in the verse that began this study, appears eighty times in the Hebrew Bible, and in every instance, it is the Hebrew phrase כרת ברית (*karat b'riyt*), which literally means "cut a covenant."

A covenant was instituted by the two parties of the covenant who would take a fattened animal, the best of the flock or herd, and "cut" it into two pieces. Then the two parties of the covenant would pass between the pieces, symbolizing their dedication to the covenant and by this action saying, "If I do not hold to the agreements of this covenant, you can do to me what we did to this animal." This methodology of "making" a covenant is clearly recorded in Jeremiah 34:18-20:

> *18 And the men who transgressed my covenant and did not keep the terms of the covenant that they made before me, I will make them like[a]*

*the calf that they cut in two and passed between its parts— **19** the officials of Judah, the officials of Jerusalem, the eunuchs, the priests, and all the people of the land who passed between the parts of the calf. **20** And I will give them into the hand of their enemies and into the hand of those who seek their lives. Their dead bodies shall be food for the birds of the air and the beasts of the earth.* (ESV)

With this understanding of a covenant, we can better understand what is going on in Genesis chapter 15:

9 He said to him, "Bring me a heifer three years old, a female goat three years old, a ram three years old, a turtledove, and a young pigeon." 10 And he brought him all these, cut them in half, and laid each half over against the other. But he did not cut the birds in half. (Genesis 15:9-10, ESV)

17 When the sun had gone down and it was dark, behold, a smoking fire pot and a flaming torch passed between these pieces. 18 On that day the LORD made (Hebrew - karat) a covenant with Abram, saying, "To your offspring I give this land, from the river of Egypt to the great river, the river Euphrates," (Genesis 15:17-18, ESV)

YHWH is cutting a covenant with Abram. However, Abram does not pass between the pieces, only the pot and torch did, representations of YHWH himself passing through the pieces. Because Abram did not pass through the pieces, the actions of Abram or his descendants are not a condition of the covenant. The only person responsible for the fulfilling of this covenant is YHWH and YHWH alone.

Besides this covenant, YHWH has made several other covenants with his people, such as the one he made with Noah and his descendants (Genesis 6:18, Genesis 9:9) and the one he made with the Israelites at Mount Sinai:

> *And Moses took the blood and threw it on the people and said, "Behold the blood of the covenant that the Lord has made (Hebrew — karat) with you in accordance with all these words."* (Exodus 24:8, ESV)

Unlike the unconditional covenants that YHWH made with Noah and Abram, this covenant will be upheld only on the condition that Israel obeys the words of YHWH:

> *14 But if you will not listen to me and will not do all these commandments, 15 if you spurn my statutes, and if your soul abhors my rules, so that you will not do all my commandments, but break my covenant, 16 then I will do this to you: I will visit you with panic, with wasting disease and fever that consume the eyes and make the heart ache. And you shall sow your seed in vain, for your enemies shall eat it. 17 I will set my face against you, and you shall be struck down before your enemies. Those who hate you shall rule over you, and you shall flee when none pursues you. 18 And if in spite of this you will not listen to me, then I will discipline you again sevenfold for your sins, 19 and I will break the pride of your power, and I will make your heavens like iron and your earth like bronze. 20 And your strength shall be spent in vain, for your land shall not yield its increase, and the trees of the land shall not yield their fruit.* (Leviticus 26:14-20, ESV)

And in Deuteronomy 31 YHWH foretells of the day when Israel will break this covenant by following after other gods:

> *For when I have brought them into the land flowing with milk and honey, which I swore to give to their fathers, and they have eaten and are full and grown fat, they will turn to other gods and serve them, and despise me and <u>break my covenant</u>.* (Deuteronomy 31:20, ESV)

It is interesting to note that when Israel does break this covenant, YHWH "cuts" Israel into "two" nations, Israel and Judah. But YHWH promises that he will make a new covenant with the children of Israel and he will unite these two nations into one nation again.

> *And I will make them one nation in the land, on the mountains of Israel. And one king shall be king over them all, and they shall be no longer two nations, and no longer divided into two kingdoms.* (Ezekiel 37:22, ESV)

> ***31** Behold, the days are coming, declares the Lord, when I will make a new covenant with the house of Israel and the house of Judah, **32** not like the covenant that I made with their fathers on the day when I took them by the hand to bring them out of the land of Egypt, my covenant that they broke, though I was their husband, declares the Lord. **33** For this is the covenant that I will make with the house of Israel after those days, declares the Lord: I will put my law within them, and I will write it on their hearts. And I will be their God, and they shall be my people.* (Jeremiah 31:31-33, ESV)

Genesis 34:30

> And it came to pass, when Moses came down
> from mount Sinai with the two tables of
> testimony in Moses' hand, when he came
> down from the mount, that Moses wist not
> that the skin of his face shone while he talked
> with him. And when Aaron and all the children
> of Israel saw Moses, behold, the skin of his
> face shone; and they were afraid to come nigh
> him. Exodus 34:29,30 (KJV)

In this verse, we find there was a physical change in Moses which created fear in the people. Was it just a light coming off him that generated this fear? No—as we shall see, the above translation "skin of his face shone," is a poor translation of the Hebrew. The Hebrew word translated as "shone" is קרן (Q.R.N), which literally means "to have horns." Interestingly, many paintings and sculptures of Moses depict him with horns such as in Michelangelo's sculpture of Moses.

It has been speculated the "horns" on Moses' face are "rays" of light that shone from his face, hence the translation we read in all English Bibles. However, there are other Hebrew words meaning "to shine," and if that was what the author had intended he would have used one of those. Instead, he deliberately chose to use the word קרן (Q.R.N) to show Moses was indeed one of power and authority. This is an example of my reasons for desiring a "mechanical" and "literal" translation of the Hebrew Bible, so the reader can read the text without the translators' bias being interjected into the text.

Genesis 37:3

> *Now Israel loved Joseph more than all his children, because he was the son of his old age: and he made him a coat of <u>many colours</u>.* (Genesis 37:3, KJV)

What many are not aware of is that about 20% of the meanings of Hebrew words in the Bible are not known. Some of them are completely unknown while the meanings of others are still obscure. Over time more and more word meanings are coming to light due to archeological discoveries. Sometimes older translations (such as the KJV) are less accurate because less is known about the words but newer translations have the advantage of recent discoveries. This is probably the case with the word פס (pas). Originally it was guessed that this word meant "diverse" or "many colors." But now it is known that this word has something to do with the palm and in this context probably means a "long-sleeved" garment, which would be an uncommon and special garment at that time.

Genesis 48:16

When Jacob blessed his son Joseph, he called God a מלאך (mela'ak), meaning "messenger," but often translated as "angel."

> *The God who my fathers Abraham and Isaac walked before, The God who shepherded me from the beginning to this day, The <u>Angel</u> who redeemed me from all evil...* (Genesis 48:15, 16)

God is able to send himself as his own messenger, which can also be seen in the following summary of God's promise to lead the nation of Israel into the Promised Land:

The Angel leads Israel

> "And I [YHWH] will come down to snatch them from the hand of the Egyptians and to bring them up from that land to a good and wide land to a land flowing with milk and honey. (Exodus 3:8)

God heard the cries of Israel's bondage in Egypt and promised that he would bring them out and lead them into the Promised Land. Once Israel was delivered and taken into the wilderness, Israel began to grumble and complain. When YHWH met Moses at the burning bush, he told Moses of his plan for Israel. YHWH delivered them out of Egypt and brought them to Mount Sinai. Throughout this journey, Israel grumbled and complained and YHWH became angry with them:

> "Look, I [YHWH] will send a _messenger_ (מלאך) before you to guard you on the way and to bring you to the place which I prepared. Be on guard from his face and hear his voice, do not make him bitter or he will not forgive your rebellion, for my name is within him." (Exodus 23:20,21)

> "And I [YHWH] will send before you a _messenger_ (מלאך) and he will cast out the Canaanites, the Amorites and the Hittites and the Peruzites, the Hivites and the Jebusites, to a land flowing with milk and honey, for I will not go up with you because the people are stiff

necked, and I will turn and devour you on the way." (Exodus 33:2,3)

After God declared that his "Angel" would lead them into the Promised Land, we read that it was YHWH who would go before them preparing their way into the land:

> *"And they will say to the dwellers of this land, as they have heard, that you YHWH are within this people who saw you YHWH, eye to eye, and your cloud stood over them and you walked before them in the pillar of cloud by day and in a pillar of fire by night."* (Numbers 14:14)

> *"And in this thing you did not believe in YHWH your God who walked before you on the way to search for you a place to camp, in a fire by night to show you the way you are to walk and in a cloud by day."* (Deuteronomy 1:32,33)

> *"And you will know today that YHWH your God is the one who will cross over before you as a devouring fire, he will destroy them and he will subdue them before you."* (Deuteronomy 9:3)

It appears from the above passages that YHWH promised to take Israel into the Promised Land, but because of their stiff necks, YHWH said that he would not go but would send his "messenger." Then we read that YHWH himself went before them to prepare the way to the Promised Land. Again, we have YHWH who did not go with them, but it was the "messenger" YHWH who did. Another apparent contradiction concerning YHWH is found in Exodus chapter thirty-three:

> *"And YHWH spoke to Moses face to face, just as a man speaks to his friend."* (Exodus 33:11)

> *"And he [YHWH] said, you cannot see my face because man cannot look on it and live... And when my glory passes by, I will set you in a cleft of the rock, I will cover over you with my palm until I pass by. I will remove my palm and you can see my back, but my face you cannot see."* (Exodus 33:20,22,23)

It is important to make a distinction between the simple reading and understanding of any text from one's interpretation of the text. It is not uncommon for people, when reading the text, to make an interpretation of the text based on their preconceived beliefs and biases. When we read the Bible and interpret it according to our beliefs, we will never discover truths within it, and, therefore, we are unable to grow in understanding. Instead, we must learn to read the Bible according to what it says and adjust our beliefs accordingly.

The simple reading of the above text states that Moses spoke with YHWH face to face, but Moses was not allowed to see the face of YHWH. There are many different ways to interpret this apparent contradiction, and it is not my intention to do so here, but only to point out that according to the texts, there is a "messenger" of YHWH called YHWH.

We will now look at another series of passages where the "messenger of YHWH" is not only called YHWH, but also God.

The Angel of the Lord

> *"And Moses was shepherding the flock of Jethro his father-in-law, the priest of Midian and he drove the flock to the back of the*

wilderness and he came to Horeb the mountain of God. And he saw the messenger of YHWH (מלאך יהוה) in flames of fire from the middle of the bush. And he saw and looked, the bush was consumed in fire and the bush was not devoured." (Exodus 3:1,2)

Throughout the scriptures, this "messenger of YHWH" appeared to individuals such as we see with Moses' encounter at the burning bush. Was this "messenger" a specific angel or God himself? In this passage, as can be seen in other passages as well, we will see that YHWH was his own messenger.

"And YHWH saw that he turned to see and God called to him from the middle of the bush and he said, Moses, Moses. And he said, I am here.... And he said, I am the God of your fathers, the God of Abraham, the God of Isaac and the God of Jacob. And Moses hid his face because he was afraid to look at God." (Exodus 3:4,6)

The "messenger of YHWH" is now identified as God, the God of his fathers. Moses knew that this was God for he was afraid to look at his face, knowing that anyone who looks at the face of God would die (see Exodus 33:20).

"And God again said to Moses, Say to the sons of Israel, YHWH, the God of your fathers, the God of Abraham, the God of Isaac and the God of Jacob." (Exodus 3:15)

We have now seen that the "messenger of YHWH" is God. In the above passage, we see that YHWH is God. From this, we can conclude that the "messenger of YHWH" was actually YHWH himself.

Exodus 3:14

> *And Moses said unto God, Behold, when I come unto the children of Israel, and shall say unto them, The God of your fathers hath sent me unto you; and they shall say to me, What is his name? what shall I say unto them?* (Exodus 3:13, KJV)

In this verse, Moses is asking YHWH what his "name" is so that he can tell the Israelites when they ask. Exodus 3:14 is YHWH's response.

> *And God said unto Moses, I AM THAT I AM: and he said, Thus shalt thou say unto the children of Israel, I AM hath sent me unto you.* (Exodus 3:14, KJV)

YHWH first tells Moses, "I am that I am," but we will come back to that phrase. Then he tells him to tell the Israelites, "I am sent me to you." The King James translators conclude that his "name" means "I am," which in Hebrew is אהיה (*ehyeh*). Many translations of the Bible translate this word, but never transliterate it. Contrast this with the following verse.

> *And I appeared unto Abraham, unto Isaac, and unto Jacob, by the name of God Almighty, but by my name JEHOVAH [YHWH] was I not known to them.* (Exodus 6:3, KJV)

In this verse, YHWH gives his name as יהוה (*YHWH*) and most translations transliterate this word. Keep in mind there is no letter "J" or "J" sound in Hebrew. Remember that when the King James Version was first written in 1611, the letter "I" was used and had a "Y" sound and still does in many languages. It is my opinion that the word אהיה (*ehyeh*) in Exodus 3:14

should be transliterated as "*Ehyeh*" and simply translated in the first person as "I am."

Because a person's character is reflected in his name in Hebrew tradition, it is important then to know what אהיה (*ehyeh*) means. The word אהיה (*ehyeh*) is a conjugation of the verb היה (*H.Y.H*) and the following are the various conjugations of this verb:

Person	Hebrew	Transliteration	Translation	Example
1st person	אהיה	*Ehyeh*	I exist (I am)	Exodus 4:12
2nd person	תהיה	*Tihyeh*	You exist (You are)	Exodus 4:16
3rd person	יהיה	*Yihyeh*	He exists (He is)	Exodus 4:16

As you can see, the word אהיה (*ehyeh*) means "I exist." There is another Hebrew verb that has the same basic meaning as the verb היה (*H.Y.H*) and that is הוה (*H.W.H*), which is conjugated in the same manner.

Person	Hebrew	Transliteration	Translation	Example
1st person	אהוה	*Ehweh*	I exist (I am)	N/A
2nd person	תהוה	*Tihweh*	You exist (You are)	Daniel 2:41

| 3rd person | יהוה | Yihweh | He exists (He is) | N/A |

Notice the third person form is יהוה, which is the name YHWH, and means "he exists." When YHWH told Moses his name he said אהיה, meaning "I exist," but then when Moses addresses Israel, he tells them that God's name is יהוה, meaning "he exists."

Now, let's get back to the phrase "I am that I am," which is a common translation for Exodus 3:14. In the Hebrew text, this is written as אהיה אשר אהיה. We have already examined the word אהיה, which appears twice. The other word אשר (asher) is the relative pronoun that, depending upon the context, can be translated as "which," "who," "what," "because," "that," etc. If we choose to translate אהיה as "I am," then this phrase would be translated as "I am who I am." But if we choose to translate אהיה as "I exist," which I believe is a more accurate translation, then this phrase would be translated as "I exist because I exist."

Exodus 8:3

In Exodus 8:3 is the word וַיַּעֲלוּ. This is the verb עלה (Ah.L.H) and may be written in the *qal* form of the verb, in which case it means "and they went up," but it can also be the *hiphil* form, in which case it means "and they caused to go up." In most places, the correct form of this verb can be determined by the context of how the word is used, but in Exodus 8:3 (verse 7 in Christian Bibles) the context could imply either.

If we assume the *hiphil* form, this verse would read: "and the magicians did so with their secrets, and they made frogs go up upon the land of Mits'rayim" and implies that the secrets of the magicians were successful.

However, if we assume the *qal* form, this verse would read: "and the magicians did so with their secrets, and frogs went up upon the land of Mits'rayim" and does not necessarily mean that the secrets of the magicians worked. The frogs may have gone up upon the land by coincidence or by some other force, such as by God.

Exodus 9:16

There are some people who claim that if you do not use the absolute correct pronunciation for the name YHWH, he will not hear you. This is based partially on Exodus 9:16 where it appears to be saying that we are to declare his name to all people and teach them how to correctly pronounce it.

> And in very deed for this cause have I raised thee up, for to shew in thee my power; <u>and that my name may be declared throughout all the earth.</u> (Exodus 9:16, KJV)

However, as the Hebrew word שם (*shem*), translated as "name" in this verse, can also mean "character," it is my opinion that this verse should be translated as, "and that my character may be declared throughout all the earth." This verse is not speaking about how to pronounce the name, but teaching others about the character of YHWH.

Exodus 12:23, 29

> For the LORD will pass through to smite the Egyptians; and when he seeth the blood upon the lintel, and on the two side posts, <u>the LORD will pass over the door, and will not suffer the</u>

> *destroyer to come in unto your houses to smite you.* Exodus 12:23

In this verse YHWH prevents the destroyer from killing the firstborn of the house with the blood on the doorposts:

> *And it came to pass, that at midnight the LORD smote all the firstborn in the land of Egypt, from the firstborn of Pharaoh that sat on his throne unto the firstborn of the captive that was in the dungeon; and all the firstborn of cattle.* Exodus 12:29

In this verse, the destroyer is identified as YHWH. Therefore, when "YHWH the preventer" sees the blood on the doorpost, he prevents "YHWH the destroyer" from killing the firstborn.

Exodus 17:12

> *But Moses' hands were heavy; and they took a stone, and put it under him, and he sat thereon; and Aaron and Hur stayed up his hands, the one on the one side, and the other on the other side; and his hands were steady until the going down of the sun.* Exodus 17:12 (KJV)

The Hebrew word translated as "steady" in this verse is אמונה (*emunah*) meaning "set firmly in place" or "supported," and clearly demonstrates the concreteness of the meaning of Hebrew words through an action. This word is a derivative of the verb אמן (*A.M.N*), *meaning* "to support."

This word is often translated as "faithful" or "faithfulness" which is defined in an English dictionary as: "Adhering firmly and devotedly, as to a person, cause, or idea; loyal." In the following passage, replace the word "faithfulness" with "firmness" and the Hebraic context of the verse comes alive:

> *I will sing of the mercies of the LORD for ever: with my mouth will I make known thy <u>faithfulness</u> (emunah) to all generations. For I have said, Mercy shall be built up for ever: thy <u>faithfulness</u> (emunah) shalt thou establish in the very heavens. I have made a covenant with my chosen, I have sworn unto David my servant, Thy seed will I establish for ever, and build up thy throne to all generations. Selah. And the heavens shall praise thy wonders, O LORD: thy <u>faithfulness</u> (emunah) also in the congregation of the saints. Psalm 89:1-5 (KJV)*

Exodus 17:14

> *And the LORD said unto Moses, Write this for a memorial in a book, and rehearse it in the ears of Joshua: for I will utterly put out the remembrance of Amalek from under heaven. (Exodus 17:14, KJV)*

This verse is an excellent example that illustrates the concrete nature of the Hebrew language and how translators have removed that concreteness and replaced it with abstracts. In this passage is the phrase "write this for a memorial in a book and rehearse it in the ears of Joshua." The Hebrew text literally reads, "Write this as a memorial in a scroll and place it in the ears of Joshua." This passage is literally saying to "take the scroll and place it in Joshua's ears." Of course, this is meant to be taken figuratively, and the spoken words of the scroll were to be heard by Joshua's ears.

It has always been my opinion that the role of a Bible translator is to translate the text true to the Hebrew and not to interpret the text for the reader. By doing so, the reader is given someone else's interpretation and is oblivious to the fact that it is an interpretation and not what the text actually states. In passages such as this, the translator should footnote the text to assist the reader with understanding the text.

Exodus 20:4-5

The Hebrew word often translated as "graven" or "carved images" is the word תמונה (temunah). This word comes from the root מין (miyn) meaning "a species." Because all animals of the same species look alike, the word temunah means a likeness:

> You shall not make for yourself a graven image [pesel], or any likeness [temunah] of anything that is in heaven above, or that is in the earth beneath, or that is in the water under the earth. Exodus 20:4 (RSV)

Does this command prohibit the making of statues, paintings, figurines, photographs, etc.? If so, how could God instruct Moses to make an image of a serpent (Numbers 21:8) or Cherubim (Exodus 25:18) on the cover of the ark? The key is the next verse which does not prohibit the forming of the images, but forming them and bowing down and serving them.

> You shall not bow down to them or serve them; for I the LORD your God am a jealous God, visiting the iniquity of the fathers upon the children to the third and the fourth

generation of those who hate me. Exodus 20:5
(RSV)

Exodus 20:7

*Thou shalt not take the name of the LORD thy
God in vain...* (Exodus 20:7, KJV)

Take

The Hebrew verb behind this English word is נשא (*N.S.A*) and is
a very generic verb used in a wide variety of ways in the text.
This word has been translated as "lift," "carry," "accept,"
"exalt," "regard," "obtain," "respect" and many other ways. In
the context of this verse, it is the "name" that is being "lifted
up." One lifts up a name by making it known to others.

Name

In our modern western culture, a name is nothing more than
an identifier, nothing different from being assigned a number.
The Hebrew word for a name is שם (*shem*), but in the Ancient
Hebrew culture, the "*shem*" was much more than just a name.
It was the "breath" of the individual. To the Hebrews the
breath was more than just the exchange of air in the lungs; it
was his "character," the internal qualities of an individual that
make him unique. This idea of the word *shem* meaning
"character" can be seen in 1 Kings 4:31, "*and his fame was in
all the nations round about.*" Here, the word "fame" is
understood as being his "character."

All Hebrew names are words with meaning and these words
reflect their characters. For instance, Eve (*Hhavah* in Hebrew)
means "life" because she is the mother of all the living (*Hhay*,
a related word to *Hhavah*, see Genesis 3:20). The names for
God are no different. The name YHWH means "he exists" and

God (*Elohiym*) means "one of power and authority." Some other names of God include "Jealous" (Exodus 34:14), "One" (Zechariah 14:9, which literally reads "his name is one"), "Holy "(Isaiah 57:15) and others. What is God's name? Most will answer "YHWH" or "God," but we must remember that a name or *shem* in Hebrew is the character of the individual. Therefore, the correct question should be: "What is God's character?"

Vain

The third word that we need to understand correctly is the word "vain." This is the Hebrew word שוא (*sheva*). This word literally means "empty," and vain actions are empty of substance. This word can also be understood as "falsely" in the sense of being empty of its true substance, as clearly seen in Exodus 23:1, *"You shall not utter a false report."* The word "false" is the very same Hebrew word שוא (*sheva*).

Now that we have a more complete understanding of the words in the passage above, we are able to make a more Hebraic interpretation:

> *You shall not represent the character of Elohiym falsely*

So, what does this mean? In Genesis 1:27 we read that *"God created man in his own image."* This verse is, in fact, saying that God had placed within us a representation of himself. This representation is his *shem* or character and we are to show this character to others. If, however, we represent that character falsely, or, in other words, live our lives contrary to the character of God, then we are violating this command and taking his name (character) in vain (representing it falsely).

Exodus 21:23-25

What does *"life for life"* and *"eye for an eye?"* mean? The King James Version translates Exodus 21:23-25 as follows:

> *And if any mischief follow, then thou shalt give life for life, Eye for eye, tooth for tooth, hand for hand, foot for foot, burning for burning, wound for wound, stripe for stripe.*

In this translation the phrase "life for life" implies that if you take a person's life, your life is to be taken. I do not believe this is what the verse is implying. The Hebrew translation for "life for life" would be *hhayim l'hhayim*, but this is not what is found in the Hebrew. The Hebrew reads *nephesh tahhat naphesh* which means "being in place of being." I interpret this to mean that if you take a life, such as that of a servant (see the previous verses) or a beast, then you must replace that life.

The KJV translation of "eye for eye" also implies that if you take the eye of another, then your eye must be taken. In the Hebrew, this phrase is written as *ayin tahhat ayin* meaning "an eye in place of an eye." If you take the eye of a person, then you must replace that eye. Of course, this cannot mean implanting a new eye, but instead, you must take whatever measures are necessary to give that person what he needs in order to compensate him for the missing eye. This might mean giving him a servant to see for him or money to replace his lost wages.

This interpretation can be supported by the following passage:

> *but if a man will hit the eye of his servant, or the eye of his bondwoman, and he damages her, he will send him to freedom in place of his eye, and if the tooth of his servant, or the*

*tooth of his bondwoman is made to fall out, he
will send him to freedom in place of his tooth.*
Exodus 21:26,27

Exodus 31:3

Wisdom

The parent root חם (*hham*), meaning "heat," is the root of the
word חכם (*hhakham*), meaning "wisdom."

The word *hham* appears as ᗯᕽ in its original pictographic
script. The letter ᕽ is a picture of a wall which "separates" one
side from another. And the letter ᗯ is a picture of "water."
Combined, these two letters literally mean "separate water."
When "heat" (*hham)* is applied to water, we have evaporation
or a "separating of water."

The following Hebrew words are all derived from the parent
root חם (*hham*):

חמת	*hheymet*	skin-bag
חמה	*hheymah*	cheese
חמה	*hhammah*	sun
חמס	*hhamas*	to shake
חמד	*hhamad*	to crave/desire
חמץ	*hhamats*	to sour

While we can plainly see the root חם (*hham*) at the beginning
of each of these words, what may not be as plainly seen is
how the meanings of each of these words are related.

Soured (חמץ) milk was placed in a skin-bag (חמת) that was set
out in the heat (חם) of the sun (חמה) and shaken (חמס). The
natural enzymes in the skin-bag caused the "water to

separate" (חם) from the milk, forming the delicacy (חסד) cheese (חמה).

So, what does all of this have to do with wisdom? חכם (hhakham) is related to the idea of "separating," as this word means "one who is able to separate between what is good and bad." This one word can be translated as either "skill," when applied to a craftsman, or as "wise," when applied to a leader or counselor:

> and now send for me a man of <u>skill</u> (hhakham) to work in gold... (2 Chronicles 2:7)

> Provide for yourselves <u>wise</u> (hhakham) men and understanding and knowing for your tribes and I will set them as rulers over you. (Deuteronomy 1:13)

A verse found in the book of Isaiah has a very interesting connection between חמה (hheymah - cheese) and a חכם (hhakham - wisdom):

> And he will eat cheese (hheymah) and honey (This Hebrew word can mean honey or dates) to know to reject the bad and choose the good. Isaiah 7:15

There appears to be a physical connection between "cheese" and "wisdom," as this passage indicates that eating cheese can bring about wisdom.

Understanding

The Hebrew word for understanding is תבון (tavun) and comes from the verbal root בין (biyn) meaning to "understand." However, the deeper meaning of this word can be found in a related verbal root - בנה (B.N.H) which means to "build." In order to build or construct something, one must have the ability to plan and understand the processes needed. This is the idea behind the verb בין (biyn) and its derivative noun תבון (tavun), "to be able to discern the processes of construction."

Knowledge

The Hebrew word for "knowledge" is דעת (da'at), which is derived from the parent root דע (dea). The name of the Hebrew letter ד is dalet, from the Hebrew word דלת (delet) meaning "door." This letter was originally written as ▽ in the ancient pictographic script. It is a picture of the tent door and can mean "to hang," as the door "hangs" down from the roof of the tent. Each Hebrew letter has more than one meaning, and this letter can also mean "back and forth" or "in and out" movement, as the door is used for moving in and out of the tent. The name of the Hebrew letter ע is ayin, from the Hebrew word עין (ayin) meaning "eye." This letter was originally written as ◉ in the ancient pictographic script and is a picture of an eye. When these two letters are combined, the Hebrew parent root דע (dea) is formed, meaning "the back and forth movement of the eye." When something is carefully examined, one moves the eye back and forth to take in the whole of what is being examined. In the Ancient Hebrew mind, this careful examination is understood as knowledge and experience on an intimate level:

> Do you _know_ (yada) the balancings of the clouds, the wondrous works of complete _knowledge_ (dea)? (Job 37:16)

The verb ידה (Y.D.H) is derived out of this parent root and carries this same meaning of an intimate knowledge. This verb is commonly used in reference to the marital relations of a husband and wife:

> *And Adam <u>knew</u> Eve his wife; and she conceived, and bare Cain...* Genesis 4:1 (KJV)

Do you know God? Not in the casual sense of awareness, as implied in the English sense of knowledge, but in a close and intimate relationship?

> *And those <u>knowing</u> your character will trust in you for you will not leave those seeking YHWH.* (Psalm 9:11)

God certainly knows us in this manner:

> *Will not God search this, for he <u>knows</u> the secrets of the heart.* (Psalm 44:21)

Do we know God in this same manner? Do we know the heart of God?

> *And by this we may be sure that we <u>know</u> him, if we keep his commandments.* (1 John 2:3 RSV)

The above verse is translated from a western perspective, but if we translate it through the mind of the Hebrews, we get a slightly different perspective:

> *And by this we may be sure that we have an <u>intimate relationship</u> with him, if we preserve his directions.*

Derived from the parent root דע (*dea*) is the noun דעת (*da'at*), meaning "knowledge." This word is derived from the verb ידע (*Y.D.Ah*) meaning "to know." The idea of "knowing" in Ancient Hebrew thought was similar to our understanding of knowing, but is more personal and intimate. We may say that we "know" someone, but simply mean that we "know" of his or her existence. In Hebrew thought, one can "know" someone only if they have a personal and intimate relationship. In Genesis 18:19 God says about Abraham, "I know him," meaning he has a very close relationship with Abraham. In Genesis 4:1 it says that Adam "knew Eve his wife," implying a very intimate sexual relationship.

Knowledge is the intimate ability to perform a specific task or function. This can be seen in Exodus chapter 31, where God had given men the ability to build the various furnishings of the tabernacle.

Exodus 32:4

> *And he received them at their hand, and fashioned it with a graving tool, after he had made it a molten calf: and they said, These be thy gods, O Israel, which brought thee up out of the land of Egypt.* (Exodus 32:4, KJV)

From a linguistic perspective, this is a problematic verse. Note that only "one" molten calf was made, but then they said, "These are your gods." The word "these" implies plurality.

However, in recent years there have been many who have visited and photographed a mountain called "Jabal Al-Laws" in Saudi Arabia and many believe this to be the real "Mt. Sinai."

Located near the base of this mountain is a pile of very large stones, which some believe to be the altar upon which the "molten calf" was placed.

But the intriguing part is that inscribed all over these stones are engravings of calves and oxen. If this is indeed the altar and the engravings are from the time of the Exodus, then the phrase, "These are your gods," now makes sense and refers to the molten calf and the engraved images of calves and oxen.

Another interesting piece to this puzzle is another nearby inscription, which, if this author's translation is correct, reads, "and he will build a molten calf."

Leviticus 10:16-20

And Moses diligently sought the goat of the sin offering, and, behold, it was burnt: and he was angry with Eleazar and Ithamar, the sons of Aaron which were left alive, saying, Wherefore have ye not eaten the sin offering in the holy place, seeing it is most holy, and God hath given it you to bear the iniquity of the congregation, to make atonement for them before the LORD? Behold, the blood of it was not brought in within the holy place: ye should indeed have eaten it in the holy place, as I commanded. And Aaron said unto Moses, Behold, this day have they offered their sin offering and their burnt offering before the LORD; and such things have befallen me: and if I had eaten the sin offering to day, should it have been accepted in the sight of the LORD? And when Moses heard that, he was content.
Leviticus 10:16-20

Summarizing this passage, Aharon's sons were supposed to eat the goat, but instead, they burned it in the fire. Moses was angry, saying they should have eaten it. Aharon then asked Moses if it would have been acceptable had he eaten it, and this was acceptable to Moses.

Now let's take a look at the Revised Mechanical Translation for this passage:

> "and Mosheh (Moses) greatly sought the hairy
> one (the goat) of the failure (sin offering), and
> look, he was cremated, and he snapped upon
> Elazar and upon Iytamar, the sons of Aharon
> (Aaron), the ones being left behind, saying,
> why did you not eat the failure in the special
> area, given that she was a special thing of
> special things, and he gave her to you to lift up
> the twistedness of the company to cover over
> them to the face of YHWH, though her blood
> was not brought to the special place within,
> you will surely eat her in the special place, just
> as I directed, and Aharon spoke to Mosheh,
> though today they brought near their failure
> and their burnt offering to the face of YHWH,
> and they called me out like this, and I will eat
> the failure today, will it do well in the eyes of
> YHWH? And Mosheh heard and it did well in
> his eyes?"

In this translation, the beginning is pretty much the same, but instead of Mosheh saying, "you should have eaten it", he said, "You will eat it." Mosheh is going to make the sons of Aharon eat the ashes of the goat! And instead of Aharon saying, "what if I had eaten it?" He says, "what if I will eat it?" Then the passage says that it did well in Mosheh's eyes, implying that he watched Aharon eat the ashes.

What an amazing sacrifice a father did for his sons.

Leviticus 16:8

And Aaron shall cast lots upon the two goats;
one lot for the LORD, and the other lot for the
scapegoat. (Leviticus 16:8, KJV)

In the realm of Biblical Books, there are four different groups of books: the Tanakh (Old Testament), the New Testament, the Apocrypha and the Pseudepigrapha.

Judaism accepts the first as canon, Christianity the first two, Catholicism the first three, but none of the major Judeo Christian religions accept the fourth within their canon of scripture. This is to their disadvantage because the books of the Pseudepigrapha can often shed light on passages in the other three. One example of this is "the scapegoat."

The following is a literal translation of Leviticus 16:7-10:

"And take the two goats and stand them up
before YHWH at the entrance to the tent of
meeting. And Aharon will give the two goats
over to the casting of lots, <u>one lot to YHWH</u>
<u>and one lot to Azazel</u>. And Aharon will bring
the goat which over him was cast the lot to
YHWH and make him a sin offering. And the
goat which was over him the lot cast to Azazel,
he will stand alive before YHWH to make
atonement to send him to Azazel in the
wilderness."

Each goat represents one type of person. The goat selected for YHWH represents the obedient servant who is committed to God; this one sacrifices his life to serve before YHWH. The other goat represents the haughty and proud who is free to live his life his own way, separate from YHWH and sent out into the wilderness.

While it would seem that the goat released into the wilderness has the better deal, this is not true; the goat that is sacrificed to YHWH is completely dedicated to YHWH, while the other is sent out into the wilderness, probably to die from starvation. The Jewish tradition actually says that the goat was taken to a high place, a cliff, and thrown over it.

What exactly is Azazel? There have been three theories. The first is that it is a combination word meaning "goat" (*az*) and "sent away" (*azel*), hence the translation in some Bibles of "scapegoat." The second is that the word is the place to which the goat was sent; a desert, solitary place, or a high place. The third is that Azazel is the name of an individual, angel or demon. The latter makes more sense, as the Hebrew says that one of the goats is "to" YHWH, while the other is "to" Azazel (one who is the opposite of YHWH). The Hebrew translated as "to" could also be translated as "for" or "belonging to."

Many times passages in the Bible cannot be understood correctly without outside sources to shed light on the ancient cultural understandings and background. While many people attempt to interpret this passage based on the Bible alone, thus creating many different interpretations, the actual meaning of Azazel can be found in the book of Enoch:

> ENOCH 8:1-3 *And Azazel taught men to make swords, and knives, and shields, and breastplates, and made known to them the metals of the earth and the art of working them, and bracelets, and ornaments, and the use of antimony, and the beautifying of the eyelids, and all kinds of costly stones, and all colouring tinctures. And there arose much godlessness, and they committed fornication, and they were led astray, and became corrupt in all their ways*

ENOCH 10:1-9 *Then said the Most High, the Holy and Great One spake, and sent Uriel to the son of Lamech, and said to him: 'Go to Noah and tell him in my name "Hide thyself!" and reveal to him the end that is approaching: that the whole earth will be destroyed, and a deluge is about to come upon the whole earth, and will destroy all that is on it. And now instruct him that he may escape and his seed may be preserved for all the generations of the world.' And again the Lord said to Raphael: 'Bind Azazel hand and foot, and cast him into the darkness: and make an opening in the desert, which is in Dudael, and cast him therein. And place upon him rough and jagged rocks, and cover him with darkness, and let him abide there for ever, and cover his face that he may not see light. And on the day of the great judgement he shall be cast into the fire... the whole earth has been corrupted through the works that were taught by Azazel: to him ascribe all sin.*

ENOCH 54:3-6 *And there mine eyes saw how they made these their instruments, iron chains of immeasurable weight. And I asked the angel of peace who went with me, saying: "For whom are these chains being prepared? And he said unto me: "These are being prepared for the hosts of Azazel, so that they may take them and cast them into the abyss of complete condemnation, and they shall cover their jaws with rough stones as the Lord of Spirits commanded. And Michael, and Gabriel, and Raphael, and Phanuel shall take hold of them on that great day, and cast them on that day into the burning furnace, that the Lord of*

Spirits may take vengeance on them for their unrighteousness in becoming subject to Satan and leading astray those who dwell on the earth."

Leviticus 25:22

The Hebrew word ישן is written two different ways in the Masoretic Hebrew text. One is יָשָׁן (*yashan*), which is the word found in the following verse and is translated as "old" (the word "store" was added to the text and is not in the original Hebrew text).

> *And ye shall sow the eighth year, and eat yet of old fruit until the ninth year; until her fruits come in ye shall eat of the <u>old</u> store.* (Leviticus 25:22, KJV)

The other is יָשֵׁן (*yasheyn*), which is translated as "sleeping" in the following verse.

> *So David and Abishai came to the people by night: and, behold, Saul lay <u>sleeping</u> within the trench, and his spear stuck in the ground at his bolster: but Abner and the people lay round about him.* (1 Samuel 26:7, KJV)

Because the Masorites believed that these were two different words, they placed different vowel pointings under the letters to make the distinction between the two words. *Strong's Dictionary* also identifies these as two different words. The word יָשֵׁן (*yasheyn*) is identified by number 3463 in *Strong's Dictionary* and is defined as "sleeping," while the word יָשָׁן (*yashan*) is identified by number 3465 and is defined as "old."

Strong's Dictionary identifies the root of both of these words as יש (*Y.Sh.N*), meaning "to sleep."

It is obvious how יָשֵׁן (*yasheyn*), translated as "sleeping," is related to the root יש (*Y.Sh.N*), meaning "to sleep," but how could יָשָׁן (*yashan*), translated as "old," be related to the same root?

The context of this word is "produce" that is "stored" for future use. The "storage" is produce that is "sleeping" and here we find the connection between יָשָׁן (*yashan*), translated as "old" and יש (*Y.Sh.N*), the verbal root meaning "to sleep."

Numbers 6:24-26

> *The LORD <u>bless</u> you and <u>keep</u> you: The LORD make his <u>face</u> to <u>shine</u> upon you, and be <u>gracious</u> to you: The LORD lift up his <u>countenance</u> upon you, and <u>give</u> you <u>peace</u>.*
> Numbers 6:24-26 (RSV)

Most people are familiar with the above translation for the Priestly Blessing. Each of the Hebrew words behind the English in this passage is filled with images that are lost when they are translated into the English language. When we examine each of these words from their original meaning and cultural context, the message in the passage comes alive:

> *YHWH will kneel before you presenting gifts, and he will guard you with a hedge of protection, YHWH will illuminate the wholeness of his being toward you, bringing order, and he will provide you with love, sustenance, and friendship, YHWH will lift up the wholeness of his being and look upon you,*

*and he will set in place all you need to be
whole and complete.*

Now, let us examine each of the words in this passage.

Bless

The Hebrew verb ברך (*B.R.K*) means "to kneel" as seen in
Genesis 24:11. However, when written in the *piel* form, such
as in the Aaronic blessing, it means to show respect (usually
translated as bless). But, because "respect" is an abstract
word, we need to uncover its original concrete meaning,
which we can do by examining other words related to this
verb. One such related word is the noun ברך (*berekh*) meaning
"knee." Another related Hebrew word is ברכה (*berakhah*
meaning "a gift" or "present." From this, we can see the
concrete meaning behind the *piel* form of the verb *barak*. It is
to bring a gift to another while kneeling out of respect. The
extended meaning of this word is to do or give something of
value to another. *Elohiym* "respects" us by providing for our
needs and we in turn "respect" *Elohiym* by giving to him
ourselves as his servants.

Keep

The Hebrews were a nomadic people raising livestock. It
would not be uncommon for a shepherd to be out with his
flock, away from the camp over the night. In order to protect
the flock, the shepherd would construct a corral of thorn
bushes. The shepherd would then guard the flock and the
corral would be a hedge of protection around them. The
Hebrew word for a thorn is שמיר (*shamiyr*) and derived from
the verb שמר (*Sh.M.R*), which literally means "to guard and
protect" and is the word used in the Aaronic blessing.

Face

The face reflects the many different moods, emotions, and thoughts of the person. The Hebrew word פנים (*paniym*), means "face," but is always written in the plural form (the ים suffix identifies this word as plural), reflecting this idea of multiple faces of each person. This word can also mean "presence" or the "wholeness of being" of an individual.

Shine

The word אור (*or*), as a noun, means "light," and as a verb, as it is used in this passage, means to "give light" or "shine" and is equated with bringing about order as light illuminates or reveals what has been dark.

Gracious

Most theologians define "grace" as "unmerited favor," but notice the abstractness of these words. The Hebrew verb translated as "gracious" in the Aaronic blessing is the verb חנן (*Hh.N.N*) and is often paralleled with other Hebrew words meaning "healing," "help," "being lifted up," "finding refuge, strength and rescue." From a concrete Hebraic perspective this verb means to "provide protection." Where does one run to for protection? The camp, which in Hebrew is חנה (*hhanah*), a word related to חנן (*Hh.N.N*).

Countenance

This is the same Hebrew word as before, meaning "face."

Give

The Hebrew verb שים (*S.Y.M*) literally means to "set down in a fixed and arranged place."

Peace

When we hear the word "peace" we usually associate this to mean an absence of war or strife. However, the Hebrew word שלום (*shalom*) has a very different meaning. The root of this word is שלם (*Sh.L.M*) and is usually used in the context of making restitution. When a person has caused another to become deficient in some way, such as a loss of livestock, it is the responsibility of the person who created the deficiency to restore what has been taken, lost or stolen. The verb שלם (*Sh.L.M*) literally means "to make whole or complete." The noun *shalom* has the more literal meaning of "being in a state of wholeness or being without deficiency."

Numbers 6:27

> And they shall put my name upon the children
> of Israel; and I will bless them. (Numbers 6:27,
> KJV)

How does one "put a name" on another person? The previous three verses cite the Aaronic blessing, a blessing that the priests would speak to all of the people of Israel. Contained within the Aaronic blessing is the character of YHWH. If we remember that the Hebrew word שם (*shem*) can mean "character" as well as "name," we will recognize that by speaking the words of the Aaronic blessing to the people, they are "receiving" YHWH's character.

Numbers 15:38-40

One of the most beautiful aspects of the Hebrew language is its clear connection between a word and its illustrative meaning. The Hebrew word צִיצִית (*tsiytsiyt*) is a good example of this relationship:

> *Speak unto the children of Israel, and bid them that they make them <u>fringes</u> (tsiytsiyt) in the borders of their garments throughout their generations, and that they put upon the <u>fringe</u> (tsiytsiyt) of the borders a ribband of blue: And it shall be unto you for a <u>fringe</u> (tsiytsiyt), that ye may look upon it, and remember all the commandments of the LORD, and do them; and that ye seek not after your own heart and your own eyes, after which ye use to go a whoring: That ye may remember, and do all my commandments, and be holy unto your God. (Numbers 15:38-40, KJV)*

From the above passage, we learn the *tsiytsiyt*, translated as "fringe," are worn on the four corners of the garments. The standard dress of the Hebrews was a rectangular piece of cloth with a hole in the center for the head and was worn similar to a modern poncho. A sash was tied around the waist to secure the garment. The fringes were then tied to each corner ("border" in the KJV translation) of this garment as reminders of God's commands for his people.

The word *tsiytsiyt* is derived from the noun צִיץ (*tsiyts*) and the verb צוּץ (*tsuts*), both of which can be found in the following passage:

> *And it came to pass, that on the morrow Moses went into the tabernacle of witness; and, behold, the rod of Aaron for the house of Levi was budded, and brought forth buds, and <u>bloomed</u> (tsuts) <u>blossoms</u> (tsiyts), and yielded almonds. Numbers 17:8 (KJV)*

When I first began studying the word *tsiytsiyt*, I pondered the connection between *tsiytsiyt*, meaning "fringe," and *tsiyts*, meaning "blossom," and wondered if the fringe originally looked like a blossom. I then reminded myself I was concentrating on the physical appearance of these objects, a Greek way of thinking, and had forgotten the Hebrews were concerned with function. When I realized the function of a blossom was to produce fruit on a tree, I was amazed to discover this was the exact same function of the *tsiytsiyt*, to produce fruit within the man:

> But his delight is in the teachings of YHWH and in his teachings he meditates day and night, and <u>he will be like a tree planted by streams of water which gives his fruit</u> in its season. Psalm 1:2,3

The function of the fringe, according to Numbers 15:38-40, is to *remember the commandments*, the teachings of God, which according to Psalm 1:2,3, is like producing fruit.

Numbers 19:1-10

> He said, "If you listen carefully to the voice of the LORD your God and do what is right in his eyes, if you pay attention to his commands and keep all his decrees, I will not bring on you any of the diseases I brought on the Egyptians, for I am the LORD, who heals you." (Exodus 15:26)

Is God's promise, given in the passage above, what we would call a miracle? Or is there something more "scientific" at work behind the commands of God? Let's take the command to wash in the ashes of the Red Heifer (Numbers 19:1-12) as an example and look at the text with a more in-depth study of the words in the text:

> 1 Now the LORD said to Moses and to Aaron, 2 "This is the statute of the law which the LORD has commanded: Tell the people of Israel to bring you a <u>red heifer</u> without defect, in which there is no blemish, and upon which a yoke has never come.

Literally, the underlined portion of the verse reads, "a heifer of red, a whole one which has no blemish in her which has no yoke lifted over her." The Hebrew poetry of the end of this verse is very beautiful - *lo alah aliyah al*. This heifer never wore a yoke, which means that it will be fat. The Hebrew word "mum" translated as "blemish" or "spot" is often thought to mean completely perfect as in without even one white hair on it. The actual meaning of the word can be seen in Deuteronomy 15:21; "And if there be any blemish (mum) therein, as if it be lame, or blind, or have any ill blemish, thou shall not sacrifice it unto the LORD thy God."

> 3 And you shall give her to Eleazar the priest, and she shall be taken outside the camp and slaughtered before him; 4 and Eleazar the priest shall take some of her blood with his finger, and sprinkle some of her blood toward the front of the tent of meeting seven times.

Portions of this procedure seem to be ritualistic in nature, such as the sprinkling of the blood seven times in the direction of the tabernacle. The number seven is often associated with an oath, because an oath was spoken seven times, probably to emphasize its importance. Ritual is always a part of everyday life, just as when we stand and salute the flag or pray before meals. These rituals are physical reminders to keep our focus on what is important. While this procedure is performed outside the camp, we are reminded that the focus is still the tabernacle. The following procedure is part of the oath or covenant between God and Israel:

> *5 And the heifer shall be burned in his sight;*
> *her skin, her flesh, and her blood, with her*
> *dung, shall be burned;*

In this verse, we have the burning of the skin, flesh, blood and dung of the animal. On a side note, the smoke from this and other sacrifices did repel insects which could carry diseases, a clear physical benefit to the sacrifices. There very well could have been chemical ingredients in the smoke from a burning animal that repelled insects far better than just wood smoke did:

> *6 and the priest shall take cedarwood and*
> *hyssop and scarlet stuff, and cast them into*
> *the midst of the burning of the heifer.*

Added to the fire were cedar wood, hyssop and a "scarlet thing." The cedar oil came from a kind of juniper tree that grew in both Israel and the Sinai. The cedar oil irritated the skin, encouraging the person to vigorously rub the solution into his hands. Hyssop oil contains 50% carvacrol, which is an antifungal and antibacterial agent still used in medicine. The "scarlet thing" was literally a scarlet worm or 'Coccus ilicis' (*kermes*), an insect used for dyeing (hence, used for the scarlet color), as well as for a medicine.

> *7 Then the priest shall wash his clothes and*
> *bathe his body in water, and afterwards he*
> *shall come into the camp; and the priest shall*
> *be unclean until evening. 8 He who burns the*
> *heifer shall wash his clothes in water and*
> *bathe his body in water, and shall be unclean*
> *until evening. 9 And a man who is clean shall*

> *gather up the ashes of the heifer, and deposit*
> *them outside the camp in a clean place; and*
> *they shall be kept for the congregation of the*
> *people of Israel for the water for impurity, for*
> *the removal of sin.*

The above ingredients, including cedar wood, ashes from the heifer, fat from the heifer, hyssop oil, and the scarlet worm, were combined with water and soap resulted. This soap was then stored (rested) in a clean place outside the camp as "water of filthiness."

> *10 And he who gathers the ashes of the heifer*
> *shall wash his clothes, and be unclean until*
> *evening. And this shall be to the people of*
> *Israel, and to the stranger who sojourns*
> *among them, a perpetual statute. 11 He who*
> *touches the dead body of any person shall be*
> *unclean seven days; 12 he shall cleanse*
> *himself with the water on the third day and on*
> *the seventh day, and so be clean; but if he*
> *does not cleanse himself on the third day and*
> *on the seventh day, he will not become clean.*

One who had been in contact with a dead body (i.e.: potential carrier of diseases received from the dead body) was first removed from the camp and taken outside to the place of the "water of filthiness" and then was washed with the above solution. Germs from a dead human body are more dangerous to another human than germs from an animal's body, because of the likelihood of transmission of disease and infection. The ingredients of this soap would be very useful in eliminating diseases that one could come in contact with from a dead body.

God promises that if we follow his teachings (*Torah*), we will be free from diseases. The above commands of the *Torah* will do just this. The ancient Hebrews may not have understood the scientific benefit to the "water of filthiness" as we can see today, but through their faith and observance of the teachings, they were made "clean."

Numbers 21:19

Ba'al, written as בעל (ba'al) in Hebrew, is one of the gods in the Canaanite pantheon. A large library discovered in the ancient Canaanite city of Ebla revealed much about their pantheon. The principal god of Ebla was Dagan and is referred to in the Eblaite texts as "Lord of Canaan," "Lord of the land" and "Lord of the gods." He is also mentioned several times in the Hebrew Bible (see Judges 16:23) where it is spelled דגון (dagon):

> And they have not cried unto me with their heart, but they howl upon their beds: they assemble themselves for grain and new wine; they rebel against me." (Hosea 7:14, ASV)

The Hebrew word for "grain" is דגן (dagan), which means "grain," but is also the name of the Canaanite god "Dagan," the god of grain. The Hebrew word for "wine" is תירוש (tirosh), which means "wine," but is also documented in the Eblaite tablets as the name of the Canaanite goddess Tirosh, the goddess of wine. With this new understanding of these words, we can read the end of the above verse as, "they assemble themselves to Dagan and Tirosh; they rebel against me."

> "Before him went the pestilence, and burning coals went forth at his feet." (Habakkuk 3:5, KJV)

The Hebrew word for "burning coals" is רשׁף (resheph), a noun meaning "flame," but is also the name of a Canaanite god, Resheph, which is found in Ugarit and now Eblaite texts. The Hebrew word for "pestilence" is דבר (daber) and it was not until it was discovered in the Eblaite texts that daber/dabir was known as one of the gods of Ebla. Knowing that these two words are in fact the names of Canaanite gods, the text can be translated as, "Before him went Resheph, and Daber went forth at his feet."

Numbers 22:22

The Hebrew word שׂטן (satan) appears 27 times in the Hebrew Bible and is a noun meaning an "adversary," one who stands against another. The following are different translations for Numbers 22:22. Note that in each case this noun is translated as "adversary:"

> And God's anger was kindled because he went: and the angel of the LORD stood in the way for an <u>adversary</u> against him. Now he was riding upon his ass, and his two servants were with him. (King James Version)

> And God's anger was kindled because he went; and the angel of Jehovah placed himself in the way for an <u>adversary</u> against him. Now he was riding upon his ass, and his two servants were with him. (English Standard Version)

> and the anger of God burneth because he is going, and a messenger of Jehovah stationeth himself in the way for an <u>adversary</u> to him, and he is riding on his ass, and two of his servants {are} with him, (Young's Literal Translation)

Some translations will treat this word as a proper name and transliterate it as "Satan," but not all do. Compare the different translations for Job 1:6:

> *Now there was a day when the sons of God came to present themselves before the LORD, and <u>Satan</u> came also among them.* (King James Version)

> *Now it came to pass on the day when the sons of God came to present themselves before Jehovah, that <u>Satan</u> also came among them.* (English Standard Version)

> *And the day is, that sons of God come in to station themselves by Jehovah, and there doth come also the <u>Adversary</u> in their midst.* (Young's Literal Translation)

In Job 1:6, the Hebrew word is written as השטן (*hasatan*). The prefix ה (*ha*) means "the" and is never used for a proper name, only a noun or verb, so in this verse, the word *hasatan* cannot be a proper name (Satan) and can only be a noun: an adversary.

2 Samuel 24 and 1 Chronicles 21 are parallel chapters recording the same events. Compare the first verse of each of these chapters:

> *And again, <u>the anger of the LORD</u> was kindled against Israel, and he moved David against them to say, Go, number Israel and Judah.* (2 Samuel 24:1)

> *And <u>Satan</u> stood up against Israel, and provoked David to number Israel.* (1 Chronicles 21:1)

In the first verse we see that it isYHWH that moves David to do the census of Israel, but in the second verse, it is Satan, according to the translation. This is a contradiction and the only way to resolve the contradiction is to translate the Hebrew word *satan* as a noun (adversary) in 1 Chronicles 21:1. With this interpretation we can now see that YHWH is the adversary, not an entity named Satan. In the Bible we have other instances where YHWH has sent an adversary in Israel's path:

> But God's anger was kindled because he went; and the angel of the LORD took his stand in the way as his <u>adversary</u>. Now he was riding on the ass, and his two servants were with him. (Numbers 22:22 RSV)

> And the LORD raised up an <u>adversary</u> against Solomon, Hadad the Edomite; he was of the royal house in Edom. (1 Kings 11:14 RSV)

An entity named "Satan" does not exist in the Hebrew Bible; there are only "adversaries."

Deuteronomy 6:4

> <u>Hear</u>, O Israel: The <u>LORD</u> our <u>God</u> is <u>one</u> LORD: And you shall <u>love</u> the LORD your God with all your <u>heart</u>, and with all your <u>soul</u>, and with all your <u>might</u>. (RSV, Deuteronomy 6:4,5)

Hear

The Hebrew verb שמע (*Sh.M.Ah*) means "to hear," but with the Hebraic idea "to pay attention to what is being spoken and act upon it." When Israel "hears" the directions of God, they agree to act upon them (they obey his words). When God "hears" the pleas of Israel in bondage in Egypt, he acts upon them (he rescues Israel).

One

The use of the word "one" in this verse is commonly interpreted to mean that there is only "one" God. However, from a Hebraic perspective, the Hebrew word אחד (*ehhad*) can mean a "unit" within a unity. This verse is stating that YHWH is in unity with himself. A good example of this is the pillar of cloud by day and a pillar of fire by night. A cloud and fire are opposites—one provides coolness and shade and the other heat and light. Yet, they work together to preserve the people during the day and the night.

In modern-day Hebrew Bibles, this passage is written as follows.

שמ**ע** ישראל יהוה אלהינו יהוה אח**ד**

Notice that the *ayin* (ע), the last letter in the first word is written oversized, as is the *dalet* (ד), the last letter in the last word. When these two letters are placed together, they form the word עד (*eyd*) meaning "witness." In Judaism, the *sh'ma* (the name given to this verse, as it is the first word in this verse) is Israel's witness, their statement of faith, if you will.

However, these oversized letters are not found in any ancient scroll, such as found in the Dead Sea Caves. They first appear in the Masoretic Hebrew texts from 1,000 A.D. Whether the Masorites added them or not we don't know; in fact, the origin of these oversized letters is a mystery.

Even though these letters do not appear to have been in the original texts, they are still excellent teaching tools.

Deuteronomy 6:5

> *You shall love the LORD your God with all your heart and with all your soul and with all your might.* (Deuteronomy 6:5, ESV)

Heart

The Hebrew word for "heart" in this verse is the Hebrew word לבב (*levav*). Another Hebrew word meaning "heart" is the word לב (*lev*), which is derived from לבב (*levav*), and can be seen in the following passage:

> *I will rejoice in doing them good, and I will plant them in this land in faithfulness, with all my heart and all my soul.* (Jeremiah 32:41, ESV)

In our modern Western world, while we associate the "heart" with "emotions," in the Ancient Hebrew world the "heart" is associated with "thought," the "mind," and we can see this in the following passages:

> *The LORD saw that the wickedness of man was great in the earth, and that every intention of the thoughts of his heart was only evil continually.* (Genesis 6:5, ESV)

> *Oh, let the evil of the wicked come to an end, and may you establish the righteous—you who test the minds and hearts, O righteous God!* (Psalm 7:9, ESV)

In the latter verse, the Hebrew word לב (*lev*) is translated as "minds." The word "hearts" in this same verse is the Hebrew word כליה (*kilyah*), which means "kidneys," not "heart." While the "heart" is seen as the seat of thought in Hebrew philosophy, the "kidneys" are seen as the seat of emotion.

Soul

Just as our Modern Western view of the "heart" is very different from the Ancient Hebrew view, the same is true for the word "soul," a very misunderstood Hebrew concept.

When you hear the word "soul," your mind most likely interprets this as, "The principle of life, feeling, thought, and action in humans, regarded as a distinct entity separate from the body, and commonly held to be separable in existence from the body; the spiritual part of humans as distinct from the physical part." This is the dictionary definition of the English word "soul," but another definition of this English word is "a human being; person," and it is this definition that more closely relates to the Hebrew word נפש (*nephesh*), as seen in the following passage:

> *All the descendants of Jacob were seventy* <u>*persons*</u>*; Joseph was already in Egypt.* (Exodus 1:5, ESV)

However, the Hebrew word *nephesh* can also be used for a "creature:"

> *And God created great whales, and every living* <u>*creature*</u> *that moveth, which the waters brought forth abundantly, after their kind, and every winged fowl after his kind: and God saw that it was good.* (Genesis 1:21, KJV)

From the Hebraic perspective, the *nephesh* is the "whole of the person" (or creature), his body, mind, emotions, organs and character."

Character

While the English word "character" does not appear in any translation of the Bible, its concept can be found throughout it. In Hebrew thought, the "breath" is associated with one's character. It is what makes a person unique. It is his personality, flaws, triumphs, etc. The Hebrew word for "breath" is נשמה (*neshemah*). This word is derived from the Hebrew word שם (*shem*), which is usually translated as "name," but more literally means "character."

In our culture, a name is nothing more than an identifier and has no real meaning. However, in the Ancient Hebrew culture, names were chosen based on the "character" of the person. For instance, Adam named his wife *Hhawah* (Eve in English) because she was the "mother of all living" (Genesis 3:20) and the Hebrew word *hhawah* means "living." *No'ahh* (Noah in English) was named this because he would "bring comfort" and the Hebrew word *no'ahh* means "comfort."

In the Hebrew mind, the "breath" is much more than the exchange of air in the lungs; it is the person's character. One could say that Deuteronomy 6:5 is the "character" of a child of God.

While we are on the subject of "breath," there is another Hebrew word that can mean "breath," or "character," the Hebrew word רוח (*ru'ahh*). This word is frequently translated as "spirit," but literally means "wind," yet can also be used for the "wind/character" of God or the "wind/character" of man.

> *The earth was without form and void, and darkness was over the face of the deep. And the <u>Spirit</u> of God was hovering over the face of the waters.* (Genesis 1:2, ESV)

> *A man's <u>spirit</u> will endure sickness, but a crushed spirit who can bear?* (Proverbs 18:14, ESV)

Might

Now that we understand the words "heart" and "soul" from a Hebraic perspective, we can better interpret it as: "You shall love the LORD your God with all your <u>mind</u> and with all your <u>person</u>…"

Now let's take a look at the word "might." This is the Hebrew word מאד (*m'od*). To get an understanding of this word, let's take a look at how it is used in other passages:

> *And God saw everything that he had made, and behold, it was <u>very</u> good. And there was evening and there was morning, the sixth day.* (Genesis 1:31, ESV)

> *Thus the man increased <u>greatly</u> and had large flocks, female servants and male servants, and camels and donkeys.* (Genesis 30:43 , ESV)

> *A mixed multitude also went up with them, and very <u>much</u> livestock, both flocks and herds.* (Exodus 12:38, ESV)

> *"Only take care, and keep your soul <u>diligently</u>, lest you forget the things that your eyes have seen, and lest they depart from your heart all the days of your life. Make them known to your children and your children's children—* (Deuteronomy 4:9, ESV)

As you can see, this word is almost always used as an adverb, but Hebrew words can play double duty. The same words used as adjectives, adverbs, prepositions, conjunctions, etc. can also be used as nouns. For instance, the Hebrew word עקב (*eqev*, Strong's #6119) is a noun meaning "heel" (see Genesis 3:15), but it is also used as a conjunction meaning "because" (but Strong's identifies this use of the word with #6118). A conjunction like the word "because" is used to identify the coming sentence or phrase as being on the "heel" of the previous sentence or verse:

> and in your offspring shall all the nations of the earth be blessed, <u>because</u> you have obeyed my voice. (Genesis 22:18, ESV)

So, the Hebrew word מאד (*m'od*) is normally used as an adverb meaning "much," "very," etc., but this word can also be used as a noun, such as in Deuteronomy 6:5, meaning… Well, there is no English equivalent, so the best we can do is create the word "muchness." What is our "muchness?" It is all of your possessions, resources and abilities.

Conclusion

What does it mean to "love the LORD your God with all your heart, with all your soul, and with all your might?" The Hebrew language loves to use parallelisms and will frequently repeat one idea two or more different ways. In the case of this verse, the words "heart," "soul" and "might" are being used as synonyms, each word increasingly more inclusive. First, the "heart," which is all your thoughts, then your "soul," which is your whole body, and then with your "muchness," which is everything you possess.

Deuteronomy 22:27

> *For he found her in the field, and the betrothed damsel cried, and there was none to <u>save</u> her.* (Deuteronomy 22:27, KJV)

The Hebrew word translated as "save" is מושיע (*moshi'a*), the hiphil participle of the verb ישע (Y.Sh.A). Most of the time, this word is translated as "savior" or "deliverer" (see Isaiah 43:11) and Deuteronomy 22:27 could better be translated as;

> *For he found her in the field, and the betrothed damsel cried, and there was no <u>savior</u> for her.*

Many who are embracing the Hebrew language of the Bible often use the Hebrew words for key Biblical words instead of the English. Some examples are, *shalom, ruach hakodesh, kehilat, Torah,* and many more. While I believe this to be a great idea, I often see some errors in how the Hebrew is applied.

A common mistake is made with the word "savior." If you look up this word in a concordance, you will find that this word is #3467 in *Strong's Dictionary* and is identified as the Hebrew word ישה that is transliterated as *yasha*. Because of this, many believe the Hebrew word *yasha* means "savior" and this is not true. The word ישה (Y.Sh.Ah) is a simple verb meaning "to deliver." When the letters י, ו and מ are added to the verb, a more complex verb is formed, specifically a *hiphil* participle verb. The *hiphil* verb is causative and means "cause to deliver." The participle is a verb of present or continuous action meaning "delivering." A *hiphil* participle verb combines both of these, meaning "causing to deliver."

In Biblical Hebrew there is a fine line between verbs and nouns and both can be used to describe an action or a person, place or thing. The word מושיע (*moshia)* can be used in the sense of an action, as in Deuteronomy 28:29 where it is translated as "save" but literally means "causing to be delivered." The same word can be used as a noun, as in Isaiah 43:11 where it is translated as "savior," but literally means "one who is causing to be delivered."

The word *moshia* (as a noun) is generally translated two different ways as shown below:

> *I, I am the LORD, and besides me there is no savior.* (RSV, Isaiah 43:11)

> *But when the people of Israel cried to the LORD, the LORD raised up for them a deliverer, Ehud, the son of Gera.* (RSV, Judges 3:15)

As the words "savior" and "deliverer" are the same Hebrew word, there appears to be a contradiction between these two verses. If God is the only savior, how can there be another savior such as Ehud? A good understanding of what the word *moshia* means is critical to proper interpretation of the Hebrew Bible. As the verb *moshia* is a *hiphil* verb meaning "to cause to be delivered," we can see that God is one who "causes to be delivered" and this can be done by the hand of God himself or by sending another to be the agent of the deliverance. Israel's deliverance is caused by God, the one and only *moshia*, who sent Ehud.

There is one other point to make concerning the word *moshia*. Remember that this verb/noun is written in the participle form. God is not one who has delivered (past tense) and he is not the one who will deliver (future tense). He is the one who "IS DELIVERING" (present tense).

Deuteronomy 32:8

When the Most High gave to the nations their inheritance, When he separated the children of men [Hebrew: Adam], He set the bounds of the peoples According to the number of the children of Israel. (Deuteronomy 32:8, ASV)

In the Hebrew Masoretic text, the Hebrew for "children of Israel" is *b'nei yisra'el*, literally meaning "sons of Israel." If we are honest with the text, this really does not make sense, as the "sons of Israel" did not exist at the time that these nations were being formed and separated. However, in the Dead Sea Scrolls we find *b'nei Elohim*, which means "sons of *Elohim*." It is pretty clear that the writers of the Masoretic text revised this passage and changed it from "sons of *Elohim*" to "sons of Israel." Why? Because the use of "sons of *Elohim*" implies a non-Monotheistic view of the Bible, so it was revised to be more Monotheistic friendly. As the evidence suggests, the Masorites edited this verse and opened up the possibility that they may have edited other verses as well, something to keep in mind as we continue our investigations into the text of the Hebrew Bible.

According to the above passage, *Elyon* (by the way, just in case you didn't notice, this is not YHWH) divided up the nations and set boundaries (borders) around them. These nations were "numbered" according to the "sons of *Elohim*." Genesis chapter 10, commonly referred to as the "Table of Nations," lists the nations descended from Noah through his three sons: Shem, Ham and Japheth. The total number of nations in this list is seventy.

In 1928 the ancient city of Ugarit was discovered in Syria. The height of the Ugaritic civilization was around the 12th Century BCE, making them contemporaries with the Israelites. Also, the religion and language of the Ugarit people are very similar to that of the Israelites. Excavations of the site revealed an ancient library filled with clay tablets. One such tablet states that *El Elyon* had seventy sons (the *Elim*) and each son was allocated to a specific people. Many of these sons of *El* are mentioned by name, including *El* of *Shaddai* and *El* of *Beriyt*.

Can you see the close parallels between Deuteronomy 32:8, Genesis 10 and the Ugarit tablets? According to these sources, *Elyon* divided up all the nations into seventy nations, one for each of his sons (*Elim*). Not a very monotheistic view of *Elohim,* is it?

Names

Aaron

Its etymology or roots make it difficult to determine the meaning of the Hebrew name Aharon (pronounced *a'ha'ron*). Many different possibilities have been proposed in many different dictionaries, some of which are: "lofty," "mountaineer," "mountain of strength," "illuminator," "light bringer" and "teacher." There are two possible parent roots from which this name can come: אר (*ar*) and הר (*har*). The parent root אר (*ar*) is the root of the word אור (*owr*) meaning "light," hence, the possibilities of "illuminator," "light bringer" and "teacher" (as one who illuminates). The parent root הר (*har*) is the Hebrew word for "hill," "mountain" "and lofty." While we cannot say for certain which root is the origin of the name, its first occurrence in the Bible may provide a clue:

> Then the anger of the LORD was kindled against Moses and he said, 'Is there not Aaron, your brother, the Levite? I know that he can speak well; and behold, he is coming out to meet you, and when he sees you he will be glad in his heart' (RSV Exodus 4:14)

It is possible that the ideas of "speaking well" and "glad in the heart" could be indicative of Aaron's character as "bright."

Abram and Abraham

In the ancient world, it was customary for the lord to name those who are under him. Such is the case in Daniel chapter one where the chief official of King Nebuchadnezzar (identified as lord in 1:10) changed the names of four Hebrew slaves.

> *"Among these were some from Judah: Daniel, Hananiah, Mishael and Azariah. The chief official gave them new names: to Daniel, the name Belteshazzar; to Hananiah, Shadrach; to Mishael, Meshach; and to Azariah, Abednego."* (NIV, Daniel 1:6,7)

Several other times names are changed such as Abram and Sarai to Abraham and Sarah (Genesis 17:5,15) and Jacob to Israel (Genesis 32:28). The most common reason given for the change in a name is a change in the character of the individual, since, as we have seen, one's character is reflected in his name.

In the case of Abraham, this is not true for reasons that I will detail here. Abraham's original name is` אברם (av'ram) formed by combining the two words, אב (av) and רם (ram). God then changed this name to אברהם (av'ra'ham), also formed by combining two words, אב (av) and רהם (raham). The word אב (av) means "father" and is the first part of both names. The difference between the two names is the second syllable, from רם (ram) to רהם (raham). The word רם (ram) means "high," "lifted up" or "exalted." The word רהם (raham) is not found in the Bible except in this name only.

While no one is certain of the meaning of the second part to the name אברהם (av'ra'ham), scholars have proposed the meaning of "father of a great multitude" supposedly from combining the two words רב (rav), meaning "many" or "great," and הם (ham), meaning "multitude." To shorten הם רב (rav ham) into the word רהם (raham) is very unlikely, as dropping a consonant, such as the ב (b), completely removes the original meaning of the word and is not a practice in Hebrew word construction.

A more plausible explanation is that the word רהם (*raham*) is the original word, being a child root from the word רם (*ram*). Several other child roots are derived from רם including: ארם (*aram*), ראם (*ra'am*), הרם (*haram*), רום (*rum*) and ירם (*yaram*), all of which also mean "high" or "lifted up." From this, we can conclude that the child root רהם (*raham*) would have the same meaning as "high" or "lifted up."

If אברם (*av'ram*) and אברהם (*av'ra'ham*) both mean "father lifted up," the reason for the change in the name is not due to a change in the character of Abraham. What then would be the reason for the change in name?

In Genesis chapter one, God, the lord over all creation, gives the names to the creation including: the day and night (1:5), the sky (1:8) and the land and seas (1:10). In Genesis chapter two, Adam (a Hebrew word meaning "man") gives names to all of the animals, birds and beasts (2:21,22) and we are told that Adam will rule over these animals, birds and beasts (1:26, 28). Adam also names his wife (2:23) and we are told that he is to rule over her, as well (3:16). From this, we discover that in the Hebraic mind, the one who gives the name is the lord over the one has been given the name. This same scenario is repeated throughout the scriptures. The founder, or lord, of a city gives the name of the city; the father, lord of the family, gives names to his children; even the gods created by men are named by the men in the hopes of having lordship over the gods. We also see this in our original discussion of the name changes of the Hebrew slaves by the chief official of King Nebuchadnezzar, who now had lordship over them.

Abram was given his name by Terah, his father and lord. It is not until after the death of Terah that God changes Abram's name to Abraham, not because of a change of character in Abram, but because of a change in lordship. God is now claiming lordship over Abraham. Abraham does not name his son, but God himself does (Genesis 17:19), showing that God was the lord of Isaac from birth. Interestingly, out of the three patriarchs Abraham, Isaac and Jacob, Isaac is the only one named by God from birth and whose lifespan is the longest. Jacob was named by his father Isaac, but it was changed by God to Israel after the death of his father (Genesis 32:28 and 35:10).

Adam

We are all familiar with the name "Adam" as found in the book of Genesis, but what does it really mean? Let us begin by looking at its roots. This name is a child root derived from the parent דם (*dam*) meaning "blood." By placing the letter א in front of the parent root, the child root אדם (*adam*) is formed and is related in meaning to דם (*blood*).

By examining a few other words derived from the child root אדם, we can see a common meaning in them all. The Hebrew word אדמה (*adamah*) is the feminine form of אדם, meaning "ground" (see Genesis 2:7). The word/name אדום (*Edom*) means "red." Each of these words has the common meaning of "red." *Dam* is the "red" blood, *adamah* is the "red" ground, *edom* is the color "red", and *adam* is the "red" man. There is one other connection between "*adam*" and "*adamah*" as seen in Genesis 2:7, which states that "the adam" was formed out of the "*adamah*."

In the ancient Hebrew world, a person's name was not simply an identifier, but was also descriptive of one's character. As Adam was formed out of the ground with blood and breath, his name identifies his origin.

Adonai

Hebrew uses a root system of words, meaning that one root can be the foundation for many different words, but all of those words being related in meaning to the original root. As an example, the root בן (*ben*), meaning a son, is the root of אבן (*even*-stone), בנה (*banah*-build) and בינה (*binah*-understanding).

Also, Hebrew uses many different prefixes and suffixes. For instance, by adding the suffix ים (*iym*) to the word בן (*ben*), we have בנים (*beniym*) meaning "sons." Or by adding the *yud* suffix (י) to בן we have בני (*beniy*) meaning "my son."

The word "Adonai" is a very complex word filled with difficulties, controversy and confusion. But let's begin with the base word, the noun אדון (*adon*) (see Psalm 114:7).

This word means "lord" and is related to the noun אדן (*eden*-- not the same spelling as the garden of "*eden*"), which means a footing or base that sustains a stable position. This meaning of *eden* can help us understand *adon* as one who provides a firm base. Both *adon* and *eden* are derived from the parent root דן (*dan*) meaning "a judge" or "moderator."

As mentioned previously, the *nikkudot* are vowel pointings that are placed above and below the letters to identify the vowel sounds. In Psalm 114:7, the word *adon* is written as אָדֹון. The first *nikkud* is placed under the *aleph* and looks like a little "t." This mark represents the vowel "a." The second *nikkud* is a dot placed between the *dalet* and the *vav* and represents the vowel "o." It is very important to remember that these *nikkudot* were not in the original Hebrew text (such as seen in the Dead Sea Scrolls), but were invented by the Masorites about 1000 years ago in order to standardize the pronunciation of the words, and also to provide clarification of word meanings (in other words, define words according to their theology, as will be apparent below).

When the *yud* suffix (י - *iy*) is added to the word אָדוֹן (*adon*), it becomes אֲדֹנִי (*adoniy*) meaning "my lord" (see Genesis 23:6). Note that the *vav* is dropped, but the "o" vowel pointing is retained. This is very common in the Masoretic Hebrew text. While the Dead Sea Scrolls will have the *vav* in the word אדון (the letter *vav* often represents the vowel sound "o"), the Masorites dropped the *vav* and added the "o" vowel pointing to represent the "o" sound. Many of you are familiar with the word אֱלֹהִים (*elohiym*). Notice that there is a dot between the *lamed* and *hey* representing the "o." In the Dead Sea Scrolls, this word is usually written as אלוהים with the *vav*, which was apparently dropped by the Masorites and replaced with the dot.

Keep in mind that before the Masorites and the *nikkudot*, the word *adoniy* would simply be written as אדוני (with the *vav* intact and without the *nikkudot*).

The plural form of אדון (*adon*) is אדונים (*adoniym*, see 1 Kings 22:17) where it is written as אֲדֹנִים. Now, if you want to say "my lords," then you would drop the *mem* and the *yud* becomes "*ai*" (in contrast to the "*iy*") and is written as אֲדֹנַי (see Genesis 19:2).

Note that אֲדֹנִי (*adoniy* – my lord) has a dot under the *nun* for the "*i*" sound, but in אֲדֹנַי there is a line under the *nun* for the "*a*" sound.

As the original Hebrew text did not include these *nikkudot*, both *adoniy* and *Adonai* would be written as אדוני. So how would you know if אדוני was "my lord" or "my lords?" By the context, but sometimes the context is not clear and for this reason, the Masorites developed the *nikkudot* to clarify the words. In other words, they decided the context for you. And when the Masoretic text was translated into English, the translator followed the context set by the Masorites and your English translation follows their interpretation of the text.

There is one other twist to this whole subject and that is the spelling אֲדֹנָי instead of אֲדֹנַי (see Genesis 15:2). Whenever the word *adonai* was used for God, the Masorites changed the line (called a *patach*) under the *nun* with the little "t" (called a *qamats*). Again, the Masorites took upon themselves to determine if the word *adonai* is being used for mere men or for God. The English translators follow their decision by using "lord" for *adonai* with a *patach* or "Lord" for *adonai* with a *qamats*. (When LORD appears in all capitals, this is for יהוה - YHWH)

Why is the word Adonai, meaning "my lords" being used for God? While some may say this is a sign of the trinity, this is not the case. Hebrew will frequently use a plural word as a title. Even *Elohiym* is a plural word meaning "gods." But it is very important to understand that even while plural nouns are used, they do not always mean a plural, and other words used in the sentence will clarify this. For instance, Genesis 1:1 reads "*bereshiyt bara elohiym.*" While *elohiym* is plural, the word *bara* means "he created," identifying the *elohiym* as a singular.

Aramnaharaim

In Hebrew, the name Aramnaharaim is written as two words: ארם נהרים (*aram naharayim*). The word ארם (*aram*) is the name for the region of Aram, modern-day Syria. The inhabitants of Aram were the Arameans, and their language is called Aramean or Aramaic. This word is not used in the Bible as a noun, but it means "elevated," "a high place."

The word נהרים (*naharayim*) is the double plural (the standard plural suffix is *iym*, but the double plural suffix is *yim*) form of the noun נהר (*nahar*) meaning "river." So the double plural form, נהרים (*naharayim*), means "two rivers."

When these two words are combined they mean "the high place between the two rivers." The place of ארם נהרים (*aram naharayim*) is known today as Mesopotamia, which is Greek for "between (*meso*) the rivers (*potamia*)."

This name appears six times in the Hebrew Bible. In the King James Version of the Bible this name is transliterated as Aramnaharaim once (Psalm 60:1), but translated as Mesopotamia the other five times (Genesis 24:10, Deuteronomy 23:4, Judges 3:8,10 and 1 Chronicles 19:6).

Asher

> And Leah said, <u>Happy</u> am I, for the daughters will call me <u>blessed</u>: and she called his name <u>Asher</u>. (Genesis 30:13, KJV)

Within this verse are three words, all from the same root. The first is the word אושר (*osher*) meaning "happiness" and is translated "happy," as in the verse above. The second is the verb אשר (*A.Sh.R*) meaning "to be happy," but is translated as "blessed" above. The third is, of course, the name אשר (*asher*), pronounced *ah-sheyr* in Hebrew.

However, Hebrew word definitions are not always so simple. In the following verse, the same Hebrew verb אשר (*A.Sh.R*) is used where it is translated as "go":

> Enter not into the path of the wicked, and <u>go</u> not in the way of evil men. (Proverbs 4:14, KJV)

93

The verb אשר (*A.Sh.R*) literally means "to go in a straight line." This can be a literal meaning, such as in Proverbs 4:14 where the image being given is one walking straight toward evil. It can also be used in a figurative way as in Genesis 30:13 in the sense that if you are being straight (doing what is right), you will be happy.

Ashterot Qarnayim

The place name Ashterot Qarnayim only appears once in the Hebrew Bible, in this verse. The root of Ashterot (*ash-te-rot*) is *ashter* meaning "the young one of the flock." The "*ot*" is the feminine plural suffix and therefore means "young ones of the flock." Ashterot is the name of the Canaanite goddess mentioned in Judges 2:13, is Ishtar in the Babylonian mythology, and is the origin of the word "Easter."

The root of Qarnayim (*qar-nah-yim*) is *qeren*, a noun meaning "horn" and is the origin of our English word "crown." In ancient times a crown was made of "horns" and the pointed tips of the crowns we are familiar with today represent those horns. The *yim* suffix identifies this noun as a double plural and therefore means "two horns."

When the two words Ashterot Qarnayim are combined, we have the meaning: "the young ones of the flock of the two horns."

Babel

To most people the name *Bavel* (or Babel) is known to us only as the name of the city where God confounded the languages:

> *Therefore its name was called Babel, because*
> *there the LORD confused the language of all*
> *the earth; and from there the LORD scattered*
> *them abroad over the face of all the earth.*
> (Genesis 11:9)

Whenever a Hebrew name is given in the text and followed by the word "because," the text is providing the connection between the name and the reason for the name. In this case the word "confused" is the Hebrew word בלל (*balal*) meaning to be mixed up, and it was here that God "mixed up" the languages. Interestingly, the name בבל (*babel*) is a mixing up of the letters from the word בלל (*balal*).

While we may only be familiar with this place name as Babel as found in Genesis, this name is used 262 times throughout the Biblical text. But, instead of translating this name the same way all the time, the translators have chosen to translate it as "Babylon" in all its other occurrences. Yes, Babel and Babylon are one and the same place; Babylon is the place of confusion.

In our English language, we also have the word "babble" meaning "To utter a meaningless <u>confusion</u> of words or sounds," a clear connection between Hebrew and English.

Benjamin

> *And it came to pass, as her soul was departing*
> *(for she died), that she called his name <u>Ben-</u>*
> *<u>oni</u>: but his father called him <u>Benjamin</u>.*
> (Genesis 35:18, ASV)

The twelfth son of Jacob was first named בן אוני (*ben oni*) by his mother Rachel. The name Ben-Oni is the word בן (*ben*) meaning "son" and the word אוני is the word און (*ohn* or *avon*) meaning "vanity," or more literally, "the effort that is put out with no results," with the suffix י (*i*) meaning "of me" or "my." The name אוני בן then means "son of my vanity" and appears to be Rachel's final words, which implies that her son, who is brought forth through much effort, would bring her life to an end.

Jacob gave a different name to his son: בנימין (*binyamin*). This is again the word בן (*ben*) meaning son, combined with the word ימין (*yamin*) meaning "right hand." The name בנימין then means "son of the right hand." When a father blessed the eldest son, he would place his right hand upon his head when giving him his blessing (see Genesis 48:18). As Binyamin is Ya'akov's youngest son, it would seem strange to call him the "son of the right hand," unless he is to be treated as the firstborn son. When it came time to divide up the family estate among the sons, the father would give a "double portion" to the firstborn. In Genesis 43:34 we see Yoseph giving Binyamin a portion "five times" as much as his brothers.

Cainan

The name Cainan in Hebrew is קינן (*qeynan*). This is not the same name Canaan, the son of Hham, which is כנען (*kena'an*). The name Qeynan comes from the verbal root קנן (*qanan*), literally meaning "to make a nest." This verbal root is derived from the parent root קן (*qeyn*) meaning a "nest."

Canaan

The name Canaan refers to the son of Ham, the son of Noah, as well as to the descendants of Canaan who settled the land west of the Jordan River. The Hebrew for this name is כנען

pronounced *kena'an*. It is derived from the root כנע (*Kena*) meaning "to be brought down by a heavy load." By extension, this word can also mean "subdue" or "humble." Canaan and his descendants are continually being "brought down." Canaan was cursed by Noah, and his descendants were subdued and conquered by Israel as God had promised in Deuteronomy 9:3:

> Know therefore this day, that Jehovah thy God
> is he who goeth over before thee as a
> devouring fire; he will destroy them, and he
> will <u>bring</u> them <u>down</u> before thee: so shalt
> thou drive them out, and make them to perish
> quickly, as Jehovah hath spoken unto thee.
> (ASV)

The phrase "Bring down" is the Hebrew word כנע (*Kena*) in the context of the conquest of the Canaanites. God used Israel to "bring down low" (*Kena*) the people who are "brought down low" (*Kena'an*).

The word כנען (*kena'an*) can also mean a "merchant" as in Hosea 12:7 (verse 8 in the Hebrew Bible). This may be because a merchant is one who carries heavy loads or it may be that the people of *Kena'an* were frequently merchants.

Dan

> And Rachel said, God hath <u>judged</u> me, and
> hath also heard my voice, and hath given me a
> son: therefore called she his name <u>Dan</u>.
> Genesis 30:6 (KJV)

The Hebrew verb דין (*D.Y.N*) means "to judge", as we can see in the verse above. This is the root of the name דן (*dan*), meaning a "judge," also found in the verse above. In Jacob's final words to Dan, he also made the connection between these two words:

> *Dan shall judge his people, as one of the tribes of Israel.* Genesis 49:16 (KJV)

Eber

Abraham is the first person called a Hebrew (Genesis 14:13) in the Biblical text. What does the name Hebrew mean and where does it come from? Abraham's fifth great grandfather was *Ever* (or Eber).

> *And Arpakshad bore Shalach who bore Ever (Genesis 10:24).*

The Hebrew spelling of the word Hebrew is עברי (*eevriy*) and the Hebrew spelling of Ever is עבר. When the letter י (*y*) is placed after a name it means "one belonging to the family of..." and in this case, a Hebrew is one who belongs to the family of Ever. By definition, a Hebrew is one who is descended from Ever and this would include Abraham, as well as his brothers Nahor and Haran. While the lineage's of Nahor and Haran seem to disappear, probably being absorbed into other cultural groups, only Abraham and his descendants remain Hebrews to this day.

The root עבר means to "cross over" or "pass through." As names play a very significant role of the ancient peoples of the Near East, this name with its meaning is indicative of Abraham and his descendants. Abraham, Isaac and Jacob were nomads who, by definition, are ones who travel or pass through many lands on their nomadic journey:

"And Abram passed through the land unto the place of Sichem, unto the plain of Moreh. And the Canaanite was then in the land." (Genesis 12:6, KJV)

The phrase "passed through" is the Hebrew verb עבר (the same word as the noun/name *Ever*).

Egypt

In almost every case, the name of a person or place in the Bible by which we know it is a transliteration of the Hebrew. For instance, the English "Jerusalem" is from the Hebrew *Yerushalem*, Israel from *Yisra'el*, and Methuselah from *Metushelach*. However, this is not the case with Egypt. The Hebrew word for Egypt is מצרים (*mitsrayim / meets-rah-yeem*). The first occurrence of this name is in Genesis 10:6:

> And the sons of Ham; Cush, and Mizraim *(mitsrayim), and Phut, and Canaan.* (KJV)

Mizraim is the grandson of Noah, and evidently settled in the land that came to be known as *Mitsrayim* to the Hebrews, and Egypt to us today.

The root of this name is צר (*tsar*) meaning "pressed in" and can be translated several different ways: "enemy" as one who presses in, "trouble" as a pressing in, "straight" as a canyon with the walls pressing in. A common method of forming nouns out of a Hebrew root is to add the letter *mem* (מ) to the front of a root. In this case, the *mem* is placed before the root forming the noun מצר (*metsar*). The prefixed *mem* can be understood as "what is...," hence *metsar* means "what is pressed in" and is usually translated as "trouble" or "straits."

The suffix of the name *mitsrayim* is the masculine plural suffix ים (*yeem*), which is the double plural suffix.

The name *mitsrayim* can be interpreted in many different ways: "two straits" (possibly referring to the two sides of the Nile river), "double straits," "two enemies," "double pressing," or even "double trouble." While we cannot determine for certain what this name originally meant, we can see some interesting parallels between Egypt and their relationship with the nation of Israel.

Elo'ah

The Hebrew word אלוה (*elo'ah*) is used 57 times in the Hebrew Bible and is almost always translated as "God." The parent root of this word is the word אל (*el*), which is also often translated as "God." While this word is frequently used in the Bible as a descriptor of YHWH, it is also used for anything of "might."

Derived from this parent root is the child root אלה (*A.L.H*) and means "to take an oath" or to "swear." Our word אלוה (*elo'ah*) is derived from this child root and more literally means "The one of the oath."

The "yoke," which is used to bind two oxen together, is a perfect illustration of an oath. It was common to pair a younger inexperienced ox with an older more experienced one and the younger one would learn from the older one. When the Israelites entered into an "oath" relationship with YHWH, they were the younger inexperienced ox being yoked to the more mature one: YHWH.

The plural form of אלה (*A.L.H*) is אלהים (*elohiym*). *Elohiym* is a plural noun identified by the *iym* suffix that is often translated as "God," "god" and "gods." I should note that plural words in Hebrew do not always work the same way they do in English, and a plural noun can be used in a singular sense.

Enoch

> *And Jared lived an hundred sixty and two years, and he begat Enoch:* (Genesis 5:18, KJV)

The name חנוך (*hhanokh*) means "dedicated" and is derived from the verb root חנך (*Hh.N.Kh*) meaning "to dedicate."

Genesis chapter five is the only place in the Tenakh (Old Testament) where Enoch is mentioned. However, the New Testament mentions him three times (Luke 3:37, Hebrews 11:5 and Jude 1:14). In Jude we read:

> *And Enoch also, the seventh from Adam, prophesied of these, saying, Behold, the Lord cometh with ten thousands of his saints.* (Jude 1:14, KJV)

Enoch's prophecy is not found in the Tenakh, but is found in "The Book of Enoch," a work that had been lost long ago, but was recently discovered in the 17th century and is included in the Pseudepigrapha.

Enosh

The name in Hebrew is אנוש (*enosh*), meaning "man." This word/name comes from the root אנש (*A.N.Sh*) meaning "mortal", in the sense of weak and sick. The word/name *enosh* is closely related to the Hebrew word איש (*iysh*), also meaning "man."

Gad

> *And Zilpah Leah's maid bare Jacob a son. And Leah said, <u>A troop cometh</u>: and she called his name <u>Gad</u>.* (Genesis 30:10,11, KJV)

The Hebrew word translated as "a troop cometh" is בגד (*begad*), which is the noun גד (*gad*) meaning "fortune" and the prefix ב (*be*) meaning "in." So, בגד (*begad*) means "in fortune." Then how does the King James Version get "a troop cometh" out of "in fortune?" First, the KJV translators created their translation almost 400 years ago. Since that time much more of the Hebrew language has been learned through etymology and linguistics and, while it was thought that גד (*gad*) meant "troop," we now know that it means "fortune." Second, many translators believe that the word בגד (*begad*) is an error and was originally written as two words: בא גד (*bo gad*) meaning "fortune (originally "troop") comes." Leah chose the word גד (*gad*) for her son because of her good "fortune" of having been given another son.

I would also like to point out that the name of the Babylonian god of fortune is the Aramaic word "*gad*." The Aramaic and Hebrew vowel "a" is not pronounced like the "a" in "bad," but like the "a" in "ball." Therefore, the Hebrew and Aramaic word/name "*gad*" is pronounced like our English word "god." It is very likely that our word "god" comes from the word גד (*gad*).

Ishmael

The name Ishmael, written in Hebrew as ישמעאל (*yish-ma-el*), is composed of three parts: י (*yi*), שמע (*sh'ma*) and אל (*el*). The word שמע (*sh'ma*) is a verb literally meaning "to listen," but can also mean "to obey" or more correctly "to respond."

This word is the title of the "sh'ma," the Jewish affirmation of faith found in Deuteronomy 6:4 that states: "sh'ma Yisra'el YHWH eloheynu YHWH echad" or, as it is normally translated, "Hear, O, Israel, the Lord our God, the Lord is one." The use of the word "sh'ma" in this verse is stating "hear and respond" to YHWH. When the letter י (yi) is prefixed to a verb, it identifies the subject of the verb as the third person, masculine and singular or "he." Therefore, the phrase ישמע (yishma) would mean "he listens." The final word is אל (el) meaning "mighty one," or as it is usually translated: "God." In Hebrew sentence structure the noun following the verb is the subject of the verb, or in this case, the "he" of "he listens." When these three components are combined into the sentence ישמע אל (yishma el), the sentence means "God listens."

Israel

The name ישראל (yisra'el) has been translated several different ways including "he wrestles with God," "Prince of God," "he struggles with God," and several others. The name "Israel" is actually a complete sentence in one word. The name has three components: י (yi), שר (sr) and אל (el). The י (y) is a prefix meaning "he." The אל (el) is the Hebrew word for "God." The שר (sr) is the part that seems to cause most of the problems in translation.

The Hebrew word שר (sr) literally means "turn the head." It is often translated as "prince" or "ruler," one who turns the head of the people. Another word related to שר (sr) is ישר (yasar) meaning "discipline." When you discipline your children, you are turning their head from a path of bad to a path of good.

Because the י (y) is in front of the word שר (sr), we know that this is a verb and not a noun (this is standard Hebrew grammar), and the name ישראל (*yisra'el*) can literally be translated as "he turns the head of God." The way I like to understand this is that when Israel (either Jacob or his descendants) speaks to God, God, the father of Israel, stops what he is doing and turns to his son and says "What do you want, my son."

Issachar

> *And Leah said, God hath given me my <u>hire</u>, because I have given my maiden to my husband: and she called his name <u>Issachar</u>.* (Genesis 30:18, KJV)

From an etymological perspective, the name יִשָּׂשכָר (*yis-sakhar*) is one of the more difficult names for which to ascertain both its pronunciation and its meaning. This name is written as יִשָּׂשכָר in the Masoretic Hebrew text. The first ש (the letter *shin*) includes the dot on the top left, indicating that it is pronounced with an "s" (if the dot were on the right it would be pronounced with a "sh"). There is also a dot inside this letter (called a *dagesh*) which doubles its sound. Therefore, the first two letters in this name are pronounced "*yis-sa...*" The second ש is a little problematic, as it does not have a dot on top (the letter *shin* always carries the dot, either on the left or the right to indicate its pronunciation as "s" or "sh"). This unusual use of the letter *shin* is a mystery with no etymological answer. The standard pronunciation of the name is *yis-sa-khar*, and the second *shin* is simply ignored as if it were spelled יִשָּׂכָר.

The second problem with this name is its meaning. It may be a form of the Hebrew word יִשְׂכָר (*yis-kor*) meaning "he will hire." However, this meaning ignores the second *shin* found in the name יִשָּׂשכָר. We must also remember that the dots and dashes added above, below and inside Hebrew letters (called *nikkud* in the singular and *nikkudot* in the plural) are a fairly recent invention and were not included in the original spelling of Hebrew words. Therefore, if we take the name as it was written: יששכר, other possible interpretations are possible. The first is the combination of two words, יש and שכר. The word יש (*yeysh*) means "there is." There are two possible translations of the word שכר. One is "liquor" (*sha-khar*), giving us the meaning of יששכר as "there is liquor." The other possibility is "wage" (*sa-khar*) giving us the meaning "there is a wage."

Jared

The Hebrew name ירד (*yered*), Romanized as Jared, comes from the verbal root ירד (*Y-R-D*) meaning "to go down." The name ירד (*yered*) means "descent," a going down.

Joseph

> *And she called his name Joseph; and said, The LORD shall add to me another son.* (Genesis 30:24, KJV)

In the verse above, the Hebrew verb יסף (*Y.S.P*) means "to add." The participle form of a verb is created by adding the vowels "o" and "e" between the three letters of the verb root. So, the participle form of יסף (*Y.S.P*) is יוסף (*yoseph*). A participle is usually translated into English by adding the suffix "ing" to the meaning of the root. So, while יסף (*Y.S.P*) means "add," the participle form יוסף (*yoseph*) means "adding." This participle form is the name יוסף (*yoseph*), which of course means, "adding."

Judah

This name is pronounced "*ye-huw-dah*" in Hebrew. Most Hebrew dictionaries define this word as "praise," but, as this English word is an abstract word, it falls short of its true Hebraic meaning. The parent root of this word is יד (*yad*) meaning "hand." Derived from this parent root is the child root ידה (*Y.D.H*) meaning "throw," and this child root is the root of the name "*yehudah*." The word "Yehudah" has the meaning "to throw your hands out." If you were standing on the rim of the Grand Canyon for the first time, you might throw your hands out and say "Wow, will you look at that." This is the Hebraic understanding of "praise."

When Judah was born to Leah (Genesis 29:35), she said, "I will '*yadah*' YHWH." She was pointing to YHWH and giving him the credit for the birth of her son. We frequently use the word "praise" in the context of worship to God. Our praise is not meant to be simply singing or praying to God, but acting upon on our belief. Our function is to point to God so that others can see him. This pointing does not have to be a literal pointing, but that in all aspects of our life our actions point to God and others will see him, as well.

Lamech

This is one of the names in the Bible that is very difficult to translate. The root of this word, למך (*L.M.K*), is not used anywhere in the Biblical text and, therefore, it is impossible to determine the meaning of this root/word/name with any degree of accuracy. One possible interpretation is that this name is the verb מוך (*mok*) meaning "low," with the, prefixed letter ל (l) meaning "to" – "to be low." Other suggested meanings for this root/word/name are "powerful," "robust," and "priest."

Levi

> *And she conceived again, and bare a son; and said, Now this time will my husband be <u>joined</u> unto me, because I have born him three sons: therefore was his name called <u>Levi</u>.* Genesis 29:34 (KJV)

The Hebrew verb לוה (*lavah*) means "to join" such as we see in the verse above. This is the root of the name לוי (*leviy*), meaning "joined," and is also found in the verse above. Both of these words are also found in the following verse:

> *And thy brethren also of the tribe of <u>Levi</u>, the tribe of thy father, bring thou with thee, that they may be <u>joined</u> unto thee, and minister unto thee: but thou and thy sons with thee shall minister before the tabernacle of witness.* Numbers 18:2 (KJV)

Mahalaleel

In Hebrew, this name is written as מהללאל (*ma-ha-la-ley-eyl*) and is a combination of two words, מהלל (*ma-ha-leyl*) and אל (*eyl*). The root of מהלל is הלל (*ha-lal*) and means "to shine." This can be the shining of a light, such as from a flame or the moon, but figuratively can be the shining of a person's character, such as his fame or pride. From this root comes the word מהלל (*ma-ha-lal*), meaning "shining" or "one who shines."

The second word is אל (*eyl*), which literally means "mighty one," but is often transliterated as "God." The meaning of the name מהללאל can be "the shining of *El*" or "the shining one of *El*."

Manasseh

> *Joseph called the name of the first-born Manasseh, "For," he said, "God has made me forget all my hardship and all my father's house."* (RSV, Genesis 41:51)

The name Manasseh is written as מנשה (*me'na'sheh*). This name/word comes from the root נשה (*N.Sh.H*) meaning to "forget" and is the root of the name/word *me'na'sheh* meaning "forgotten."

Methuselah

In Hebrew this name is מתושלח and is pronounced "*meh-tu-sheh-lahh*" (the "*hh*" is pronounced hard like the "*ch*" in the name "*Bach*"). This name is a combination of two words: *metu* and *shelahh*. *Strong's Dictionary* (#4968) states that this name means "man of the dart." According to Strong's, the root for "*metu*" is the word "*mat*" (#4962), which means "man," and the word "*shelach*" (#7973), which means a "weapon" or "missile," hence the translation of "dart."

But there is another possible meaning for this name. The word "*metu*" may be derived from the word "*mot*" meaning "death" and the "u" is a suffix that means "their" - "their death." There is no way to know for certain if the final vowel in "*metu*" was an "*o*" or an "*u*," as the vowel pointings that make that distinction are of fairly recent origin. If it was originally an "*o*," then the suffix would change to "his" - "his death."

The word *shelach* (missile or weapon) is the noun form of the verb *shalach* meaning "to send" (a missile or weapon that is sent). *Shelach* has the more literal meaning of "to send something."

We now have the possible meaning of "their death sends" or "his death sends." Sounds like an incomplete sentence doesn't it? Well, it is interesting to note that the year Methuselah died something very big was sent: the Flood. Methuselah's name may be a prophecy that on the day of his death, "his death will send" the Flood.

Moab

This name is pronounced "*mo-ahv*" in Hebrew. The base word is "*ahv*" meaning "father." The prefix "*mo*" means "from." Combined these mean "from father." Mo'av was the son of Lot's oldest daughter and Lot himself (Genesis 19:35), the product of an incestuous relationship.

According to the *Torah*, no descendent of Mo'av is allowed in the assembly of Israel (Deuteronomy 23:3). Why does God not allow this? Character traits are passed down from generation to generation and the Moabites had passed down the character trait of incest through its generations, strictly forbidden in *Torah*.

If no Moabite is allowed into the assembly, why was Ruth, a Moabitess, allowed in the assembly of Israel?

An Ancient Hebraic understanding of what a "descendant" is, is important for understanding this apparent contradiction. While a descendant is one who is physically descended from a group of people, it can also be used for one who holds the character of a group of people. In Jeremiah 23:14, God saw Israel as Sodom and Gomorrah, not because they were physically descended from the inhabitants of Sodom and Gomorrah, but because their actions were the same as those in Sodom and Gomorrah.

Ruth was a Moabitess but was allowed in the assembly of Israel because she was no longer considered a Moabitess. Her character had been changed to become like Israel when she said "your God will be my God and your people will be my people." Ruth had become an Israelite through her actions, leaving behind the character of the Moabites.

Molech

Molech was the name of the chief god within the Ammonite (another Semitic nation) pantheon. In Hebrew, this name is written as מלך /מולך (molekh). This word is a derived form of the verb מלך (M.L.K) meaning "to rule." The name Molekh is the participle form of this verb and can mean "ruling" or "ruler." Other than the participle molekh, there is another way to say "ruler" or "king" and that is with the noun (melekh), which is also derived from the verb מלך (M.L.K).

Moses

The name Moses is written in the Hebrew Bible as משה (mosheh). This name is derived from the Hebrew verb משה (M.Sh.H) meaning "to draw out." Mosheh was named such because the Pharaoh's daughter "drew him out of the water" (see Exodus 2:10).

How did the name Mosheh become Moses? Most names in English Bibles are derived from the Greek Septuagint (a 2,000 year old Greek translation of the Hebrew Bible) and not from the Hebrew Bible itself. In the Septuagint, this name is written as Μωυσῆς (Moses).

Naphtali

> *And Rachel said, With great <u>wrestlings</u> have I wrestled with my sister, and I have prevailed: and she called his name <u>Naphtali</u>.* Genesis 30:8 (KJV)

The Hebrew word translated as "wrestlings" in the verse above is נפתול (*naphtul*) meaning "to entwine," as when twisting cords together to make a rope, or to be entwined together through wrestling. The name Naphtali is this same word with a י (*y*) suffix meaning "my," so the name Naphtali means 'my wrestling.'

Nimrod

The name Nimrod is not Hebrew but it is a Semitic name and is therefore closely related to Hebrew. The name comes from the Semitic root מרד (*M.R.D*) meaning "to rebel." In the Ancient Hebrew/Semitic cultures a person's name was closely related to their character, and, therefore, Nimrod's name fits well with his personality.

Nimrod is only mentioned in Genesis 10:8 & 9 but these two passages speak volumes about the character of Nimrod. The standard translation for verse 9 is something like *"He was a mighty hunter before the LORD; therefore, it is said, 'Like Nimrod a mighty hunter before the LORD.'"* It would appear that there is nothing out of the ordinary about Nimrod. So, why is he so often seen as such an evil person?

Only two persons in the Bible are identified as "hunters," Nimrod and Esav, the twin brother of Ya'aqov. From the story of Esav and Ya'aqov we know that Esav was not the most respectful person. Not only did he despise his birthright, but to spite his parents, married foreign women. From this, we could conclude that from a Hebraic perspective, hunters are seen in a negative light. In verse 8 it states "*he was the first on earth to be a mighty man.*" The Hebrew phrase may also be translated as "he made a profaning by being a mighty one in the land." To add to this, verse 9 states that he was a "mighty hunter 'before' YHWH." The word for "before" in Hebrew is "*liph'ney*" and literally means "to the face of" and in this case "to the face of YHWH" and can mean that he was a mighty hunter in place of YHWH, implying that he, rather than YHWH, is the provider for the people.

One final clue into the character into the personality of Nimrod is how the Semitic root MRD has been used even into our own time. The Ancient Semitic root מרד (*M.R.D*) is the origin of our words MaRauDer and MuRDer.

Noah

In Hebrew the name Noah is pronounced *No'ahh* (the "*hh*" is pronounced hard like the "*ch*" in the name Bach) and is written נוח (*no'ahh*). This name is closely related to the noun נוח (*nu'ahh*), which means "rest," so the name *no'ahh* means "rest." Both of these words, *no'ahh* and *nu'ahh*, are derived from the root word נוח (*N.W.Hh*), which means "to give rest."

What type of "rest" was *No'ahh* to bring? Our English words often lack the ability to convey the full meaning of the Hebrew words and the word "rest" is no exception. In order to understand these Hebrew words better, we need to examine other words that are related to it.

The verbal root נחם (*N.Hh.M*) means to give "comfort" and is found in the following passage where it is used to describe the title of *No'ahh*.

> *and he called out his title No'ahh saying, this*
> *one will <u>comfort</u> us from our work, and from*
> *the hardship of our hands, from the ground*
> *which YHWH spitted upon, (RMT, Genesis*
> *5:29)*

The verbal root word נחה (*N.Hh.H*) is usually translated as "guide" or "lead," but has the broader meaning of "to lead to rest."

The role that *No'ahh* played prior to the Flood was as a leader; one who will guide others to rest and comfort from the toils and troubles of the days prior to the Flood.

Philistine

The Anglicized word "Philistine" means "a native or inhabitant of ancient Philistia," and comes from the Hebrew word פלישתי (*p'liysh'tiy*). To define this word we need to examine the root of this word.

The root word פלש (*P-L-Sh*) is a verb meaning "to wallow" or "to roll." Derived from this verb is the noun פלשת (*peleshet*). This noun is not used in the Biblical text, except as the name of a place (Philistia), and its meaning is uncertain, but probably means a "wallower" (one who wallows) or something to that effect.

The word פלישתי (*p'liysh'tiy*) literally means "one of *peleshet*/Philistia." The plural form is פלישתים (*peliyshtim*) and literally means "ones of *peleshet*/Philistia."

Rebecca

The Hebrew name Rebekah, also spelled Rebecca, is written as רבקה (*riv'qah*) in the Hebrew Bible. This name is related to only one Hebrew word, the noun מרבק (*marbaq*), which means "stall:"

> And belonging to the woman is a calf of the stall... (1 Samuel 28:24)

> ...and he will go out and spring about like calves of the stall. (Malachi 4:2)

The verbal root of this noun, and the name *Riv'qah,* is רבק (*R.B.Q*). While this verbal root word is not found in the Biblical text, it is found in other Semitic languages and means "to tie fast" or "secure," just as a calf is "secured" in the "stall."

Some translations of the name רבקה (*riv'qah*) to be suggested are "ensnarer" or "tied firmly," but "secured," seems to be a very good candidate for the meaning of this name.

Red Sea, The

After the Israelites were delivered out of Egypt, they camped at the "Red Sea." When the chariots of Pharaoh arrived, the waters of the "Red Sea" were parted, and the Israelites crossed over into safety on the other side.

The "Red Sea" is actually a misnomer from the translation of the Hebrew. The Hebrew is סוף ים (*yam suph*). The Hebrew word ים (*yam*) means "sea" and when used alone often refers to the Mediterranean Sea.

The word סוף (*suph*) literally means "edge." This can be the edge of a country (border), the lips as the edge of the mouth, or an outline of something. In the Biblical text, this word is used for "reeds" which line the banks, or edge, of rivers, ponds and seas. Hence, the *"yam suph"* is literally the "Sea of Reeds" or "Reed Sea." Somewhere in time, the "Reed Sea" became the "Red Sea."

Interestingly, this same word, *"suph,"* is used in Jewish theology in the term *"eyen soph"* (with just a vowel change). The word *"eyn"* means "without" and *"soph"* means "edge" or "definition" (as an outline). The phrase *"eyn soph"* means "without definition" and is used for God, the one who has no definition, outline or form.

Reuben

The name Reuben means "behold a son" and is given to the firstborn of Jacob through Leah. She gave his name: *"Because YHWH has looked upon my affliction"* (Genesis 29:32).

The name is a combination of two Hebrew words: ראו (*re'u*) and בן (*ben*). ראו is the imperative form of the verb ראה (*R.A.H*) meaning "to see," whereas the imperative means "look," "see" or "behold." The word בן means "son," hence "behold a son."

Sarah

The Hebrew word שר (*sar*) is translated various ways including: prince, captain, chief, ruler, governor, keeper, principal, general, lord and master. The word *"sar"* is a parent root that literally means "to turn the head." In the original pictographic script, the "s" is the letter "sin," a picture of a thorn—ﬨ. When traveling and coming across a thorn thicket, one must "turn" directions. The "r" is the letter *resh* and is a picture of the head of a man (ﬡ). A prince, captain, master, etc. is one who turns the head of the people. The word "*sarah*" is the feminine form of the word "*sar*."

Did Sarah "turn the head" of the people? Yes, but not in the same sense as a captain or master. In Genesis 12:14 we read:

> *When Abram entered Egypt, the Egyptians saw that the woman (Sarah) was very beautiful.*

Sarah turned the head of the people because of her beauty, not her commands.

Seth

Seth was the third son of Adam. In Hebrew, his name is שת (*sheyt*) and is a root word meaning "to set something in place." Adam's family was continued through his son Seth, because Abel (*hevel*) was killed and Cain (*qayin*) was expelled from the family. This idea of "continuing" is often expressed as "established" in English translations and concepts, but is understood as "setting something in place" in Hebrew thought. If I establish a business, I am setting something in place. But there is another possibility to the meaning of the name *Sheyt* (Seth). The more literal meaning of the word "*sheyt*" is "buttocks," the place where you sit. This poses an interesting question. Did Adam name this portion of the body after his son or did he name his son after this body part? Could this be a clue into the personality of Seth? This was meant more as fun than actual literalness, but I am always reminded of what a rabbi once said, "If you are studying the Bible and not laughing, you are doing something wrong." In my studies with friends, we often get some really good laughs. I believe laughing aids in Biblical learning, as it helps you to remember things, as well as enjoy it.

Shem

We are not given much history of Shem or what type of person he was, but his name does provide us with a clue. Unlike our names, a Hebrew's name was a word with meaning. This meaning was a reflection of the person himself and his character. The Hebrew word שם (*shem*) is most often translated as "name," and the name of Shem in English is "Name."

The word *shem* means much more than just a name. A related word in Hebrew is the word "*neshemah*" meaning "breath." In the Hebrew mind, the breath was much more than the exchange of air in the lungs, but was the seat of one's character. The word "*shem*" was also used in the manner as seen in the passage below where the word "fame" is the Hebrew "*shem*:"

> For he was wiser than all other men, wiser than Ethan the Ezrahite, and Heman, Calcol, and Darda, the sons of Mahol; and his <u>fame</u> was in all the nations round about. (1 Kings 4:31 RSV)

This is similar to our desire to "have a good name." This has nothing to do the actual name but the character of the one with the name.

As Shem's name means "character," we can conclude that he was a man of character and this is what we see in the one story about him. Shem and his brother Japheth (*yaphet*) go backwards into the tent of his father with a robe to cover the nakedness of his father, after it had been exposed by Ham. It should also be noted that "the uncovered nakedness of the father" is not the nakedness of the father but is an idiom for sexual relations with the mother, as mentioned in Leviticus 18:8

> You shall not uncover the nakedness of your father's wife; it is your father's nakedness.

It had always bothered me that Ham was the one who uncovered the nakedness of his father, but it was his son Canaan that was cursed for it. That is, until I discovered that Canaan was the product of the union between Ham and his mother. This demonstrates how a simple reading of the text does not always reveal what the text is actually stating.

Shinar

> "And they set out from the east and they found a valley in the land of Shinar and they settled there." (Genesis 11:2)

This is the land of Babylon also called "Mesopotamia" (Greek meaning "between the rivers," *meso* meaning "between" and *potamia* meaning "river").

When the names of places are transferred from one language to another, it is common for the sounds of the name to be mixed up a bit. We see this in names like *Yerushalem* in Hebrew to "Jerusalem" in English, and "*Amorah*" in Hebrew, but "Gomorrah" in English.

Sounds formed in the same region of the mouth are sometimes exchanged for another. Some common examples are a "b" and "p", "r" and "l", "m" and "n" and "s" and "sh".

When the "sh" in Shinar is changed to an "s" and the "n" is changed to an "m," you have Samar which is "Samaria" another common name for Mesopotamia.

Simeon

This name is derived from the Hebrew verb שמע (*shama*) meaning "to hear."

In Deuteronomy 6:4, discussed above in the Modern Hebrew and Middle Semitic (Paleo-Hebrew) scripts, the first word is "sh'ma," the imperative form of the verb meaning "hear!" This word is kind of a motto to Israel.

In Genesis 29:33 Leah, the wife of Jacob, says, *"Because YHWH has heard (shama) that I was hated and he gave me this one also"* and she gives her infant son the name שמעון (*Shimon*), a Hebrew word meaning "heard."

Sinai

Mount Sinai is the mountain on which Israel met with God upon leaving Egypt. The Hebrew word סיני (*Siy'nai*) means "thorny" and is derived from the parent root סן (*S.N*) that means "thorn." This parent root is also the root of the word סין (*siyn*) meaning "thorn," which is the name of the wilderness where Mount Sinai is located, the "Wilderness of Sin" or the "Thorn Wilderness." Another word derived from this parent root is סנה (*seneh*), which means "thorn bush" and is the word used for the bush that Moses saw burning in Exodus 3:2. It was not just a burning bush, but a burning "thorn" bush. The "burning thorn bush" is located on "Mount Thorny" in the "Thorn Wilderness."

Mount Sinai is also called Mount Horeb (see Exodus 3:1). The Hebrew word חורב (*hhorev*) comes from the root חרב (*Hh.R.B*), meaning "to lay waste," "be dried up," as well as "to fight." By definition, the words *sinai* and *hhorev* are synonymous, as a dry wasteland is often filled with thorn bushes. But there is also an interesting connection between the Garden of Eden and Mount Sinai.

When Adam and Eve were expelled from the Garden, God placed a "flaming sword" at its entrance. The Hebrew word for "sword" is חרב (*hherev*) and is a cognate of the place name Horeb. As both a sword and a thorn are pointed and sharp, we can see a close connection between the "flaming sword" and the "burning thorn bush." Is it possible that the burning bush and the flaming sword are one and the same thing? Was Mount Sinai the entrance into the Garden of Eden?

Zebulun

> *And Leah said, God hath endowed me with a good dowry; now will my husband <u>dwell</u> with me, because I have borne him six sons: and she called his name Zebulun.* (Genesis 30:20, ASV)

The Hebrew word זבלון (*zeh-voo-loon*) means a "resident" and comes from the root זבל (*Z.B.L*) meaning "to reside," and is translated as "dwell" in the passage above. Hebrew nouns are commonly formed by adding letters to the root. In this instance, the suffix ון (*on*) is added to the root זבל. Nouns with the ון ending generally mean "one who does the action of the root" and in this case is, "one who dwells."

Topical

Ark of the Testimony

> *There I will meet with you, and from above the mercy seat, from between the two cherubim that are upon the ark of the testimony, I will speak with you of all that I will give you in commandment for the people of Israel.* (RSV, Exodus 25:22)

The Hebrew word behind the English word "testimony" is עדות (*edut*) and is closely related to the word עד (*eyd*), meaning, "someone or something that provides or serves as evidence." This word is also found in the following verse:

> *Take this book of the law, and put it by the side of the <u>ark</u> of the <u>covenant</u> of the LORD your God, that it may be there for a <u>witness</u> against you.* (RSV, Deuteronomy 31:26)

Did YHWH give the "book of the Law (*Torah*)" to Israel to be a witness "against" them? The Hebrew for "a witness against you," is לעד בך (*b'kha l'eyd*) and literally means "with you a witness." The prefixed letter *beyt* (ב) means "in" or "with," but can also mean "against," but only in the sense of being "next" to something. As you can clearly see, the translators chose to use the word "against" here, but this is misleading, as the context does not mean "next to something," but instead as "an adversary."

A perfect witness is a mirror and the *Torah* (the law) was meant to be a mirror by which Israel could measure themselves and their actions to determine if they were following YHWH's directions.

Another word found in the passage above is the word "covenant," which is the Hebrew word ברית (*beriyt*). The verbal root of this word is ברה (*B.R.H*) and means "to have meat." Literally, ברית (*beriyt*) means "meat:"

> They said, "We see plainly that the LORD is with you; so we say, let there be an oath between you and us, and let us <u>make a covenant</u> with you, (RSV, Genesis 26:28)

The Hebrew for "let us make a covenant" is ברית ונכרתה (*v'nikh're'ta beriyt*) and literally means "let us cut the meat." Cutting meat is how covenants were established. By extension, the word *beriyt* can also simply mean a "covenant."

Another word found in Deuteronomy 31:26 is the "ark," which in the Hebrew is ארון (*aron*) and simply means a "box." This box was to be made of acacia wood (see Exodus 25:10), which is a tightly grained dark wood:

> And you shall overlay it with pure gold, within and without shall you overlay it, and you shall make upon it a molding of gold round about. (RSV, Exodus 25:11)

Gold is a very malleable metal; in fact, one ounce of gold could be molded into a wire that would be 50 miles long. One ounce of gold could be hammered out thin enough to cover about 100 square feet. When gold is hammered this thin it becomes translucent. What happens if you place a translucent sheet, such as made from gold, over a dark surface, such as the acacia wood? You have a mirror.

> And they made the plate of the holy crown of pure gold, and wrote upon it an inscription, like the engraving of a signet, "Holy to the LORD." (RSV, Exodus 39:30)

A signet was a ring that had the name of the bearer engraved in it, but in reverse, so that when the image was in wet wax, it would leave the name of the bearer within the wax. According to Exodus 39:30, the words "Holy to the LORD" were to be written on a plate that was attached to the high priest's head covering. I had always wondered why it was to be written in reverse as on a signet. If, in fact, the ark was a mirror, then when the High Priest stood before it, he would see the reflection of the plate with the words in the correct order.

Cardinal Directions

In the modern world we use "north" as the primary orientation, but in the Ancient Near East "east" was the primary orientation. The Hebrew word for "east" is קדם (qedem), which is from the root word קדם (Q.D.M) meaning "to meet," and the rising sun is "met" each morning in the "east."

South

There are two words used for "south." The Hebrew word תימן (teyman) meaning "south," is derived from the verb ימן (Y.M.N) and means "to the right." If you are facing "east," the primary orientation, then to your "right" is to the "south." The other word used for "south" is נגב (negev), a word meaning "desert," and refers to the desert region located in "southern" Israel.

West

The Hebrew word ים (yam) means "sea," but is also used for the direction "west," as the great sea, the Mediterranean, is "west" of Israel.

North

The word for "north" is צפון (*tsaphon*), which comes from the Hebrew root word צפן (*Ts.P.N*) and literally means "hidden," probably alluding to the idea that the northern regions were unknown to them.

Circular Time

The modern western mind views time as linear with a beginning and end. Whether you subscribe to the theory of evolution, creation or another theory for the origin of all things, the timeline for planet earth is the same, a beginning and an end. The creationist views this span of time in the thousands of years, with the beginning being the creation of all things by the hand of God and its end being the destruction of all things also by the hand of God. The evolutionist views this span in the billions of years, with the beginning being the creation of all things through a cataclysmic event called the Big Bang and its future destruction through another cataclysmic event.

Beginning   End

Within this timeline, both creationists and evolutionists see the introduction and eventual destruction of mankind. The creationist sees a matter of days between the beginning and the introduction of man and days between the destruction of man and the end. The evolutionist sees billions of years between the beginning and the introduction of man and an unknown period of time between the destruction of man and the end.

The span of time between the introduction and destruction of mankind includes the advancement of man through various ages. Again, the creationist and evolutionist ascribe different lengths of time to each segment, but agree on the degree of advancement.

Time spans of days and years can also be represented on a similar timeline with a beginning and end.

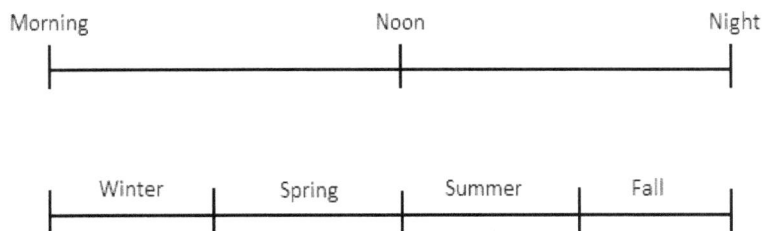

Time is not linear; it is circular. A clock is not a timeline but a circle for the simple reason that time does not begin or stop; it continues without beginning or end. In the same fashion, days and years are also circular.

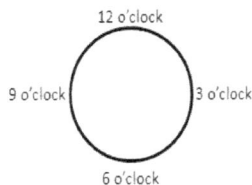

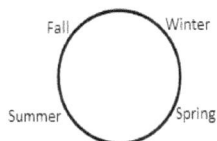

If the timeline above for the span of the earth and man is bent back onto itself we create a circle of time. With a circular view of time, our perspective on the beginning and end of the earth, and man, changes. No longer is the beginning the beginning and the end the end, but a continual cycle of beginnings and endings. While this view of time is contrary to our western way of thinking, it is consistent with other views from other cultures. The ancient Hebrews of the Bible and the people of the Orient have always understood time, the past, present and future, as circular.

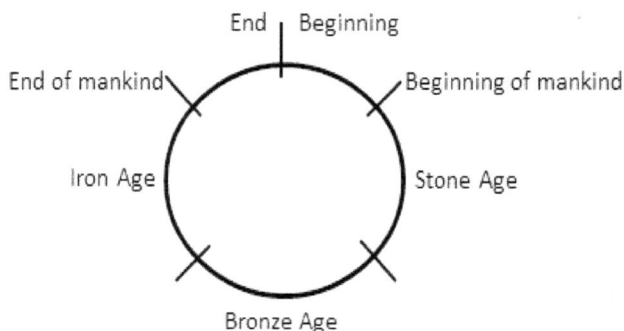

How many of these cycles, or eras, have existed in the earth and man's past? In the Biblical text there are actually five cycles:

1. Genesis 1:1-2 suggests that something existed prior to Genesis 1:1.
2. The creation of Genesis 1:3 to the fall of man in Genesis
3. From the expulsion of man from the Garden of Eden to Genesis 6 and the Flood.
4. Genesis 10 with Noah and proceeding to beyond the modern time.
5. The "New Heavens and New Earth" as prophesied by the prophets.

In each of these cycles, we see a common theme: the creation, or restructuring of the earth, the advent of man who populates and advances on the earth, the eventual downfall of man through his evil inclination and the destruction of the earth.

Beyond these five we can speculate on previous eras of man based on physical, textual and geological evidence. Physical evidence of man's achievements, on a limited basis, has been preserved in the archeological record. Textual evidence, which has been handed down from generation to generation, has been preserved through oral and written accounts of man's history. Geological evidence preserved within the earth provides us with catastrophic events that have restructured the earth on numerous occasions.

Documentary Hypothesis

The documentary hypothesis of the *Torah* states that there were five authors of the *Torah*, each one with a unique style of writing. One of the authors is called the Elohist and he uses the word *Elohiym*, as seen throughout the first chapter of Genesis. Another of these authors is called the Yahwist and he uses the name, YHWH, as seen throughout the second chapter of Genesis.

The event where God gives Jacob the name Israel is recorded twice, one by one author who mentions that Jacob called the place of this event "Peniel" (Genesis 32:30) and another author who mentions that Jacob called the place of this event "Bethel" (Genesis 35:15).

Throughout the text, one author will continue to use "Jacob," while another author will continue to "Israel." Here is an example where the first verse is written by one author who uses the name Israel, and the second verse is written by another author who uses the name "Jacob"

> *And Israel dwelt in the land of Egypt, in the country of Goshen; and they had possessions therein, and grew, and multiplied exceedingly.* Genesis 47:27

> *And Jacob lived in the land of Egypt seventeen years: so the whole age of Jacob was an hundred forty and seven years.* Genesis 47:28

We all speak and write differently, and the styles of writing can be compared to determine the authors of different texts. As an example from English, one might say "I talked to Mom;" while another person might say "I spoke to my mother." We can easily see that these two sentences are from two different people. We frequently see the same thing in the *Torah*. For instance, in Numbers 21:16 we read למשה יהוה אמר (*amar yhwh l'mosheh*) which means "YHWH said to Moses." But in Exodus 4:30 we find the phrase, דבר יהוה אל משה (*diber yhwh el mosheh*), which means "YHWH spoke unto Moses." These differences in writing style are found throughout the text. In fact, we can even see the writing of one person throughout the text that is intermixed with the style of writing from another person. This is the result of what is called the "Redactor." This Redactor took different writings from different people and mixed them together to create one account.

Here is a story written by "John:"

> *In the morning Fred drove to work.*
> *He stopped at the coffee shop for an espresso.*
> *When he arrived at work he began to work on his projects.*

The second story is by "Jim" who is telling the same story from his perspective.

> *Fred went to work early to get a coffee.*
> *When Fred got to work he attended a meeting.*
> *Fred drank his coffee while working the project.*

Then "Bill," who is the redactor, combines the two stories (underlined) of John and Jim, but also adds a few words (bolded) to add to the narrative.

> *In the morning Fred drove to work.*
> **He left** <u>*early to get a coffee.*</u>
> *He stopped at the coffee shop for an espresso.*
> <u>*When Fred got to work he attended a meeting.*</u>
> **Then** *he began to work on his projects.*
> <u>*Fred drank his coffee while working the project.*</u>

Notice that the two stories are very similar, but they have differences, and these differences can be seen in the redacted story. For instance, John uses the word "espresso," while Jim uses the word "coffee." John mentions Fred's "projects," but Jim mentions a "project." Jim mentions a "meeting," but John doesn't.

Earth Age

Which came first, the Earth or the Sun, Moon and Stars?

In our western minds, we are accustomed to relating all things to a chronological order. A novel is assumed to be a chronological order of events, we tell stories in chronological order, etc. If Genesis chapter one is read as a chronology, we would conclude that the earth was made first, then later came the sun, moon and stars. But, there is a problem with this perspective.

On day one God separated light from darkness (Genesis 1:4: *And God saw the light, that it was good: and God divided the light from the darkness.*) but on day four God again separates the light from the darkness (Genesis 1:18: *and to divide the light from the darkness: and God saw that it was good*). From a chronological perspective this makes no sense, how can God separate light from darkness on two different days?

The Ancient Hebrews did not think in chronological order as we do. In fact, they perceived time in much the same way as space; in fact, Hebrew words that are related to time are the same words used for space.

For example the word *qedem* is literally "where the sun rises" and is used for "the east," but is also used for an "ancient time." Imagine yourself standing in the desert of the Near East facing the rising sun (In ancient time all things were oriented to the east, whereas Westerners use the north). What lies before you is "the east" and it is "the past," all there for you to see. (While Westerners see the past as behind, the Ancient Hebrews saw the past as being in front and the future behind). But the farther east you look, the hazier it is and more difficult to see. What is obscure or unseen at the horizon is called the *olam* (usually translated as "eternity"). The origins of the world to the Ancient Hebrews are like the fuzzy horizon in front of you that is difficult to see.

The Ancient Hebrews did not attempt to clear up the image of the past; instead, they just understood it as *olam* (at or beyond the horizon). It is only our western mind that needs to clear up this image; we need to know precisely how the origins of the world came about. The Ancient Hebrews did not care; they just knew that it was.

As I mentioned, Genesis 1 is not a chronological order of events. The Ancient Hebrews think in blocks of events. Let me demonstrate with the following paragraph from a western perspective.

> *"I got up and ate breakfast and read the newspaper. I then drove to work. While at work I read yesterday's reports. At noon I walked across the street for lunch. While there I read a magazine. Back at work I read my emails. After work I drove home and had dinner."*

Now let me rearrange this paragraph in block form, the way the Hebrews would have conveyed this same story.

> *"I drove to work and walked across the street and I drove home and I ate breakfast and I ate lunch and I ate dinner and I read the newspaper and I read the reports and I read a magazine and I read my emails."*
>
> *It seems that I read this same or a similar account somewhere above.*

There is no way you can make any chronological sense out of this narrative. Instead you can easily see what I "did." Genesis 1 is written in the same fashion of "blocks."

When I read the Bible I try not to read it from a modern Western perspective. Instead, I try and read it from an ancient Eastern one. The question, "Which came first, the earth or the sun and moon?" is an irrelevant question to the Ancient

Hebrews, and, therefore, not a question that can be answered from the Biblical text.

Ebla

> *"Lord of heaven and earth: the earth was not, you created it, the light of the day was not, you created it, the morning light you had not yet made exist."*

The above quotation may sound very similar to Biblical passages like Exodus 20:11, but it is, in fact, a passage found in three literary texts inscribed on clay tablets that were discovered in the Royal Archives of the ancient city of Ebla.

In 1964 the Italian Archeological Mission led by Paolo Matthiae began a dig at Tel Mardikh in Syria. In 1968 the team uncovered a statue of Ibbit-Lim, King of Ebla, which included an Akkadian (Eastern Semitic language) inscription detailing Ibbit-Lim bringing an offering to the goddess Ishtar. Up until this time, the ancient city of Ebla was known from other Ancient Near Eastern texts, but its location was completely unknown. With the discovery of the statue, it was suspected that this may be the elusive Ebla. Then in the years 1974 through 1976, the Royal Library was discovered and these revealed that, in fact, this was the city of Ebla. The texts of the library, which dated to about 2500 BC, included about 2,000 complete tablets ranging in size from 1" to over a foot, 4,000 fragments and over 10,000 chips and small fragments, making this the largest library ever discovered from the 3rd Millennium BC.

The tablets were written with a cuneiform script, like Ugarit, but the language, as discovered by Giovanni Pettinato, the chief epigrapher for the Ebla excavation, was a Semitic language related to Canaanite, Phoenician, Ugarit and Hebrew, and came to be called Eblaite.

It was revealed from the artifacts uncovered by the excavation of Ebla and through the study of the tablets that Ebla was a major economic power, a cultural center of the land of Canaan and a large metropolis of 260,000 people. The majority of the texts in the Royal Archive are related to the economic and administrative details of Ebla. However, the texts included historical information, religious texts, academic texts, agricultural details, laws, treatises and, of most interest to the study of Semitic languages, dictionaries (monolingual and bilingual) and encyclopedias, the oldest dictionaries and encyclopedias in history.

Until the discovery of the Eblaite tablets, the only Semitic language known to exist in 3rd Millennium BC was Akkadian. Now with this discovery, another Semitic language was found to be in use in the 3rd Millennium BC and has a very close relationship with the Hebrew language of the Bible.

Et – the Untranslatable Hebrew Word

The most common word in the Hebrew Bible is the word את (et) and is never translated, as there is no equivalent word in the English language. The first letter in the word is the א, called an *aleph*, and is the first letter of the Hebrew alephbet. The second letter in the word את (et) is the ת, called a *tav*, and is the last letter of the Hebrew alephbet. These two letters are the "first and the last," the "beginning and the end" and the "*Aleph* and the *Tav*" (which is translated as "the alpha and the omega," the first and last letters of the Greek alphabet, in the book of Revelation).

Beat your plowshares into swords, and your pruning hooks into spears; let the weak say, "I am a warrior." (Joel 3:10, RSV)

The word "plowshares" in the above passage is the Hebrew word את (*et*). A plowshare is the metal point of the plow which digs into the soil creating a furrow for planting seeds. When we examine the original pictographic script used in ancient times to write Hebrew, we can see a clear connection between the letters of this word and its meaning.

The Modern Hebrew form of the letter *aleph* is א, but is an evolved form of the original pictograph 𐤀, a picture of an ox head. The ancient pictographic form of the letter ת is ✝, a picture of two crossed sticks which are used as a marker. When these two pictographs are combined we have the meaning "an ox toward the mark." Fields were plowed by an ox or a pair of oxen pulling a plow behind them. In order to keep the furrows straight, the driver of the ox would aim toward a mark, such as a tree or rock outcropping in the far distance. As we can see, this meaning of driving the ox toward a mark can be seen in the letters of the Hebrew word את (*et*)

The word את is also used over 7,000 times in the Hebrew language such as can be seen in the very first verse of the Bible.

בְּרֵאשִׁית בָּרָא אֱלֹהִים אֵת הַשָּׁמַיִם וְאֵת הָאָרֶץ׃

Because the word את has no equivalent in the English language, it is not translated, but to demonstrate its meaning in this verse I will translate Genesis 1:1 into English, but retain the word את in its correct position.

In the beginning Elohiym shaped את *the sky and* את *the land*

The untranslated word את is used as a grammatical tool to identify the definite object of the verb. In the example of Genesis 1:1 the verb is the Hebrew word ברא (*bara*), meaning "to shape," and the definite objects, the ones receiving the action of the verb, are the sky and the land. Just as the "ox" moved toward the "mark" when plowing, the word את (the plowshare) plows the path from the verb of a sentence (the ox) to the definite object (the mark).

Just as the phrase "heaven and earth" is an idiomatic expression meaning "all of creation," the phrase "*aleph* and *tav*" are an idiomatic expression meaning "the whole of the alephbet."

Eternal Torah

Was the *Torah* given to Israel at Mount Sinai, a new *Torah* from God? Or a reminder of his *Torah* which was given to man before Israel? Is it possible that this *Torah* was given previously to Abraham, Noah or possibly Adam? We can look at the book of Genesis and say that the *Torah* did exist prior to Israel and that Adam, Noah and Abraham followed it.

> *I will make your descendants as numerous as the stars in the sky and will give them all these lands, and through your offspring all nations on earth will be blessed, because Abraham obeyed me and kept my requirements (mishmeret), my commands (mitzvot), my decrees (hukah) and my Torah.* (Genesis 26:4,5)

We can see that even Abraham kept God's *Torah* over 400 years before Israel came to Mount Sinai. In the passage above, three words are used paralleling the word *Torah*, *mishmeret*, *mitzvot* and *hukah*. These are the same words used through the rest of scripture to describe the *Torah* of God. According to this passage, Abraham kept the same type of *Torah* that God gave Israel.

Throughout the Book of Genesis, we see example after example of God's commands being kept and broken. These same commands can be found in the *Torah* given to Israel. In most cases, we read of an individual keeping or breaking a command, but the command itself is not recorded. With this in mind, we cannot say with certainty when the command was given, just that it did exist.

Let us look at some of the commands found within the *Torah,* then look at cases in the book of Genesis where they are obeyed or disobeyed.

Murder

> *You shall not murder.* (Exodus 20:13)

This command is first given at Mount Sinai with the giving of the 10 commandments. This command was broken in Genesis:

> *While they were in the field, Cain attacked his brother Abel and killed him.* (Genesis 4:8)

You cannot condemn a man for an action unless that action has been determined to be wrong and the command not to do that action is communicated to the people. If my son takes a piece of candy from a store without paying for it, I cannot punish him unless I have previously taught him that this is a wrong action.

In order for God to punish Cain for taking the life of his brother, he had to have been taught at one point by either

God or his father Adam (who would have been instructed by God) that murder is a sin.

Altars

> *"Make an Altar of earth for me and Sacrifice on it your burnt offerings and fellowship offerings, your sheep and goats and your cattle. Wherever I cause my name to be honored, I will come to you and bless you. If you make an altar of stones for me, do not build it with dressed stones, for you will defile it if you use a tool on it. And do not go up to my altar on steps, lest your nakedness be exposed on it."* (Exodus 20:24,26)

This is the first command given in the Bible for the construction and regulations concerning altars. Compare the similarities with the above passage and the ones below from the book of Genesis:

> *Then Noah built an altar to the LORD and taking some of all the clean animals and clean birds, he sacrificed burnt offerings on it.* (Genesis 8:20)

> *The LORD appeared to Abram and said, "To your offspring I will give this land." So he built an altar there to the LORD, who had appeared to him. From there he went on toward the hills east of Bethel and pitched his tent, with Bethel on the west of Ai on the east. There he built an altar to the LORD and called on the name of the LORD.* (Genesis 12:7,8)

> *That night the LORD appeared to [Isaac] and said, "I am the God of your father Abraham.*

> *Do not be afraid, for I am with you; I will bless you..."Isaac built an altar there and called on the name of the LORD.* (Genesis 26:24,25)

> *Then God said to Jacob, "Go up to Bethel and settle there, and build an altar there to God, who appeared to you when you were fleeing from your brother Esau."* (Genesis 35:1)

> *Moses built an altar and called it 'The LORD is my Banner.' (Exodus 17:15)*

Here we have five incidents where, in each case, we can see a portion of the command in Exodus 20 being observed: Sacrifices of burnt offerings are placed on the altar, altars are erected where the name of God is honored, and erected where the presence of God and his blessings appear.

Tithes

> *I give to the Levites (the priests of Israel) as their inheritance the tithes (a tenth) that the Israelites present as an offering to the LORD.* (Numbers 18:21)

Now let us look at this command in the book of Genesis:

> *Then Melchizedek king of Salem brought out bread and wine. He was priest of God Most High, and he blessed Abram...Then Abram gave him a tenth (tithe) of everything.* (Genesis 14:18,20)

> *This stone that I (Jacob) have set us as a pillar will be God's house, and of all that you give me I will give you a tenth.* (Genesis 28:22)

Abraham and Jacob understood the command to tithe their possessions to God and his priests, just as God commanded Israel in the *Torah*.

Sacrifices and Offerings

> When you sacrifice a thank offering to the LORD, sacrifice it in such a way that it will be accepted on your behalf. (Leviticus 22:29)

> [Jacob] offered a sacrifice there in the hill country. (Genesis 31:54)

> When [Jacob] reached Beersheba, he offered sacrifices to the God of his father Isaac. (Genesis 46:1)

Animal offerings

> "All the firstborn are mine.... whether man or animal. They are to be mine, I am the LORD." (Numbers 3:13)

> If he offers an animal from the flock as a fellowship offering to the LORD, he is to offer a male or female without defect ....All the fat is the LORD's. (Leviticus 3:6,16)

> Abel brought fat portions from some of the firstborn of his flock. (Genesis 4:4)

Abel's offering must have been done in obedience because it was accepted by God as stated in verse 4: "The LORD looked with favor on Abel and his offering."

Food offerings

> A tithe of everything from the land, whether grain from the soil or fruit from the trees, belongs to the LORD; it is holy to the LORD. (Leviticus 27:30)

> Cain brought some of the fruits of the soil as an offering to the LORD. (Genesis 4:3)

Evidently, Cain's offering was done in disobedience because verse 5 tells us; "but on Cain and his offering he did not look with favor."

The Bible does not explain why he looked with favor on one but not the other. If God did not outline the requirements for the giving of offerings prior to this, he could not have held either of them accountable for their offerings. Therefore, Cain and Abel must have known what the requirements were for the offerings. Prior to the giving of the commands concerning sacrifices and offerings to Israel at Mount Sinai, there is no mention of sacrificial requirements. We can assume that, since Cain was held accountable for his disobedient sacrifice, the requirements were known prior to Mount Sinai but were not recorded in the book of Genesis.

Clean and Unclean

> "These are the regulations concerning animals, birds, every living thing that moves in the water and every creature that moves about on the ground. You must distinguish between the unclean and the clean, between living creatures that may be eaten and those that may not be eaten." (Leviticus 11:46,47)

Leviticus chapter 11 is a complete list of all the clean and unclean animals. Although this is the first time the distinction is made between the clean and the unclean, it is not the first time they are mentioned:

> The LORD said to Noah,"Take with you seven of every kind of clean animal, a male and its mate, and two of every kind of unclean animal, a male and its mate." (Genesis 7:1,2)

> Then Noah built an altar to the LORD and taking some of all the clean animals and clean birds, he sacrificed burnt offerings on it. (Genesis 8:20)

Blood

> Any Israelite or any alien living among you who hunts any animal or bird that may be eaten must drain out the blood and cover it with earth, because the life of every creature is its blood. That is why I have said to the Israelites, "you must not eat the blood of any creature, because the life of every creature is its blood; anyone who eats it must be cut off." (Leviticus 17:13,14)

Compare this with the following passage:

> "But you must not eat meat that has its lifeblood still in it." (Genesis 9:4)

Sabbath

> Remember the Sabbath day by keeping it holy. Six days you shall labor and do all your work, but the seventh day is a Sabbath to the LORD

your God. On it you shall not do any work.
(Exodus 20:8-10)

The Sabbath command is first found here, but it was observed prior to Mount Sinai. The Sabbath day of rest is recorded as being observed on two occasions prior to the giving of the *Torah*. One occurrence is recorded in Exodus 16. Here we see that Israel observed the Sabbath day during their journey from Egypt to Mount Sinai. The other is when God himself rested from his work on the seventh day of creation (Genesis 2:2).

Summary

In all the passages above we can see evidence that the commands concerning: murder, altars, tithes, sacrifices and offerings, clean and unclean animals, abstaining from the eating blood, and the Sabbath were in existence long before Israel arrived at Mount Sinai. The observance of *Torah* commands in the book of Genesis are few compared to a great number of commands found in the *Torah*. But we can see hints of *Torah* keeping also in the book of Genesis, such as: Honor your Father and Mother, do not steal, do not worship false gods, and many others. There is no way of saying with certainty just how many commands and requirements of the *Torah* were kept during the time of the book of Genesis, but it is not impossible that all of the *Torah* was given to man long before the nation of Israel ever existed. We did see that Abraham kept all of God's *Torah*, so is it not possible that Adam and Noah also kept God's *Torah*?

> *"I remember your ancient laws."* (Psalms 119:52)

> *"Long ago I learned from your statutes that you established them to last forever."* (Psalms 119:152)

"All your words are true; all your righteous laws are eternal." (Psalms 119:160)

Friend and Bad

> *... he hath humbled his <u>neighbour's</u> wife: so thou shalt put away <u>evil</u> from among you.* (Deuteronomy 22:24, KJV)

In this passage are the words 'neighbor' and 'evil.' Both of these words are the Hebrew word רע. How is it possible that one Hebrew word could have two very different meanings?

There are several Hebrew words that include the letter *ayin* (ע), but have two very different meanings. Here are a few examples.

רע / friend / bad
יעל / profit / goat
סער / hair / storm
עול / infant / wicked
עור / skin / blind
עיף / weary / darkness
עיר / colt / city
ענה / heed / answer
ערב / weave / dark
ערם / naked / crafty
ערף / neck / rain
רעה / shepherd / break

In Biblical Hebrew and Modern Hebrew, there are 22 letters in the alphabet. However, at some time in the very ancient past, a time before the Bible was written, there were more than 22 letters in the Hebrew (Semitic) alphabet. One of these letters was the *ghayin* (identifying this letter as the *ghayin* is simply an educated guess, as we really do not know what the name of it was). The letter *ayin* had the sound like an 'a', but the *ghayin* had a sound like a 'g'. And then at some point, again, before the Bible was written, the *ayin* and *ghayin* were combined into one letter, the *ayin*. Therefore, the Hebrew word רע was originally two words, one pronounced 'ra' (meaning friend) and the other 'rag' (meaning bad).

As I mentioned before, when the Bible was written, the letter *ghayin* had been absorbed by the letter *ayin*, but the pronunciation did not change. How do we know this? By examining Hebrew names that include the letter *ayin*, and how they were transliterated in the *Greek Septuagint*.

The following three Hebrew names, followed by their transliteration in the *Greek Septuagint*, include the letter *ayin* and notice that in the Greek the *ayin* is assigned an 'a' sound. From this we can conclude that these names were in fact written with the letter *ayin*:

בעל / *baal*
בלעם / *Balaam*
עשתרות / *Astaroth*

The next three Hebrew names also include the letter *ayin*, but this time, when they are transliterated into Greek, they now have a 'g' sound, evidence that the *ayin* in these names were originally spelled with a *ghayin*:

עמרה / *Gomorras*
עזה / *Gazan*
פעור / *Pogor*

Gender Pronouns

In the original King James Version of Exodus 25:31, the pronoun "his" is used five different times to describe the Menorah. Why was "his" changed to "its" in every other Bible version I could find?

It is interesting that the KJV would use "his." Let me begin by explaining how pronouns work in Hebrew. All nouns in Hebrew are either masculine or feminine. For instance, father (*av*), light (*or*) and tree (*ets*) are masculine and mother (*eym*), faith (*emunah*) and soul (*nephesh*) are feminine. Pronouns used for these words would also be masculine or feminine. Below are some examples:

> *hu av* = he is a father
>
> *hiy eym* = she is a mother

These translations make sense in English but when working with nouns that have no gender in English it is a little different. For instance, the phrase *"hu ets"* would literally be translated as "he is a tree," but because this is poor English, the translators would change it to "it is a tree."

Now let's look at Exodus 25:31. The noun that the pronouns refer to is the Hebrew word "menorah." Menorah is a feminine word. The KJV has "his branches, his bowls, his knops, and his flowers." The Hebrew is *"yereykhah, veqanah, geviyeyah, kaphtoreyah, uphraheyah."* Notice that each of these words end with "ah" and is the pronoun "her." So, it should be translated as "her branches, her bowls, her knops, and her flowers" or "its branches, its bowls, its knops, and its flowers."

Why the KJV chose to use the masculine pronoun "his" is beyond me.

God or gods

In Genesis 1:1, we read, "*In the beginning God created...*" The word for "God" is *elohim*, a plural noun, and many might ask why this verse isn't translated as, "In the beginning gods created?" The word *elohim* is the subject of the verb "created." In Hebrew most verbs identify the number (singular or plural) of the subject. In this case, the verb "*bara*" (translated as created) identifies the subject as singular. Therefore, the grammar of the verse dictates that the word *elohim*, be understood as a singular (God) and not a plural (gods).

When the verb identifies the subject as a plural, then the noun is grammatically identified as a plural. An example can be seen in 2 Kings 19:12 which reads in the KJV, "Have the gods (*elohim*) of the nations delivered them?" The word "delivered" identifies the subject as plural and therefore the word *elohim* must be translated as a plural (gods).

In most cases the translators correctly translate such grammatical occurrence; however, at other times they ignore it, especially when the correct grammatical translation does not align with the monotheistic belief system of the translators. An example of this can be found in Genesis 20:13, which in the KJV reads, "*God (elohim) caused me to wander from my father's house.*" In this verse the verb wander identifies the subject as plural and should be correctly translated as, "the gods caused me to wander from my father's house." Because this translation supports a view that is contradictory to monotheism, the translators "fix" the text for the reader. This is not an isolated case; here are a few others where the verb in the Hebrew identifies the subject as plural:

Genesis 35:7

- King James Version: *God appeared unto him*
- Literal Translation: *gods appeared unto him*

2 Samuel 7:23

- King James Version: *God went to redeem for a people to himself*
- Literal Translation: *gods went to redeem for a people for him*

Psalm 58:11

- King James Version: *he is a God that judgeth in the earth*
- Literal Translation: *there are gods that judge in the earth*

Good and bad

Very few sermons in our Western synagogues and churches would include the passage "*I [God] form the light and create darkness, I make peace and I create evil, I am the LORD who does all of these*" (Isaiah 45:7). Our Western mind sees these two forces as opposing opposites, while the Eastern mind sees them both as equals and necessary for perfect balance. In the Western mind, God is only good and therefore unable to create evil. The Eastern mind sees God as a perfect balance of all things including good (*tov* in Hebrew) and evil (*ra* in Hebrew).

It should be noted that the English word "evil" has no Ancient Hebrew equivalent. Most English translations will use the word "evil," usually for the Hebrew word "*ra,*" which simply means "bad." In the Ancient Hebrew mind, there is no such thing as an "evil" person or thing. To understand the words "good" and "bad" from a more Hebraic understanding, these words should be understood as "functional" and "dysfunctional." God is both functional (such as seen in the Creation story of Genesis one) as well as dysfunctional (such as the destruction of the Flood).

Our Western mind classifies all things in two categories, either it is "good" or it is "bad." One is to be sought, cherished and protected, the other is to be rejected, spurned and discarded. Let us take light and darkness as an example. We see light as good and darkness as bad. The idea of light brings to mind such things as God, truth and love. Darkness, on the other hand, invokes Satan, lies and hate. To the Orientals, including the Hebrews, both are equally necessary, as one cannot exist without the other. In the Bible, God is seen as a God of light as well as darkness "And the people stood at a distance and Moses approached the heavy darkness where God was." (Exodus 20:21). If you stare at the sun, which is pure light, what happens? You become blind. If you are standing in a sealed room with no light, what happens? You are again blind. Therefore, both light and darkness are bad and yet, both are good. In order to see, we must block out some of the light as well as some of the darkness.

The two poles of a magnet are north and south. These two poles create balance; they are not morally good or bad, but necessary ingredients of physics that complement each other. Good and bad are more like the north and south poles of a magnet rather than our Western conception of good and bad.

Can good exist without the bad? Absolutely not. How could you judge something to be good if you could not compare it to something bad? The same is true for all other concepts. Cold cannot exist without heat, or short without tall, far without near, or large without small. Our Western mind usually ignores these extremes and seeks to always find the "good" or the "bad." The Eastern mind is continually seeking both the "good" and the "bad" in order to find the balance between the two. Even Solomon recognized this when he said: "Do not be overly righteous" (Ecclesiastes 7:16).

Throughout the scriptures, this search for balance is found, yet ignored by Westerners who do not understand the significance of balance.

Heaven or Heavens?

Is there a difference between "heaven" and "heavens?" Is one spiritual and the other physical? Is one used for the sky and the other for God's abode?

The first thing to keep in mind is that in Ancient Hebrew thought there is no separation between the physical and non-physical; they are one and the same. An example of this is in Psalm 24:4, where "clean hands" and "pure heart" are one and the same thing. A common form of Hebrew poetry uses the word "and" to connect two phrases, which mean the same thing, together. Clean hands are a sign of a pure heart, and vice versa.

The "heavens" are the physical skies and also the place of God, one and the same thing. It is the western Greek thinking that separates the two realms. We often see the "spirit" as spiritual and the "body" as physical, but in Hebrew thought they are one and the same thing. Without the spirit (actually "breath" in Hebrew) the body cannot survive, and without the body, the spirit cannot survive.

In Hebrew, the word *shamayim* is in the plural (the *"yim"* ending is the plural suffix) and this word is always written in the plural. You may see "heaven" or "heavens" in your Bible, but they are both the word *shamayim*. There are several Hebrew words that are always written in the plural: water is *mayim* and face is *paniym* (*yim* and *iym* are both plural endings). Personally, I prefer to translate the Hebrew word *shamayim* as "skies." This eliminates any confusion between heaven, heavens and sky.

The Ancient Hebrews, who knew nothing about giant balls of burning hydrogen, understood the lights in the night sky as a "sheet" that covers the earth, just like the Hebrews' nomadic tent that covers the family. In fact, from the inside of a nomadic tent, the cover looks just like the night sky, stars and all.

I believe the connection that the Hebrews made between God and his "host" is that they can see the "sheet" of the skies, but they cannot see beyond it, nor can they see or even speculate on what is beyond that sheet. The Ancient Hebrew mind did not concern itself with things they could not see, hear, feel, smell or touch. It is Greek thinking that delves into the philosophy of the unknown. The Hebrew word *"olam"* is usually translated as "eternity" or "forever." This word literally means "what is beyond the horizon" or "hidden." To the Hebrews, God is *"olam,"* not eternal but "unknown" or "hidden."

Idioms

> then thy heart be lifted up, and thou forget
> Jehovah thy God, who brought thee forth out
> of the land of Egypt, out of the house of
> bondage; (Deuteronomy 8:14, ASV)

An idiom is defined as a manner of expression peculiar to a given language, culture or people whose meanings cannot be understood through the context of the words alone. We use idiomatic words and phrases all the time without realizing that we are doing it. Below are just a few examples of idioms peculiar to the English language of America involving parts of the body.

> I bent over backwards. (I tried everything.)
> Let me give you a hand. (Let me help.)
> I put my nose to the grindstone. (I worked hard.)
> I spilled my guts. (I told everything.)
> You're pulling my leg. (You're joking.)
> He's shooting his mouth off. (He's saying too much.)
> Break a leg. (Good luck.)
> My ears are burning. (Someone is talking about me.)
> My head is spinning (This is too much for me to think about.)
> I have a hollow leg. (I eat a lot.)
> I'm dragging my feet (I'm procrastinating.)
> I'm pulling my hair out. (I'm frustrated.)
> Hold your tongue. (Don't say anything.)

When someone from another culture hears or reads these idioms, there is no way for them to comprehend the meaning unless they consult an outside source for interpretation. To demonstrate how difficult it is to interpret an idiom, consider the following idiom from Mexico, "The farmer went into the field and hung up his tennis shoes."

When we read this, we see a farmer going out into the field and hanging his shoes up in a tree, fence post or something like that. There is no possible way for us to understand this passage without an outside source. The phrase "hung up his tennis shoes" is equivalent to our idiom, "kicked the bucket." In other words, he died.

In Deuteronomy 8:14 the phrase "heart lifted up" is an idiom for being "proud." Below are only a few of the idioms found in the Bible.

face fell = sad (Genesis 4:5)
knew no quiet in the belly = greedy (Job 20.20)
open the ear = inform (Job 33.16)
right hand = mighty (Psalms 89.13)
hide the face = refuse to answer (Psalms 102.2)
bad eye = stingy (Proverbs 28.22)
good eye = generous (Proverbs 22.9)
hard forehead = stubborn (Ezekiel 3.7)

The first idiom found in the Bible is in Genesis 1:1. The phrase, "heaven and earth," is a Hebrew idiom meaning "all things." It should be remembered that the ancient Hebrews who wrote the Biblical text did not have a conception of the Milky Way Galaxy or the universe. Also, they saw the heavens and stars as a canopy or tent covering the earth. Genesis chapter one is not meant to be a scientific discussion on the origins of the solar system, but rather a poetic story about God's involvement with his whole of creation.

It is quite possible that there are many Hebrew idioms in the Bible; however, the definition of an idiom is a phrase that has no real meaning and is only understood because of the culture from which it is derived. What this means is that there may be many other idioms, but because we do not know them from the culture of that day, we would never recognize them to be idioms. Therefore, we often understand them as literal when they were never meant to be literal. Some idioms are known only because they have survived as idioms to this day. In Israel, the expressions "good eye" and "bad eye" are still used to mean "generous" and "stingy." Both can be found in both the Old and New Testaments (Proverbs 22:9, Proverbs 23:6, Matthew 6:22,23).

Keeping and Breaking

The Bible often refers to the keeping and breaking of a covenant, and it is usually interpreted as obedience or disobedience to the covenant. If disobedience were the meaning of "breaking," Israel would never have been able to remain in covenant relationship as long as they did because of their continual disobedience to the terms of the covenant. Let us examine these two words within their Hebraic context beginning with the word for "keep":

> *Now, if you will intently listen to my voice and* *keep* *my covenant, they will be for me a treasured possession from all the people, for all the land is mine.* (Exodus 19:5)

In the above passage, the Hebrew word behind the English word "keep" is the verb שמר (*Sh.M.R*). If we interpret this word as "obedience," we can easily interpret this passage to mean, "Obey the covenant." But as we shall see, this translation is not always suitable for the context of the passage:

> *"The LORD bless you and* *keep* *you."* (Numbers 6:24, NIV)

Obviously, the word שמר (*Sh.M.R*), also translated as "keep" in this verse, cannot be interpreted as "obey;" otherwise it would read, "The LORD bless you and obey you." We can clearly see that the word "obey" is a poor interpretation for the Hebrew word שמר (*Sh.M.R*).

The original use of this word means a corral constructed out of thorn bushes by the shepherd to protect his flock from predators during the night. The שמר (*Sh.M.R*) was built to "guard" the flock and we can see this same imagery in the passage above by interpreting it as "The LORD bless you and guard you." We now see that "keeping the covenant" is not strictly about obedience, but "guarding the covenant." The individual's attitude toward the covenant is the issue: does he guard it as a shepherd does his flock, or does he "break" the covenant.

Just as the word "keep" has been misunderstood in the context of the original Hebraic meaning, the word "break" has also been misunderstood, as the word does not mean "disobedience."

> *"If you reject my decrees and if you cast away my judgments and you do not do all my commands, breaking my covenant, then, I will do this to you; I will bring upon you sudden terror, disease and fever."* Leviticus 26:15,16

The Hebrew translated as "break" in the above passage is the verb פרר (*P.R.R*). The original use of this word was the "treading" over grain. The harvested grain was thrown onto the threshing floor where oxen would trample over the grain breaking the hull open, releasing the edible seeds inside. The "breaking" of a covenant means the total disrespect for the covenant where one literally throws it to the ground and tramples on it. As we can see, the keeping or breaking of a covenant is the respect or lack that one has for the covenant.

Learning

There are several Hebrew words which can be translated into English as "learn." When we read the English text we often come across words like "learn"," teach," "instruct," "discipline" and "chastise," but, as we will see, these words do not give us an accurate meaning of these words from a

Hebraic perspective and some of their meaning is "lost in the translation."

The Hebrew language is centered on the life of desert dwellers that lived their lives as shepherds and farmers. In order to really understand the Hebrew words for learning, we will be looking at them as they did 4000 years ago.

Learn by direction

> *Specially the day that thou stoodest before the LORD thy God in Horeb, when the LORD said unto me, Gather me the people together, and I will make them hear my words, that they may <u>learn</u> to fear me all the days that they shall live upon the earth, and that they may <u>teach</u> their children.* (Deuteronomy 4:10, KJV)

The Hebrew verb למד (*L.M.D*) appears twice in this verse. The first time it appears in the simple form of the verb and is translated as "learn." The second time it appears in the intensive form and is translated as "teach." The origin of this Hebrew verb is the noun מלמד (*malmad*), meaning a "goad," a stick with a pointed end for driving livestock.

The verb למד (*L.M.D*) literally means "to learn through direction."

Learn by example

Oxen were very important to desert dwellers as a source of power, much as the tractor is to the modern farmer today. The Hebrew word for an ox is אלף (*eleph*) and is derived from the verb אלף (*A.L.P*), meaning "to yoke together."

When two oxen were placed together in a yoke for plowing, an older, more experienced ox was placed alongside a younger inexperienced ox. The younger would then learn by association and example from the older. Hence, the word *eleph* can also mean "to associate with" or "to learn by example."

A man yoked to another will learn by example from the other. A child will also learn from his parents only by observing the actions of the parent. This can be either in a positive or a negative way.

> *Make no friendship with an angry man; and with a furious man thou shalt not go: Lest thou learn his ways, and get a snare to thy soul.* (Proverbs 22:24,25)

To learn by showing

The next word we will look at is the verb ירה (*Y.R.H*) meaning, "to throw" like a rock or arrow, as in the following passage:

> *And I will shoot three arrows on the side thereof, as though I shot at a mark. (1 Samuel 20:20)*

This can also be a figurative "throwing of the finger" meaning to point, as in the following passage:

> *And the people murmured against Moses, saying, What shall we drink? And he cried unto the LORD; and the LORD showed him a tree, which when he had cast into the waters, the waters were made sweet: there he made for them a statute and an ordinance, and there he proved them.* (Exodus 15:24,25)

It can also mean "to learn by pointing out the way:"

And the LORD said unto Moses, Come up to me into the mount, and be there: and I will give thee tables of stone, and a law, and commandments which I have written; that thou mayest <u>teach</u> them. (Exodus 24:12)

To learn by exercise

The next word which we will look at which is usually translated as "learn" or "teach" is שנן (*Sh.N.N*). This verb literally means "to make pointed," or "to sharpen" such as a knife or sword:

When I <u>sharpen</u> my flashing sword and my hand grasps it in judgment, I will take vengeance on my adversaries and repay those who hate me. (Deuteronomy 32:41)

A dull knife will not cut. Hence, we take our knife and sharpen it on a stone so that it will be ready to perform the work it must do properly. This sharpening process is careful and sometimes time-consuming. *"Shanan"* can also refer to the careful sharpening of your children's skills:

And these words, which I command thee this day, shall be in thine heart: And thou shalt <u>teach them diligently</u> unto thy children, and shalt talk of them when thou sittest in thine house, and when thou walkest by the way, and when thou liest down, and when thou risest up. (Deuteronomy 6:6-7)

To learn by discipline

The word יסר (*Y.S.R*) literally means "to turn the head" or "to turn to another direction." This word can be translated as "chastise" or "discipline:"

*Correct thy son, and he shall give thee rest;
yea, he shall give delight unto thy soul.*
(Proverbs 29:17)

Lend and Borrow

*The LORD shall open unto thee his good
treasure, the heaven to give the rain unto thy
land in his season, and to bless all the work of
thine hand: and thou shalt <u>lend</u> unto many
nations, and thou shalt not <u>borrow</u>.*
(Deuteronomy 28:12, KJV)

If you look up the word "lend" in a *Strong's Dictionary*, you will find that it is identified as Strong's #3867, the Hebrew verb לוה (*L.W.H*). If you look up the word "borrow" in a *Strong's Dictionary* you will find that it is identified as the very same number, #3867, and the very same word, the Hebrew verb לוה (*L.W.H*). How can the same word have two completely opposite meanings?

My standard comment about *Strong's Dictionary* is that it is one of the best tools invented for people for studying the Hebrew language, but it is also the worst tool invented for people for studying Hebrew. *Strong's* is great for people who do not know Hebrew to gain a little exposure to it and learn a little more about the deeper meaning of Hebrew words. On the flip side, *Strong's* has its limitations and if those limitations are not known, it can create some problems. It is true that the same Hebrew word is used for "lending" and "borrowing," but what *Strong's* cannot show you are the different tenses, prefixes, suffixes, moods and voices of each Hebrew verb. The words "lend" and "borrow" are translations of the Hebrew verb לוה (*L.W.H*), which means "to join."

The Hebrew word behind "borrow" is the "*qal*" or simple form of the verb לוה (*L.W.H*) and in the context of Deuteronomy 28:12 means to "borrow" in the sense of "joining yourself to another." The Hebrew word behind "lend" is the "*hiphil*" or causative form of the verb לוה (*L.W.H*) and, in the context of this verse, it means "to lend" in the sense of "causing another to join themselves."

Livestock

While the Hebrew word מקנה (*miqneh*) is often translated as "cattle," this word more literally means "livestock." The Hebrews were master herders and shepherds and possessed a variety of stock.

Camel

These large and powerful animals are well suited for travel in the desert because of their ability to travel long distances without water. They were often used to carry family members as well as their belongings when they traveled from pasture to pasture.

The Hebrew word for "camel" is גמל (*gamel*), the origin of our word "camel." This word is from the root גמל (*gamal*) meaning "wean" or "ripen." This "adopted root" is derived from the parent root גם (*gam*) meaning "gather to the water." When a child is "weaned" he no longer derives liquid from the mother but from the watering hole. A camel is one that "gathers to the water to drink."

Cattle

The ox was a common labor animal used to pull plows and wagons. Because of these abilities, only on very rare and special occasions, such as a large group of visitors or a festival, was one of these animals slaughtered for a meal.

There are several Hebrew words used for cows, bulls, oxen and cattle.

Sheep

One of the principal animals found in the nomad's flock is the sheep. The wool of the fleece was used for clothing. The milk of the sheep was a part of their diet and was also made into a cheese. One was occasionally slaughtered for a meal, especially when visitors arrived or for a festival. The horns of the rams were used to make trumpets called *shofars*. The skin of the slaughtered animals was made into clothing or bags for storage.

Goat

The goat served many of the same functions as the sheep including milk, cheese, leather and· meat. The horns of the goats, smaller than the rams, were made into flasks for carrying olive oil, a common food ingredient or a medicine for wounds. The hair of the goat was also vital in the construction of the nomad's tent.

Donkey

This animal was mostly used for transporting people and materials.

Living Soul

Living

The Hebrew word חַי (*hhai*), usually translated as "life," is pronounced like the English greeting "Hi," but the "H" is pronounced hard, like the "ch" in the name "Bach."

The concept of "life" is an abstract thought, meaning that "life" cannot be seen, heard, smelled, tasted or felt. As the Hebrew language does express abstract thought, it is always expressed through concrete ideas. In order to demonstrate this process of concrete and abstract thought, let us examine the meaning of the word "heart," which in Hebrew is the word לֵב (*lev*). First, the heart is the concrete and physical "heart," the organ in the chest. Second, this Hebrew word represents the idea of the "mind," for the ancient Hebrews understood the "heart" to be the seat of thought (in contrast to our understanding of thought being associated with the brain).

When we come to the word חַי (*hhai*), we understand the abstract concept behind the word as "awareness," "existence," etc., but what was the concrete background to the word? The following passage (quoted from the KJV) can help us unravel this mystery:

> "Wilt thou hunt the prey for the lion? or fill the appetite of the young lions" (Job 38:39, KJV)

The word "appetite" in this verse is the translator's translation of the word *hhai*. The word "appetite" is also an abstract word and was probably chosen for the translation as it best fits with the idea of "life." But, if we replace "appetite" with "stomach," a more concrete Hebraic concept, we find that the verse makes much more sense.

*"Wilt thou hunt the prey for the lion? Or fill the
<u>stomach</u> of the young lions"*

Just as the heart is the seat of thought, according to Hebrew thought the stomach is the seat of life. If we think about this, we can easily understand why. First, remember that the Hebrews were nomads who traveled from pasture to pasture with their flocks in search of food and water. This was their primary goal in "life." If food and water were in plenty, life was good; if they were not, life was very bad.

Soul

The Hebrew word נפש (*nephesh*) is usually translated as "soul," but what is the soul? *Webster's Dictionary* gives the following definition: "The spiritual nature of humans, regarded as immortal, separable from the body at death, and susceptible to happiness or misery in a future state." In most cases, people will understand the soul through this definition. But, as I have so often stated, our interpretation of Biblical words should be from a Hebraic perspective, not a modern western viewpoint such as we find in the English dictionaries.

If we look at the various ways this word is translated in an English translation such as the KJV, we see a wide variation in its interpretation. Some of these translations include *soul, life, person, mind, heart, creature, body, dead, desire, man, appetite, lust, thing, self, beast, pleasure, ghost, breath* and *will*. What exactly does this word mean?

I had always assumed that only humans had a soul, but it was during a study of the word "soul" that I discovered that translations often influence how we interpret Biblical concepts. In the KJV translation of Genesis 2:7 we find that man is a "living soul" and in Genesis 1:21 we find that animals are "living creatures." When I first started using a concordance to look up the original Hebrew words, I was amazed to discover that these two phrases were identical Hebrew phrases: *nephesh chayah*. Why would the translators translate *nephesh chayah* as "living soul" in one place and "living creatures" in another? It was this discovery that prompted me to learn the Hebrew language.

In the Hebrew mind, we are composed of three entities; body, breath and mind. The body is the vessel composed of flesh, bones and blood. The mind, or the heart in Hebrew thought, is one's thoughts. The breath is one's character; it is what makes a person who they are.

The soul is the whole of the person, the unity of the body, breath and mind. It is not some immaterial spiritual entity; it is you, all of you, your whole being or self.

Moses the Servant

Each individual is designed to follow a passion. A passion that is pursued as a hobby, such as sports, collecting, etc., results in great satisfaction but little is gained. When that passion is your occupation, there is great benefit, as you will more than likely succeed and grow because of the passion.

Any form of art, whether it is a painting, writing, etc., done without passion is drab and lifeless. But once passion is interjected into the art, it comes to life as the heart and soul of the individual is transplanted into the art.

Within a kingdom, there are two types of people: those who are subjects to the king, and those who are servants of the king. The subjects confine their passions to their family and business and are virtually oblivious to the needs and desires of the king. On the other hand, the servant is continually occupied with the needs and wishes of the king. His sole purpose in life, his passion, is to recognize and fulfill the needs, desires, wishes and will of the king. A good servant will learn from and study the king until he knows the king so well he can anticipate the needs and wishes of the king. A servant knows what the king wants because the will of the master is in him; the servant becomes *echad* (one, or in unity) with the king.

According to Amos 3.7, the prophets are the servants of YHWH. The Hebrew in this passage literally states that YHWH makes his foundations (the Hebrew word here "sod" also means the mysteries) naked before the servant prophets. He literally lays completely bare all his plans and mysteries to the prophets, who in turn will carry the plans and mysteries to the people. A prophet who performs his function with passion will be a mighty servant for YHWH.

The majority of Israel, as well as today's followers of God, are subjects. We continually live our lives to ourselves, following after our needs and desires with little regard for the desires of the King. Moshe and a few other prophets in the history of Israel have shown us what a true servant of God is capable of doing and being.

Name Changes

When it comes to giving names in the Bible, we find something very interesting. God gave Adam his name. Adam named the animals, and after the fall he named Eve and their children. The one who has authority over another chooses that one's name.

Isaac gave the name Jacob to his son, but after Isaac died and Jacob met with God, his name was changed to Israel. God did this because now he had authority over Jacob and not Isaac.

When it comes to Abraham and Sarah, their names were originally Abram and Sarai, but in Hebrew, these names are אברם (ABRM) and שרי (SRY).

These names were given to them by their fathers, but when God met with them he changed their names to Abraham and Sarah, which in Hebrew are written as אברהם (ABRHM) and שרה (SRH).

Note that there is only one letter added to both names, the letter ה (H). The name of this letter is "hey," which is a Hebrew word that means "look!" Now that God has authority over Abraham and Sarah, he changed their names by adding this one letter, and now their descendants, the Jewish people, "look" to them as their fore-parents just as he promised them in Genesis 15:5.

Names

Any study in the various names of the Bible should begin with an understanding of how names are formed in Hebrew. The name of a people, their land and their language begins with a patriarch, an individual who is considered the "father" of a people.

In Genesis 10:22 we read that ארם (Aram) was the son of Shem.

A male descendantof Aram is called ארמי (aramiy), such as in Genesis 25:20. Some translations, such as the RSV, translate this name as "Aramean," while other translations, such as the KJV and ASV, use the name "Syrian," which comes from the Greek Septuagint.

A female descendant of Aram is called ארמיה (aramiyah, see 1 Chronicles 7:14). Some translations, such as the KJV and ASV, translate this name as "Aramitess," while others, such as the RSV, translate it as "Aramean."

The descendants of Aram are called ארמים (*aramiym*), simply the plural form of ארמי (*aramiy*), such as can be seen in 2 Kings 8:28. While the NRS translates this as "Arameans," most translations use "Syrians."

The land of the Arameans is called ארם (Aram), the same as the name of the Patriarch, such as in Numbers 23:7. Some translations use "Aram" and "Syria" for the Hebrew ארם (Aram) interchangeably. For example, in the KJV the name ארם (Aram) is written as "Aram" in Numbers 23:7, but is translated as "Syria" in 1 Kings 10:29. Other translations use "Syria" exclusively.

The language of the Arameans would be called ארמית (*aramiyt*), as seen in 2 Kings 18:26. This name is translated as "Aramaic" in some translations or as "Syrian" or "Syriac" in others.

When doing studies in the New Testament, it is helpful to know how the Greek language deals with each of these names. The best way to examine this is through the Greek *Septuagint* which in some cases, as pointed out above, uses some very different methods for translating names.

Natives, Strangers, Immigrants and Foreigners

In the Old Testament, we have four different people groups: the natives, strangers, immigrants and foreigners.

Attempting to differentiate between these different people groups can be very difficult if you are using a translation, as it is not uncommon for a translation to use the same English word for different groups. For instance, the King James Version uses the word "stranger" for זור (*Z.W.R*, a stranger, see Leviticus 2:10), גר (*ger*, an immigrant, see Exodus 2:22) and נכרי (*nakhriy*, a foreigner, see Deuteronomy 17:15). This is why it is imperative that one use a Hebrew dictionary, such as Strong's, when doing a study of Biblical words.

Native

The natives (sometimes translated as "home-born") are those who are born to one of the twelve tribes of Israel. The Hebrew word for a native is אזרח (*ezrahh*). This word comes from the verbal root זרח (*Z.R.Hh*), which means to "come up" or "come out of." So an *ezrahh* is one has "come out of" Israel.

> All that are <u>home-born</u> shall do these things after this manner, in offering an offering made by fire, of a sweet savor unto Jehovah. (Numbers 15:13, ASV)

Stranger

The Hebrew verb זור (*Z.W.R*) means "to be separated out." The participle form of this verb means a "stranger," one who is separated out. This word is frequently used in the Torah for someone who is not from one's own tribe:

> to be a memorial unto the children of Israel, to the end that no <u>stranger</u>, that is not of the seed of Aaron, come near to burn incense before Jehovah; that he be not as Korah, and as his company: as Jehovah spake unto him by Moses. (Numbers 16:40, ASV)

> "If brothers dwell together, and one of them dies and has no son, the wife of the dead shall

167

*not be married outside the family to a
stranger; her husband's brother shall go in to
her, and take her as his wife, and perform the
duty of a husband's brother to her.*
(Deuteronomy 25:5, RSV)

Immigrant

The Hebrew word for an immigrant (often translated as
"stranger" or "sojourner") is גר (*ger*) and is derived from the
verb גור (*G.W.R*), which means to "dwell with" or "dwell
among." So an immigrant is one who is not a native-born
Israeli, but lives with the natives. According to the Torah, the
immigrants are to live according to the same customs and
laws as the natives:

> *One law shall be to him that is home-born,
> and unto the stranger (גר) that sojourneth
> (גור) among you.* (Exodus 12:49, ASV)

And they are to be treated the same way as a native because
the Israelites were once immigrants:

> *And a sojourner shalt thou not wrong, neither
> shalt thou oppress him: for ye were sojourners
> in the land of Egypt.* (Exodus 22:21, ASV)

However, there are still some differences between a native
and an immigrant, as is apparent in the following verse:

> *Ye shall not eat of anything that dieth of itself:
> thou mayest give it unto the sojourner that is
> within thy gates, that he may eat it; or thou
> mayest sell it unto a foreigner...* (Deuteronomy
> 14:21, ASV)

Foreigner

A foreigner is one who was born in a foreign land, but unlike an immigrant, is not bound to the customs and laws of the native or immigrant:

> Unto a *foreigner* thou mayest lend upon interest; but unto thy brother thou shalt not lend upon interest. (Deuteronomy 14:21, ASV)

There are two Hebrew words for a foreigner; נכרי (*nakhriy*) and נכר (*nekhar*). Both of these words are derived from the root נכר (*N.K.R*) meaning "to be recognizable," probably because a foreigner is easily recognizable due to their very different culture and lifestyle.

Nomads

Many Biblical characters, such as Abraham, Isaac, Jacob, Moses, David and others lived a nomadic lifestyle. A nomad lived in tents and traveled from location to location in search of water and pastures for their livestock.

The Wilderness

The home of the nomad was the wilderness, often dry and arid, but with an occasional oasis, river, water basin and pasture. The nomad was as much at home in the wilderness as we are in our own environment. He also knew the area in which he traveled very well. He knew where all the water sources were, where pastures were located at different times of the year and all the landmarks which directed him on his travels.

Rain is the most important element to the nomad, as without it, he, his family, his flocks and herds could not survive. Each area received rain at different times of the year and in different locations. It was the chief's responsibility to ensure that they were at the right places at the right times. The rains may be local providing water and pasture, but may also be very distant. These distant rains would flood the rivers, causing them to overflow and water the grounds near the rivers within their area of travels.

Possessions

Nomads lived a very simple life and because of their constant travels, they could not carry a great amount of supplies and equipment. Their major possession was the tent made of goat hair, the poles, stakes and ropes for supporting the tent, a curtain to divide the tent into two parts (male and female sides) and a carpet for the floor. The nomad's wealth was measured by the size of his flocks and herds which supplied him with most of his needs including milk, meat, skin, hair for tents, horns for trumpets and liquid containers and many other odds and ends.

His cooking supplies and equipment consisted of bags made of skins for carrying food reserves such as grains and dried fruits; a few utensils such as spoons, knives and bowls; and a grinding mill for making flour out of grains. He also carried harvesting supplies such as sickles and mattocks to gather crops when available. For defense, he carried weapons such as the bow and arrow, spears and knives. Many of his weapons were everyday tools that could be used as a weapon. For instance, the tent poles, which were sharp at one, were also used as spears.

Family

A nomadic camp consisted of about 25 to 50 members. Any less and it would be difficult to protect the family and any more would be difficult to feed. Usually, the oldest member of the family was the head, or chief, of the clan. The remainder of the clan would consist of his brothers, sons, nephews and grandsons as well as their wives. Each clan was an independent entity with the chief as judge and ruler. He had the ultimate authority in all manners including where they went, discipline, management of the flocks and herds and the daily tasks of the camp.

When a clan became too large to support itself, it was divided and separated with all of the clans belonging to one tribe. The name of the tribe was generally that of the original family patriarch and each clan carried the name of its original patriarch.

Foods and Medicines

The nomad's diet consisted of bread, fruits (when available), milk and cheese and meat. Grains, such as barley and wheat, were gathered and ground into flour and mixed with water and placed on hot rocks to make bread. Some of the fruits available were grapes, pomegranates, olives and dates. These were often dried for later use and sometimes mixed with flour for cake type bread. Milk was taken from the sheep and goats and also was used to make cheese. Animals from the flock were occasionally butchered, especially for special events such as when guests arrived but not on a regular basis.

Olives were not only used as a food source, but for medicinal purposes, as well. Olive oil was drunk for stomach and intestinal problems and applied to wounds as an antiseptic. The fat of animals was made into soap for washing and bathing.

Social Activities

The men often would gather together, usually at mealtimes, to discuss past events, needs, locations and other details of operating the camp. The women gathered together to prepare foods, make clothing and make tent repairs. Storytelling was probably one of the most important forms of entertainment. The older members of the clan would tell the stories of their history to the children in order to pass on the experiences of the tribe and clans to the next generation.

One of the major responsibilities of the clan was to provide hospitality to anyone who came to them. This may be a member of a related clan or even an enemy of another tribe. In both cases, it was the responsibility of the clan to provide food, shelter and protection as long as they were within their camp.

Religion

The religion of the nomads was very different from our understanding of religion. The whole of the nomad's life was his religion. As his very existence was dependent upon rain, he understood that his life was in God's hands at all times. The nomad saw the power, justice, love and mercy of God in all things and all of his activities, from eating to making shelter, were seen as a service to God. The nomad lived in harmony with his surroundings and understood his being one with God who created all things. In short, his life was one long prayer to God.

Office of Priest

> And you shall put them upon Aaron your brother, and upon his sons with him, and shall *anoint* them and *ordain* them and *consecrate* them, that they may *serve me as priests*. (Exodus 28:41, RSV)

In this verse are four verbs describing Aaron and his sons' installation as priests: anoint, ordain, consecrate and serve as priest. While these words describe this installation, they do so from an abstract perspective. The Hebrew verbs in the Hebrew text describe this installation from a more concrete perspective that is hidden by the English translation.

The verb משח (M.Sh.HH) is translated as "anoint," which unlike the other three translations, is a concrete concept. The verb literally means to "smear," as can be seen in Jeremiah 22:14 where it is translated as "paint," "to smear on a color." Aaron and his sons were "smeared" with oil as a sign of their installation.

The RSV translates the verb מלא (M.L.A) with the word "ordain" and in the KJV it is translated as "consecrate," both being abstracts. In the Hebrew, there is more than just the verb, but a phrase, which reads ומלאת את ידם (umileyta et yadam) which literally translates as "and you will fill their hand." The actual meaning of this phrase is uncertain, but may be related to an Akkadian (another Semitic culture) custom of handing a scepter to the king at his ordination, "a filling of his hand."

The verb קדש (Q.D.Sh) is translated as "consecrate" in the RSV, and in the KJV it is translated as "sanctify," again abstracts. The Hebrew word means to "set apart" or "to separate" from the whole for a special purpose. Aaron and his sons have been separated from the rest of the community for the special purpose of taking care of and administering the tabernacle.

The Hebrew verb כהן (K.H.N) is variously translated as "minister in the priest's office," "serve as priest" or "be a priest." The literal concrete meaning of this word can be found in Isaiah 61:10 which reads, in part, "A bridegroom decks himself with ornaments." In this passage, the word "decks" translates the verb כהן, which literally means to "adorn." Aaron and his sons were adorned with special garments and ornaments. The noun כוהן (*kohen*) usually translated as "priest," literally means "adorned one."

Below is the literal and more concrete translation of this verse:

> And you will clothe them, Aharon your brother and his sons with him, and you will smear them, and you will fill their hand, and you will set them apart, and they will be adorned for me.

Past and Future

In the Hebrew Bible, the "past" is expressed with the Hebrew word תמול (*temol*), which literally means "yesterday." This noun is derived from the Hebrew verb מול (*mul*), which means "to be in front."

In the Hebrew Bible, the "future" is expressed with the Hebrew word מחר (*mahhar*), which literally means "tomorrow." This noun is derived from the Hebrew verb אחר (*ahhar*), which means "to be behind."

In our modern Western philosophy, we associate the "past" as being "behind" us and the "future" as "in front" of us. The reason for this is that we view time linearly. But the Hebrew philosophy is just the opposite, the reason being that they perceived time from their vantage point. To them, the "past" was "in front" of them because it was "known," they could see it, but the "future," which was unknown, is behind them and could not be seen.

Paragogic Nun

Hebrew verbs can have a variety of prefixes and/or suffixes added to the verb root. For instance, when the letter ת (*tav*) is added to the front of the verb עבד (*Ah.B.D*), the conjugated verb תעבד (*ta'aved*), meaning "you (masculine singular) serve," is formed. When the letter ו (*vav*) is then added to the end of this verb, it becomes תעבדו (*ta'av'du*), meaning "you (masculine plural) serve." On rare occasions, one will find the letter ן (*nun*) added to the end of a verb conjugation and it is this *nun* that is the paragogic *nun*. This word can be found in the following verse where the phrase "shall serve" is the translation of תעבדון (*ta'av'dun*), the final letter, the paragogic *nun*, which is being translated as "shall."

> *He said, "But I will be with you, and this shall be the sign for you, that I have sent you: when you have brought the people out of Egypt, you shall serve God on this mountain." (Exodus 3:12, ESV)*

So, while תעבדו (*ta'av'du*) means "you will serve," תעבדון (*ta'av'dun*) means "you SHALL serve."

Pillar of the Cloud

> *And it came to pass, as Moses entered into the tabernacle, the cloudy pillar descended, and stood at the door of the tabernacle, and the LORD talked with Moses. (Exodus 33:9, KJV)*

In some translations, including the KJV, the word "LORD" is written in italics, meaning that it has been added to the text. Why did the translators feel it was necessary to add the word "LORD?" Did they believe that the text needed to be fixed?

This verse is translated as follows in the author's *Revised Mechanical Translation:*

> *and it will come to pass, when Mosheh is about to come unto the tent, the pillar of the cloud will go down, and he will stand at the opening of the tent, and he will speak with Mosheh,*

Notice that the second half of this verse includes three verbs; go down, stand and speak. When two or more verbs are written, only the first verb will identify the subject of the verb, which is then applied to the following verbs. Here is an example from Exodus 2:15, also from the author's Revised Mechanical Translation:

> *And Mosheh fled away from the face of Paroh, and he settled in the land of Mid'yan and he settled upon the well.*

Note that only the first verb identifies Mosheh as the subject the verb and the following two verbs use the pronoun "he," in reference to Mosheh. We can see the same structure in Exodus 33:9 where the first verb states, "the pillar of the cloud will go down," and the following two verbs simply say, "he will stand," and "he will speak." It should be noted that in Hebrew, all nouns are either masculine or feminine and since the word עמוד (*amud*) is a masculine word, it would be identified with the masculine pronoun (he).

From the grammar in Exodus 33:9, we can see that it was the "pillar" that spoke with Mosheh. The standard translations have revised the text so that the "pillar" remains an inanimate object and YHWH, as a separate entity, becomes the active participant. Does this mean that YHWH is taking an inactive role here? Not at all. In verse 11 we read that it is YHWH who is speaking to Mosheh." Therefore, we can conclude that YHWH is not "in" or "with" the pillar, he "is" the pillar.

Poetic License

Hebrew authors love to make word puns. The first one appears in Genesis 1:2, where it says, *"tohu v'vohu,"* which is usually translated something like, "without form and void." When you read the Hebrew text, you come across these word puns all the time.

The second part of Genesis 36:31 is a good example of an author taking poetic license to create a word pun:

> *...before there reigned any king over the children of Israel.* (KJV)

Here is a transliteration of the Hebrew text of this passage.

> *liph'ney m'lakh melekh liv'ney yis'rael*

The words *m'lakh* (reign) and *melekh* (king) are one set of word puns and *liph'ney* (before) and *liv'ney* (to the sons) is another.

The poetic license is the word *liv'ney*. The proper way to say "reign over the sons of Israel" is *"m'lakh al b'ney Yisra'el"* and we see many examples of this throughout the Hebrew Bible. However, only in this one verse, the author chose to write this as, *"m'lakh liv'ney Yisra'el,"* which literally translates as "reign to the sons of Israel." The author chose to not use the proper form in order to have the word *liv'ney* be a pun with the word *liph'ney* (before).

Poetry of the Creation Account

It is generally understood that the creation account of Genesis chapter one is a chronological order of events. It should be understood that Hebrew writers were not as concerned about chronology as we are in our modern culture. To prove that the seven days of creation are not written in chronological order, we can compare day one with day four.

On day one God divided the light from the darkness (Genesis 1:4). On day four God made the sun and the moon and placed them in the firmament to "divide the light from the darkness" (Genesis 1:18). If God separated the light from the darkness on day one, how can he do the same thing on day four? The reason is that Genesis chapter one is written in a form of Hebrew poetry and day one and day four are describing the same event.

As Hebrew poetry is written much differently than our own Western style of poetry, many do not recognize the poetry, which can cause problems when translating or interpreting these passages.

Approximately 75% of the Tanakh (Old Testament) is poetry. All of Psalms and Proverbs are Hebrew poetry, and even the book of Genesis is filled with poetry. There are several reasons the Hebrews used poetry: much of the *Torah* was sung and poetry is easier to sing; also, poetry and songs are easier to memorize than straight texts. Parallel poetry (as in Genesis 1) emphasizes something of great importance, as the creation story is. The rabbis believed that "if something is worth saying, it is worth saying beautifully." There is much more poetry in the Bible than most recognize, because most people do not understand it.

Parallelism is the expression of one idea in two or more different ways. Parallelism is most commonly found in the book of Psalms and Proverbs, but is found throughout the whole of the Hebrew Bible:

"Thy word is a lamp to my feet and a light to my path." (Psalms 119:105, RSV)

The above is an example of a simple parallel and can be written in this manner:

Your word is:

1. a lamp to my feet
2. a light for my path

Here we see that the words "lamp" and "light" are paralleled as well as the words "my feet" and "my path." Below is another example of this style of poetry:

"My son, do not forget my teaching, but let your heart keep my commandments." (Proverbs 3:1)

In this verse the words "my teachings" is paralleled with "my commands" and "you shall not forget" is paralleled with "your heart shall guard" and can be written as follows:

My son:

1. do not forget my teaching
2. let your heart keep my commandments

Below is Psalm 15:1-3 broken down into its poetic sequences. In this example, each thought is represented by the letters A, B, C and D. Each expression of a thought is represented by the numbers 1 and 2:

A1. Lord, who may dwell in your sanctuary?
A2. Who may live on your holy hill?
B1. He whose walk is blameless.
B2. and who does what is righteous.
C1. who speaks the truth from his ear.

C2. and has no slander on his tongue.
D1. who does his neighbor no wrong.
D2. and casts no slur on his fellow man.

In the following example from Isaiah 6:10, three thoughts are given, each using a part of the body. Then the same three thoughts are repeated, but in reverse order:

A1. Make the *heart* of this people fat,
B1. and make their *ears* heavy,
C1. and shut their *eyes*;
C2. lest they see with their *eyes*,
B2. and hear with their *ears*,
A2. and understand with their *heart*, and return, and be healed."

Another common form of parallelism is the use of negatives where two opposing ideas are stated, as we see in Proverbs 11:19-20:

A1. Righteousness brings one to life
B1. Pursuit of evil brings one to his death
B2. a twisted heart is an abomination of YHWH
A2. a mature path is his pleasure

The Creation account of Genesis 1:1 through 2:3 is written in this very same style of Hebrew Poetry. As you read the following narrative, notice that days 1 and 3 are describing the same event of separating and filling the sky and land, days 2 and 4 are describing the separating and filling of the water and sky and days 3 and 6 describe the separating and filling of the land.

A. *Elohiym* filled the sky and the land because it was empty and it was all in chaos so the wind of *Elohiym* settled upon the water (1:1 to 1:2)
A1. Day 1 - *Elohiym* separates (1:3 to 1:5, Day one)

a. light

b. dark

> A2. Day 2 - *Elohiym* separates (1:6 to 1:8, Day two)
>
> a. water
>
> b. sky
>
> > A3. Day 3 - *Elohiym* separates (1:9 to 1:13, Day three)
> >
> > a. land
> >
> > b. plants spring up from the land

B1. Day 4 - *Elohiym* fills (1:14 to 1:19, Day four)

a. the light with the sun

b. the dark with the moon

> B2. Day 5 - *Elohiym* fills (1:20 to 1:23, Day five)
>
> a. fills the water with fish
>
> b. fills the sky with birds
>
> > B3. Day 6 - *Elohiym* fills (1:24 to 1:31, Day six)
> >
> > a. the land with animals and man
> >
> > b. plants are given as food

B. *Elohiym* Finishes his separating and filling of the sky and the land and respects the seventh day because in it he ceased from his occupation (2:1 to 2:3, Day seven)

Genesis chapters 2 and 3 also appear to have a poetical structure.

1a. Garden (2:8-14)

    1b. Man (2:15-21)

        1c. Woman (2:22-25)

            1d. Serpent (3:1-5)

                2. Man & Woman (3:6-13)

            3d. Serpent (3:14-15)

Pond, Pound, Ponder

In the English language the word "pound" has two meanings. The first is something with weight (as in a "pound of salt") and the second is an enclosure (as in a "dog pound"). Etymology scholars agree that these are two different words from two different sources and this may very well be the case, but there is some very interesting evidence to suggest that there may actually be a connection between the two.

It is assumed that the word "ponder" is derived out of the word pound (weight), in the sense of giving weight to an idea or thought or "weighing the options," so to speak. However, the word "ponder" is also defined as "reflecting" on an idea or thought. A reflection is what is seen on the surface of the water, such as a "reflecting pond." The word "pond" is derived from the word "pound" (enclosure) in the sense that a pond is enclosed by its banks. In Eastern cultures, ponds are a very common place for meditating (reflecting/pondering).

In the Hebrew language, the idea of "pondering" is also closely related to bodies of water, as can be seen in the following verse:

> ...He will ponder (meditate) on his teachings day
> and night, and he will be like a tree planted by a
> channel of water..." (Psalm 1:2-3)

There are several Hebrew words meaning to meditate. One of these is the word שיח (si'ahh), which is closely related to the word שחה (sahhah) meaning "to swim."

The purpose of meditation is to generate strength inside one's self. This strength may be manifested in an emotional or psychological response, such as in creating courage or confidence. The strength may also be revealed in a physical sense, such as in creating the ability to stand up to an enemy, trouble or burden.

In addition, water is involved in most of the miracles of the Bible:

- Creation begins with the Wind of God hovering over the waters (Genesis 1:2).
- The destruction of all mankind, save Noah, was done with a flood (Genesis 6:17).
- The infant Moses is saved from Pharaoh's decree to kill all the children by being placed in the river of the Nile (Exodus 2:5).
- The water in Egypt was turned to blood (Exodus 4:9).
- Moses' parting of the Red Sea (Exodus 14:21).
- Moses brought water to the thirsty Israelites by striking the rock (Exodus 17:6).
- Quail from the sea fed the Israelites (Numbers 11:31).
- *Manna* appeared on the ground after the dew dried up (Exodus 16:14). The stopping of the flow of the Jordan River (Joshua 3:13).
- Elijah drowns his offering with water and it still ignites (1 Kings 18:38).
- Naaman is healed of leprosy in the Jordan River (2 Kings 5:14).
- Jonah was saved from drowning in the sea by a fish (Jonah 1:17).

Positive and Negative

When I speak of the positive and negative nature of *Elohim*, I am not speaking about a "moral" positive and negative, but the "forces" of positive and negative, much like the two poles of a magnet or the forces of the protons (positive) and electrons (negative) of an atom. God is a perfect balance of positive and negative: Good and Bad, Light and Dark, Large and Small, Make and Break, Loud and Quiet, Far and Near, One and Many, Male and Female, etc.

This concept of "balance" is virtually unknown in our western philosophy, but it is a very important one in the ancient philosophy of the Israelites and other ancient peoples. From this ancient perspective, "balance" is "order" and anything out of balance is chaos. In the following two verses we can see this balance of positive and negative within the actions of *Elohim*:

> In the beginning Elohim *created* the heavens and the earth. (Genesis 1:1, Author's Translation)

> I (Elohim) will *destroy* all [flesh] with the earth. (Genesis 6:13, Author's Translation)

In the first verse we see *Elohim* creating (positive) the world, but in the second verse, we see him destroying (negative) it.

> And Elohim said, Let there be light, and there was light. (Genesis 1:3, Author's Translation)

> And Moses drew near to the thick darkness where Elohim was. (Exodus 20:21, Author's Translation)

In these two verses, we see *Elohim* being associated with light (positive) and darkness (negative). It is interesting to note that

Jews and Christians always associate *Elohim* with light and Satan with darkness. However, almost every time *Elohim* appears to the Israelites, he is in the darkness.

In Genesis 1:4 we read that "*Elohim* separated the light from the darkness." The word for light is feminine, while the word for darkness is masculine. Not only is this verse about the balance of light and darkness, but it is also about the balance of the masculine and the feminine.

In the next two verses we see two contrasting attributes of YHWH, mercy (positive) and a consuming fire (negative):

> *YHWH your Elohim is a merciful El.* (Deuteronomy 4:31, Author's Translation)

> *YHWH your Elohim is a consuming fire.* (Deuteronomy 4:24, Author's Translation)

In Genesis 1:26 we find that the image of *Elohim* is male (positive) and female (negative). In Genesis 3:5 and 3:22 we see that *Elohim* is good (positive) and bad (negative). In Joshua 23:15 we read that YHWH does good things (positive) and bad things (negative). In Deuteronomy 30:1 YHWH provides blessings (positive) and curses (negative). In Isaiah 45:7 we are told that God makes peace (positive) and evil (negative).

Below is one of the most vivid passages in the entire Bible that demonstrates this positive and negative aspect of ancient philosophy:

> *For everything there is a season, and a time for every purpose under heaven: a time to be born, and a time to die; a time to plant, and a time to pluck up that which is planted; a time to kill, and a time to heal; a time to break down, and a time to build up; a time to weep,*

and a time to laugh; a time to mourn, and a time to dance; a time to cast away stones, and a time to gather stones together; a time to embrace, and a time to refrain from embracing; a time to seek, and a time to lose; a time to keep, and a time to cast away; a time to rend, and a time to sew; a time to keep silence, and a time to speak; a time to love, and a time to hate; a time for war, and a time for peace. (Ecclesiastes 3:1-8, ASV)

Power and Authority

When we read the Bible we must read it from the mindset of the writer and not from our own way of thinking. The authors of the Bible lived in a culture that was very different from our own and they perceived the world from a different perspective. If we truly want to grasp what the authors were trying to say, we must remove our westernized thinking caps and replace them with the thinking cap of one from the ancient Near East (Orient).

Have you ever heard that the ancients considered their rulers as gods? This is true for the Egyptians who saw the Pharaohs as gods, the Babylonians who saw the Kings as gods and the Romans who saw the Caesars as gods.

In the Biblical text, the most basic word for a 'god' is אל (*el*). This Hebrew/Semitic word is found throughout the Near East and literally means "one of power and authority." The Semitic people did not view a 'god' as strictly a supernatural deity, but simply as "one of power and authority." Even in the Biblical text, the word אל is used for Laban in Genesis 31:29: "אל is in my hand to do you harm." Laban was the one in power and authority over Jacob and was, by the true sense of the meaning of the word, an אל.

From the ancient perspective, a 'god' is anyone or anything that has power and authority over another. Who has power and authority over us? If our government, then our government is our אל. In the same way, Abram's אל was the King of Babylon, which is why God had him leave and go to the wilderness where there was no king. Also, Moses' אל was the pharaoh of Egypt, and God removed him from there and brought him into the wilderness, as well.

At this point most of you will be saying, "No, the God of the Bible is my אל." Is that true? While I believe it is possible for this to be true in most cases, it is not. Let's examine a scenario. Let's say that in one way or another you were prevented from worshiping God or praying to him and you are no longer able to read or study the Bible. While I do believe this would have a negative impact on you and society as a whole, would it destroy you? No, you will continue to exist, you will still have grocery stores, gas stations, law enforcement and military for protection, electricity, garbage pick-up, etc. But let's change the scenario a little bit and say that our government, for one reason or another, no longer exists. Without a government, we lose our entire monetary system, we lose our law enforcement and military. Without a monetary system there are no more grocery stores, gas stations, power houses, etc. In short, you are completely on your own. Could you survive? Most could not, and within a few short weeks a major portion of our population would be dead. Now, which "power and authority" is more influential on your life today?

Religion

The concept of "religion" is a purely Greco-Roman (Western) concept as it divides a person's life into a religious aspect and a secular aspect. This form of dualism is foreign to the Ancient Hebrew mind, which instead saw all aspects of life as one and the same. Prayer was considered just as important as eating and worship, just as important as work. The Modern Hebrew language, which is just as Western as the English language is, uses the Biblical Hebrew word דת (*dat*) for the concept of "religion," but this Biblical Hebrew word originally meant "edict" or "decree" in Biblical Hebrew.

Resources

The early Hebrews were a nomadic people, living in tents traveling from pasture to pasture with their flocks and herds. Their flocks provided much of their needs. The black hair of their goats was spun into panels for making tents. Their tents, black in color, kept the air inside the tent cool. It was constructed with a very low profile because of the strong desert winds. The meat from the goats and sheep were used for food and was always served when visitors came to the tent. Milk from the goats and sheep was commonly drunk and also made into cheese. The skins of the livestock were turned into leather used for various things such as water bags, sandals, bags, etc. The wool from the sheep was used for clothing and blankets. Grains were also a large staple of the Hebrews. The people would often stay in one area long enough to plant and harvest grains that were made into bread. Other foods harvested included grapes, dates, pomegranates, and melons. One of the best passages in the Bible showing the life of the nomadic Hebrew is found in Genesis 18:1-8.

Righteous and Wicked

> *The eyes of the LORD are toward the righteous, and his ears toward their cry.* (Psalm 34:15 RSV, verse 16 in the Hebrew Bible)

Who are the righteous and what is righteousness? As our verse above indicates, God sees and listens to the righteous, so it would be in our best interest to know for certain what righteousness is. Every Hebrew word in the mind of the Ancient Hebrews painted a picture of action. By doing a little investigation this picture can be found.

The first step in finding a more concrete meaning to a word is to find it used in a concrete context. For example, the word *barak* was almost always translated as "bless," but being an abstract word, we need to find it being used in a more concrete manner, which we do in Genesis 24:11. There it means "to kneel." This gives us a more concrete picture of the word. The problem with the word *tsadiyq*, the word that is often translated as "righteous," is that it was never used in a concrete manner.

The next method is to compare its use in Hebrew poetry where words were commonly paralleled with similar meaning words. A common form of Hebrew poetry is the expression of one idea in two different ways, as we can see in the passage below where the word righteous is paralleled with the word upright:

> *Be glad in the LORD, and rejoice, O <u>righteous</u>, and shout for joy, all you <u>upright</u> in heart!* (Psalm 32:11 RSV)

The Hebrew words *tsadiyq* (righteous) and *yashar* (upright) are paralleled many times in the Bible, indicating that in the

Hebrew mind these two words were similar in meaning. While the word "upright" can be understood as a concrete word meaning "straight up," the Hebrew word more literally means "straight," as in a straight path, as can be seen in the following passage:

> I will cause them to walk by the rivers of waters in a straight way, wherein they shall not stumble (Jeremiah 31:9, KJV)

Another common form of Hebrew poetry is to use opposites in parallel, such as in the following verse:

> For the arms of the <u>wicked</u> shall be broken; but the LORD upholds the <u>righteous</u>. (Psalm 37:17 RSV)

Here we find the word *rasha* (wicked) being used as an antonym (opposite in meaning) to the word *tsadiyq* (righteous). These two words are also commonly used together in the Bible, indicating the Hebrews saw these two words as opposites. While the word "wicked" is an abstract, we can find its concrete meaning in the verb form, which is found in the following passage:

> For I have kept the ways of the LORD, and have not <u>wickedly departed</u> from my God. (Psalm 18:21, KJV)

The verb form means to "depart" and the noun form means "one who has departed."

We now have a few clues into the meaning of a *tsadiyq*. He is one who is straight and does not depart from the way of God. The next step is to understand these concepts from the Ancient Hebraic culture, lifestyle and thought.

The Ancient Hebrews were a nomadic people who often traveled the same paths to pastures and campsites. Anyone leaving these straight paths can become lost and wander in the wilderness. A wicked person is seen as one lost on a crooked path, while a righteous person is one who remains on the straight path.

The next question is: how do we know what the path is in our lives as we attempt to remain on God's path?

> *And what great nation is there, that has statutes and ordinances so righteous as all this law (Torah, meaning teachings) which I set before you this day?* (Deuteronomy 4:8 RSV)

The teachings of God are the path. When we remember to show love, honor and respect to others and their property, we are on the path of righteousness; but when we forget the ways of God, we are leaving the path, and if we do not get back onto that path, we are in danger of becoming lost.

> *For YHWH knows the path of the <u>ones who follow the path</u> (tsadiyq), but the path of the <u>ones who depart from the path</u> (rasha) will perish.* (Psalm 1:6)

Roads, Streets and Paths

A common question is, "Is it really helpful to look at the Hebrew words behind a translation?" While many will say, "No, the English is sufficient," I have found that those who have no comprehension of Hebrew are the ones who say this. But those who know Hebrew, or have studied the Hebrew words of the Bible, understand that no translation can really convey the meaning of Hebrew words accurately. Case in point: in Biblical Hebrew there are multiple words for an object or animal depending on its function. By learning the meanings of these different words, deeper understanding of the text is achieved. As an example there are three Hebrew words for the moon:

1. ירח (y'rey'ahh & #3394) is used in reference to its path in the sky, as it comes from an unused root meaning "to follow a prescribed path."

2. חודש (hhodesh) is used in reference to a "new moon," as it comes from the root word חדש (Hh. D.Sh), which means "to be new" or "to be renewed."

3. בנה (lavanah) is used in reference to its "whiteness," as it is derived from the root לבן (L.B.N) meaning "to be white."

In the case of the different Hebrew words for a "path," "road" or "street," the Biblical Hebrew language has many words, each with its own nuance of meaning that will help in interpreting the text:

1. רחוב (rahhov) is derived from the root רחב (R.Hh.B), which means "to be wide," so this word is used for a "wide" road probably used for carts and wagons.

2. דרך (derekh) is derived from the root דרך (D.R.K) meaning "to take footsteps," so this word is used for "footpath" or "a trail."

3. שביל (shaviyl) appears to be derived from the root שבל (Sh.B.L, but written as שבר), which means "to exchange," as in trading; and this word for a road is probably used for a "trade route."

4. נתיב (*natiyv*) is derived from the root נתב (N.T.B, which is not found in the Hebrew Bible) meaning "to tramp," and this word for a road is probably used in reference to "a well-trodden path."

5. מסילה (*mesiylah*) is derived from the root סלל (S.L.L) meaning "to build up" or "to mound up," and this word for a road is probably used for a road that has been built up higher than the surrounding landscape, "a highway."

6. אורח (*orahh*) is used in reference to a path that is frequently taken and is from an unused root meaning "to follow a prescribed path," the same root word used for ירח (*y'rey'ahh* & #3394) meaning "the moon."

7. משעול (*mishol*) is "a narrow path" or "a path in a valley."

Sons of Israel

Why do some translations have "sons of Israel," but other translations have "children of Israel?" The Hebrew word for "son" is בן (*ben*) and "sons" is בנים (*benim*). The Hebrew word for "daughter" is בת (*bat*) and "daughters" is בנות (*banot*). However, if there is a group of "sons" and "daughters" the Hebrew will use the masculine plural בנים (*benim*). When I am translating the Hebrew, I will always translate it literally, so I always translate בנים (*benim*) as "sons." Usually the context of the passage will dictate if this masculine plural is referring to only male children or male and female children. However, in some cases, such as in the command that all the "sons of Israel" are to place fringes on their garments (Numbers 15:38), there is no context to help with this interpretation. Traditional

Judaism has decided that this is only referring to sons and not daughters, which is why Jewish women do not wear the fringes. Outside of Judaism, some believe that it is referring to only sons, and others believe it is referring to sons and daughters. This is a decision each person or group must make.

Spirit of God

The parent root of the word רוח (ru'ahh) is רח (rahh). In the ancient script, the first letter in this parent root is his (r), which is the picture of a man's head. The head is seen as the top of the body and can be the top or head of anything such as the body, time, mountaintop, rank, etc. This letter can also represent a man. The second letter is ﬡ (hh) and is a picture of the wall of a tent or enclosure that separates and protects what is inside from what is outside, such as inclement weather or predators. When these two letters are combined, they mean "the man of the enclosure."

The responsibilities of the nomadic man outside of the tent included the feeding, watering and caring for the livestock. Livestock are healthier and more productive when on a routine; therefore, the man followed a routine or "a prescribed path" each day when caring for his livestock.

There are several words derived from this parent root. The word ירח (Ye-Re-aHh) is "the moon," which follows a prescribed path each night from horizon to horizon:

> *And from the excellent produce of the sun and from the excellent yield of the moon (ירח - yere'ahh). Deuteronomy 33:14*

The word ארח (A-RaHh) is a traveler, one who follows a prescribed path to arrive at a specific destination:

A stranger did not lodge outside, I opened my door to the traveler (ארח - orehh). Job 31:32

The word רחה (*re-hheh*) is a millstone, a large circular stone that is revolved in a "prescribed path" on top of another stone to grind grain into flour:

All the firstborn in the land of Egypt will die, from the firstborn of Pharoah sitting on the throne to the firstborn of the maidservant who is behind the millstones (רחה - rehhah), and all the firstborn of the livestock. Exodus 11:5

The word רוח (*ru'ach*) is the wind. The Hebrew nomads were very familiar with the wind patterns, as they would follow a prescribed path indicating the coming season. From this word comes the idea of 'breath," as it is the wind of man which also follows a prescribed path of inhaling and exhaling. This word is often translated as "spirit," but Hebraically is the "breath." The ancient Hebrew saw the breath as an essential part of the man, just as much as the mind is.

The רוח (*ruahh* - wind) cannot be seen, but the effects of the wind can be. We can see the leaves of the tree moving in the wind and we can feel the wind against our bodies. In the same manner, God cannot be seen but we can see his effects all around us in his creation. Just as the winds follow a prescribed path through the seasons, God also follows a prescribed path; he is the same yesterday, today and forever.

Our life is a journey along the road that will lead to righteousness or wickedness. Just as the wind of the sky follows a prescribed path, our wind follows a prescribed path. When God gives us a new wind, his wind, he will cause us to follow his path:

And I will give to them a new heart and a new <u>*wind*</u> *I will give within them, and I will remove the heart of stone from their flesh and I will give to them a heart of flesh, and I will give within them* <u>*my breath and I will cause them*</u> <u>*to do my statutes they are to walk*</u> *and my laws they will guard and do them.* Ezekiel 36:26,27

Only by receiving the wind of God can we follow the correct path.

Tents

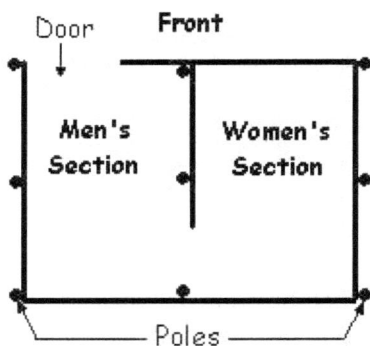

The tent was divided into two parts. The main section, behind the tent door, was the men's section. The other section was the women's section, with a wall dividing the two parts. The only persons allowed into the women's section were the father of the tent and children. Notice the similarity to the pictographic Hebrew letter *beyt* - ⌂. The word "*beyt*" is not only the name of a letter, but is also a common Hebrew word meaning "home." This letter is a representation of the floor plan of the tent, the "home" of the nomadic Hebrews.

The entrance to the tent was covered by a curtain which hung down from the top of the entrance. The Hebrew word *"dal"* means "hang down" and is the root for the word *dalet* meaning "door." This word is also the name of another Hebrew letter ד, a representation of the tent door. The door of the tent was the most important part of the tent, not because of its appearance, but by its function as the entrance into the tent:

> *He [Abraham] was sitting at the entrance of the tent as the day grew hot* (Genesis 18:1)

The door of the tent could be equated with the throne of a king. In the Hebrew culture, the father of the family was the "king," the one who held full authority over the family. The father would often sit at his door much like a king would sit on a throne. All family legal matters were performed at the tent. During the strong heat of the day, the father would often sit at his door watching his family, livestock and the road for travelers (Genesis 18:1, 2). The nomadic rules of hospitality were very strict and complex.

Tents were woven of black goat hair:

> *Dark am I....dark like the tents of Kedar, like the tent curtains of Solomon.* (Song of Solomon 1:5)

The hair was spun into strands which were then woven together forming panels approximately three feet wide and the length of the tent. Over time, the panels began to bleach from exposure to the sun and were periodically replaced. As much work was invested in their materials, very little was discarded, including the tent. The pieces of the tent that were removed were recycled into walls or mats.

Another Hebrew letter derived from the tent itself is the letter *hhet*, a word meaning "wall." This letter in the ancient pictographic script is 𐤇, a picture of a wall, as can be seen in the above picture.

The size of the tent depended on the size and wealth of the family. As the family grew, additional panels were added to increase the size of the tent:

> *Enlarge the place of your tent, stretch your tent curtains wide, do not hold back; lengthen your cords, strengthen your stakes.* (Isaiah 54:2)

The goat hair tent was unique in that it was perfectly suited for the desert regions of the Near East. A tent provided shade from the sun. The walls of the tent could be lifted to allow the breeze to pass through the tent. The black tent absorbed heat, keeping the tent warm. A fire was also built just inside the door for warmth.

Like any other cloth, there were tiny openings in the hair fabric. Light coming through holes in the black roof appeared as stars in the night sky:

> *He stretches out the heavens like a canopy, and spreads them out like a tent to live in.* (Isaiah 40:2)

When the hair fibers got wet from the rains, the fibers expanded, forming a watertight roof.

Strong ropes, secured by pegs driven into the ground, supported the poles which held up the tent:

I will drive him like a peg into a firm place; he will be a seat of honor for the house of his father. (Isaiah 22:23)

The word "firm" in the previous passage is the Hebrew word אמן (*A.M.N*) and is often translated as "believe." The walls of the tent are laid on the top of the ropes, thus allowing the wind to pass over the tent.

The nomadic family consisted of the *beyt* (house, family), *mishpechah* (clan) and *matteh* (tribe). All the family: children, parents and grandparents, resided in one tent. The clan consisted of the extended family: grandparents, aunts, uncles, cousins, etc., all residing in one camp and might have contained as many as 50 to 100 tents laid out in a circular pattern. When the clan became too large for one area to support it, the tribe split into two clans (see Genesis 13). All the clans (all being descended from one ancestor) may have covered hundreds of square miles making up the tribe. As an example: the house of Moses, of the clan of Levi, of the tribe of Israel.

Hhanan is a Hebrew word often translated as "grace," but is Hebraically understood as a "camp." The camp is a place of beauty, love, warmth and comfort.

Verb Forms

Hebrew verbs have seven different forms: *qal* (simple active), *niphal* (simple passive), *hiphil* (causative active), *hophal* (causative passive), *hitpa'el* (simple reflexive), *piel* (intensive active) and *pual* (intensive passive). Each form slightly changes the application of the verb, as will be demonstrated with the verb "to cut." The *qal* form is simply "cut." The *niphal* form would be "was cut." The *hiphil* form would be "made cut." The *hophal* is "was made cut." The *piel* is "slashed." The *pual* is "was slashed."

The Hebrew verb ראה (*ra'ah*) is identified in *Strong's Dictionary* as number 7200 and states that this word can mean "see" or "appear." This is a little misleading and one of the weaknesses of *Strong's Dictionary,* as it does not differentiate between the different forms of the verbs. The word ראה (*ra'ah*) means "to see," but when used in the *niphal* form it would be "was seen" which we can translate as "appear."

Voice and Assembly

The parent root קל (*qal*), written as ⟨P in the ancient pictographic script, is formed by combining the picture of the sun at the horizon, meaning "draw in," with the picture of a shepherd staff. The combined meaning is "to draw to the shepherd staff." The child root קול (*qol*) is translated as "voice," and it is the voice of the shepherd that calls the flock to be drawn toward his staff (the sign of his authority). Another child root derived from this parent root is קהל (*qahal*) meaning, "assemble." This word is used throughout the Bible for the "assembly" or "congregation" of Israel, the sheep who hear the voice of their shepherd YHWH:

> "These words YHWH spoke to all your
> <u>assembly</u> (קהל - a gathering flock) with a
> great voice (קול - voice of the shepherd) from
> in the midst of the fiery cloud on the
> mountain." Deuteronomy 5:22

In this passage, we can clearly see the imagery of the shepherd calling his sheep. When the voice of YHWH (the shepherd) came from the mountain, all of Israel (the sheep) gathered in front of the mountain (the staff) to hear his words.

Way, The

A common theme throughout the Old Testament is "the way of YHWH :"

> I have chosen him, that he may command his children and his household after him to guard the way of YHWH by doing righteousness and justice. (Genesis 18:19)

The word "way" is the Hebrew word דרך (*derekh*) literally meaning a "road" or "path." Israel's journey on the path of YHWH is frequently addressed, but often hidden behind the English translations.

Pointing out the road

From the root ירה (*Y.R.H*) comes the verb ירה (*Y.R.H*) meaning to "cast" or "throw," as seen in the following passages:

> Pharaoh's chariots and his host he <u>cast</u> into the sea. Exodus 15:4

> And I will <u>shoot</u> three arrows to the side of it. 1 Samuel 20:20

This same verb can also be translated as "teach" in the sense of "throwing the finger," or pointing the one who is being taught to walk in a particular direction:

> Teach me your way (Psalm 86:11)

This last verse could be translated literally as *Point me in the direction of your path*.

Derived from the root ירה (*Y.R.H*) is the noun תורה (*torah*), meaning "the direction that is pointed out" or a "teaching" as in Proverbs 1:8:

> *Hear, my son, your father's instruction, and reject not your mother's <u>teaching</u>.*

This same word is used throughout the Old Testament for the "teachings" of God our father:

> *but his delight is in the <u>teachings </u>of YHWH , and on his <u>teaching </u>he meditates day and night.* (Psalm 1:2)

The Nomadic migration through the wilderness

The Hebrew language is composed of a series of roots. The most basic, the parent roots, are formed by combining two letters together. In some cases, parent roots sharing a common letter are related in meaning, such as in the roots צא, צו and צי which are all related to the nomadic migration. When a third letter is added to the parent root, a child root is formed and the definition of this child root is going to be closely related to the parent.

The migration

The parent root צא (*Ts.A*) represents the migration of the nomad from one location to another. The child root יצא (*Y.Ts.A*) also has the definition of the migration. The verb יצא (*Y.Ts.A*), derived from this child root, can be found in Exodus 20:2:

> *I am YHWH your God, who <u>migrated </u>you out of the land of Egypt, out of the house of bondage.*

This is the beginning of Israel's migration from Egypt to the land he has promised them.

The directions

The parent root צו (Ts.W) represents the directions the nomad took on his migration. This same meaning is applied to the child root צוה (Ts.W.H), and its verbal form, צוה (Ts.W.H), can be seen in Deuteronomy 1:19:

> And we set out from Horeb... as YHWH our God _directed_ us.

God provided Israel with their directions during their migration toward the land he had promised them.

The directions can be directions for a physical journey through a land or for a journey through life. The noun מצוה (mitswah), derived from the child root צוה (Ts.W.H) by adding the letter מ (m), is used for this journey through life, as seen in Deuteronomy 6:25:

> And it will be righteousness for us, if we are careful to do all this _direction_ before the LORD our God.

The verb צוה (Ts.W.H) is commonly translated as a command, but this definition does not reflect the Hebraic background to the word. When we read about the "commands" of God in the Bible, we have this image of a general giving his commands to his troops. But the Hebraic concept behind these "commands" is the direction from God for our journey through life, so that we will not get lost from the correct path.

The wilderness

The parent root צי (*Ts.Y*) represents the place of the nomad's journey, the wilderness. From this parent root is derived the noun, ציי (*tsiyiy*), meaning "a wilderness" as in Psalm 72:9:

> They that dwell in the <u>wilderness </u>shall bow
> before him; and his enemies shall lick the dust.

The wilderness was filled with landmarks that the nomads followed to guide their way. The noun ציון (*tsiyuwn*), derived out of the parent root צי (*Ts.Y*) by adding the letters ון (*on*), means a landmark as seen in Jeremiah 31:21:

> Set up <u>Landmarks </u>for yourself, make yourself
> guideposts; consider well the highway, the
> road by which you went.

God had given Israel their directions to take them from landmark to landmark. As an example, God directed Israel to rest on the seventh day. The seventh day is not the direction; rather, it is the landmark to guide them on their journey through life from one Shabbat to the next. Each of the feasts was given as a landmark, and the *Torah* provides the directions to recognize and find these landmarks. Just as there were many different kinds of landmarks in the wilderness such as, mountains, rock outcroppings, wadis and rivers, God placed a wide variety of landmarks to guide Israel on their journey: a person in need or a lost animal, for instance. The *Torah* provided the directions to these landmarks, as well as what direction to take once one had arrived at the landmark.

On the path and lost from the path

When traveling the wilderness, it is important to stay on course in order to find the next landmark as well as the pastures and water sources. If one were to lose their way, they would become lost and may die if they did not return to the proper route. The idea of being on course and lost from the course is found in two Hebrew words, צדיק (*tsadiyq*) and רשע (*rasha*). The word *tsadiyq* literally means "to stay on course," "to remain on the path," while *rasha* means "to be lost from the path." *Tsadiyq* is usually translated as "righteous" and *rasha* as "wicked," but these English words do not convey the original meaning behind the Hebrew very well.

One who is *tsadiyq* remains on the road, following God's directions, but, on the other hand, one who is *rasha* is lost and in jeopardy of death. Consider Proverbs 10:11 which states:

> The mouth of the tsadiyq is a source of life but
> violence covers the mouth of the rasha.

Once one realizes that he has become lost (*rasha*), his goal is to turn around and return to the correct path. This idea is expressed in the Hebrew verb שוב (*Sh.W.B*). This same verb is used in the context of repenting (returning to the path) from wrongdoing (lost from the path) and returning to the commands (directions) of God:

> And thou shalt return and obey the voice of
> the LORD, and do all his commandments
> which I command thee this day or, from a
> more Hebraic perspective - and you will return
> to the path and you will listen to the voice of
> YHWH and you will follow all his directions
> which I have pointed out to you today.
> (Deuteronomy 30:8)

The guiding light

In ancient times the stars would guide one on their journey. The Hebrew verb הלל (*H.L.L*) is a verb meaning "to shine" or "to give light."

His candle shined upon my head... (Job 29:3)

This same word is used in the following passage this word is used for the shining of the stars.

> *For the stars of the heavens and their constellations will not <u>give</u> their <u>light</u>.* (Isaiah 13:10)

This same word is also translated as "praise" in the following verse:

> <u>Praise</u> *the LORD; for the LORD is good: sing praises unto his name; for it is pleasant.* (Psalm 135:3, KJV)

Hebraically, the verb הלל (*H.L.L*) literally means to "look toward another as a shining light." When the Psalms say, *Praise Yah (halelu-Yah)*, as in Psalm 135:3, it is literally saying "Look to Yah as the light that will guide you on your journey."

Zion

Zion is another name for Jerusalem, but is more specifically the mountain within the city (Isaiah 2:3). The Hebrew word for Zion is ציון (*tsiyown*), the very same word above meaning "landmark" with just a slight change in pronunciation (*tsiyuwn* instead of *tsiyown*). Zion is not just a mountain; it is the central landmark for Israel. Three times a year all of Israel was to travel to the landmark where God had placed his name (Exodus 23:17, Deuteronomy 16:16). This landmark was Zion (Isaiah 18:7).

Conclusion

Our life is supposed to be a migratory journey on God's road. The Bible is the 'map' that shows us the directions, paths and landmarks which he has pointed out to us. The Bible is also the guide to show us how to stay on the path and how to find it again if we become lost on our way. If we are not reading (*a.k.a.* studying) this book, how can we expect to find our way to the road of YHWH?

Years old

The nomadic tent was constructed by weaving black goat's hair into panels about three feet wide and the length of the tent. If the tent was required to be made larger, they would sew in additional panels. As each panel aged and began to break down from exposure to the sun, it was replaced with a new panel. As a general rule, one panel was replaced each year.

Many similarities exist between these panels of the tent and the family members themselves:

> *Sing, O barren, thou that didst not bear; break forth into singing, and cry aloud, thou that didst not travail with child: for more are the children of the desolate than the children of the married wife, saith the LORD. Enlarge the place of thy tent, and let them stretch forth the curtains of thine habitations: spare not, lengthen thy cords, and strengthen thy stakes;*
> Isaiah 54:1,2 (KJV)

The phrases underlined in the passage above literally describe what happened when the family size became larger by the addition of children. Just as new members were added to the family to increase its size, new panels were also added to the tent to increase its size.

The new tent panels were black in color, just like the hair on the children. The hair on the head of older members turned white after many years, just as the panels of the tent began to turn white over the years from exposure to the sunlight.

Just as the older members of the family died and were replaced with newborns, the older strips of the tent were removed and replaced with new panels.

Because the tent was continually being renewed year after year with the addition of new panels as needed, the tent literally lasted forever; and, in the same way, the lineage of the family residing within the tent continued generation after generation.

> And Isaac was _forty years old_ when he took Rebekah to wife... Genesis 25:20

The phrase "forty years old" is an English translation of the Hebrew phrase בן ארבעים שנה (ben arba'iym shanah) which is literally translated as "a son of forty years." Because of the many similarities between the tent panel and the sons of the family, it appears that the Hebrew word בן (ben) meaning "son" may also be the Hebrew word for the tent panel. If this is true, then the Hebrew phrase ben arba'iym shanah could be translated as "forty years of tent panels" and, as one panel was replaced each year, it could serve as a type of calendar.

Yesterday and Tomorrow

The hand gesture usually referred to as the "thumbs up," conveys the idea of "good," while the "thumbs down" means "bad." You are probably aware that these gestures have their origin in the gladiatorial games when Caesar would give one of these gestures to the conquering gladiator to convey his desire for the fate of the defeated, but you may not be aware of the original meanings behind these gestures.

If Caesar gave the "thumbs up," which was actually pointing to the throat, and not up as we mistakenly think, it signaled to the gladiator standing above the defeated to put his sword through the loser's throat, to kill him. On the other hand, if he gave the "thumbs down" he was signaling the gladiator to throw his sword to the ground, to spare the defeated.

As you can see, over the last two thousand years, the meanings of "thumbs up" and "thumbs down" have reversed in meaning. We have already seen a few examples of how different Hebrew thought was from our own Modern Greek way of thinking, but is it possible that at times our modern way of thinking is opposite of Hebrew thought? Let's look at an example that shows that it can be:

In our way of recollecting time, we view time as a line or road. On this road, the past—where we have already walked—is behind us, and the future—where we have not yet walked—is in front of us.

If we examine some Hebrew words related to time, we can get a clue as to how the Ancient Hebrews perceived the past and the future.

The Hebrew word for tomorrow is מחר (mahhar) from the root אחר (ahhar) meaning "to be behind." The Hebrew word for yesterday is תמול (temol, from the word מול (mul) meaning "in front." As you can see, in Hebraic thought, they perceived the past (yesterday) as in the front, while the future (tomorrow) as behind. It is not that they saw themselves walking the road of time backwards—in fact, they did not see time as linear, but as cyclical. They perceived their history, the past, as events that can be seen, therefore in front, while the future cannot be seen. Therefore, it is behind and out of view.

Words

Alone

> *And the LORD God said, It is not good that the*
> *man should be* <u>*alone*</u>*; I will make him an help*
> *meet for him.* (Genesis 2:18, KJV)

The base word of the word לבדו (*le'vado*) is בד (*bad/vad*) meaning a "strand" or a "stick." The ל (*le*) is a prefix meaning "to" and the ו (*o*) is a suffix meaning "his." So לבדו literally means "to his stick." A stick is a piece of a tree that is separated from the tree. The phrase "to his stick" is a Hebrew idiom meaning to be "alone."

Amen

The subject we are going to cover here is a prime example of how Hebrew teaches concepts. If you wanted to teach your children what it means to believe, how would you do it? If you think about it, it is a very difficult thing to do.

In our culture, concepts, words and ideas are taught by using other concepts, words and ideas. Often this is a very difficult task to accomplish. Since the Hebrew language is a task-oriented language, teaching these concepts, words and ideas is much easier.

The Hebrew language developed in a nomadic agricultural culture. Because of this, much of the language is centered on this lifestyle. The more we understand their way of life and culture, the more we can understand their language. This benefits us as Bible students, because we can better understand the author's message if we better understand their language.

The Nomads

In Genesis 4:20 we read about the first Nomad, Jabal, a descendent of Adam through Cain:

> *"And Adah bare Jabal: he was the father of such as dwell in tents, and of such as have cattle."*

We know that Jabal and his descendants were nomads from the simple fact they lived in tents and raised livestock. A tent (*ohel* in Hebrew) is a portable shelter for the purpose of moving from one grazing place to another. The Hebrew word used in the above for cattle is "*miqneh*" which actually means any livestock property. This could be cattle, sheep, goats, donkeys, etc. When the livestock consumed the edible vegetation in one area, the herder would then pack up his tent and his belongings and move on to better grazing land.

Probably the most famous nomad is Abraham. He traveled a great deal through the land of the Near East living in tents and raising livestock.

The Tent

The tent was a very important part of the nomad's life. By looking at the many words derived from this shelter we have tangible, hands-on tools with which to teach our children the basic concepts in the Bible. In this study we will be looking at a tent stake. For those who have camped before, you are probably familiar with these stakes. What is the most important factor when placing your tent stakes? The ground. If you drive in soft ground, the tension on the rope will pull the stake right out. You need very firm ground to hold the stake in. The ideal ground would require a hammer to pound in the stake. In the ground like this the stake will remain secure in its position even in a strong wind. Let us now look at a passage of Scripture that uses this "concept."

> I will drive him like a peg into a <u>firm</u> place, he will be a seat of honor for the house of his father. Isaiah 22:23

Here we have the stake (peg) being driven into a "firm" place. The Hebrew word translated as "firm" is the verb אמן (A.M.N) which literally means "to be firm or sure." When setting up our tent, we desire to find a spot where the ground will be firm.

Believe

This verb "aman" is used 110 times in the Old Testament. Let us now look at another passage using this same verb and see what it says:

> Abram <u>believed</u> the LORD, and he credited it to him as righteousness Genesis 15:6

The word "believed" is the very same Hebrew verb "aman." The picture we have from this is that Abram was firm in his devotion to God. Just as a stake planted in firm ground supports the tent even in a storm, Abram will support God even in the storms of life. The question we now ask is, "How did Abram remain firm?" The verse just before states:

> '[God] took [Abram] outside and said, "Look up at the heavens and count the stars--if indeed you can count them." Then he said to him, "So shall your offspring be." Abram <u>believed</u> the LORD, and He credited it to him as righteousness. Genesis 15:5,6

We usually read this to mean that Abram believed God's promise in verse 5. The problem with this is that the Hebrew verb "*aman*" means more than just knowing something to be true. Why did God give this promise to Abram?

> *I will make your descendants as numerous as the stars in the sky and I will give them all these lands, and through your offspring all nations on earth will be blessed, because Abraham obeyed me and kept my requirements, my commands, my decrees and my laws.* Genesis 26:4,5

God made this promise to Abram because he was firm in his obedience to God. The Hebrew in Genesis 15:6 does not say Abram believed God, it says he was firm in God. From Genesis 26:5 we see that he was firm in his obedience to God and his *Torah*.

Angel

The word מלאך (*mela'ak*) is translated two different ways as can be seen in the following examples:

> *And they sent a <u>messenger</u> unto Joseph, saying, Thy father did command before he died, saying....* Genesis 50:16 (KJV)

> *Behold, I [YHWH] send an <u>Angel</u> before thee, to keep thee in the way, and to bring thee into the place which I have prepared.* Exodus 23:20 (KJV)

The word מלאך (*mela'ak*) is formed by adding a מ (*m*) in front of the child root לאך (*la'ak*). This child root is derived from the parent root לך (*lak*), which is written in the ancient pictographic script as (ש)ל. The ל (*l*) is a staff, while the (ש) (*k*) is a picture of the palm of the hand. The parent root (ש)ל has an original Hebraic meaning of "staff in the palm" or "to walk," as a staff was a common tool carried by the traveler. Another child root formed from the parent root לך is הלך (*halak*), also means "to walk." The noun מלאך (*mela'ak*) is "one who walks for another," a "messenger." This can be one who walks for another man and is translated as "messenger" as seen in the first verse above. This word can also be one who walks for God, which is translated as "angel" in the second verse.

Anger

Greek thought views the world through the mind (abstract thought). Ancient Hebrew thought viewed the world through the senses (concrete thought):

Concrete thought is the expression of concepts and ideas in ways that can be seen, touched, smelled, tasted and/or heard. All five of the senses are used when speaking and hearing and writing and reading the Hebrew language. An example of this can be found in Psalms 1:3:

> He is like a _tree_ _planted_ by _streams of water,_
> which yields its _fruit_ in season, and whose _leaf_
> does not _wither._

In this passage, we have concrete words expressing abstract thoughts, such as a tree (one who is upright or righteous), streams of water (grace), fruit (good character) and an unwithered leaf (prosperity).

Abstract thought is the expression of concepts and ideas in ways that cannot be seen, touched, smelled, tasted or heard.

Hebrew never uses abstract thought as English does. Examples of abstract thought can be found in Psalms 103:8:

> The LORD is <u>compassionate</u> and <u>gracious,</u> Slow
> to <u>anger,</u> abounding in <u>love.</u>"

As you may have noticed, I said that Hebrew uses concrete and not abstract thoughts, but here we have abstract concepts such as compassionate, gracious, anger, and love in a Hebrew passage. In reality, these are abstract English words translating the original Hebrew concrete words. The translators often translated this way because the original Hebrew makes no sense when literally translated into English.

Let us take one of the abstract words above to demonstrate how this works. Anger, an abstract word, is actually the Hebrew word אף (*awph*) which literally means "nose," a concrete word. When one is very angry, he begins to breathe hard and the nostrils begin to flare. A Hebrew sees anger as "the flaring of the nose (nostrils)." If the translator literally translated the above passage "slow to nose," it would make no sense to the English reader, so אף, "a nose," is translated to "anger" in this passage.

Appear

For those who do not know Hebrew, the only tool available for studying the Hebrew text of the Bible is *Strong's Hebrew Dictionary*. While this dictionary is a valuable resource, it has many limitations.

In the King James Version of Exodus 3:16 we read, "The LORD God of your fathers... appeared unto me..." A person might read this and ask, "How can the LORD 'appear' to someone when he has no form?" This person then takes out his *Strong's*

Dictionary and looks up the word "appear" in this verse and finds the following entry:

H7200 ראה râ'âh
Translations - see 879, look 104, behold 83, shew 68, appear 66, consider 22, seer 12, spy 6, respect 5, perceive 5, provide 4, regard 4, enjoy 4, lo 3, foreseeth 2, heed 2, misc 74; used 1313 times

The reader then sees that the Hebrew word ראה (*ra'ah*) means "see" and "look." Armed with this bit of "knowledge," the reader then retranslates this verse as, "And the LORD God of your fathers... looked unto me..." and then says, "ah-ha, the LORD didn't 'appear' to him, the LORD 'saw' him." Then to confirm his theory, he goes back a few verses and reads Exodus 3:4, "And when the LORD saw that he turned aside..." Taking out his trusty *Strong's Dictionary* he looks up the word "saw" and finds the following entry:

H7200 ראה râ'âh
Translations - see 879, look 104, behold 83, shew 68, appear 66, consider 22, seer 12, spy 6, respect 5, perceive 5, provide 4, regard 4, enjoy 4, lo 3, foreseeth 2, heed 2, misc 74; used 1313 times

He then says, "There it is, the Hebrew word translated as 'saw' is the very same Hebrew word *ra'ah*!"

Have you ever heard the expression, "A little knowledge is a dangerous thing?" Well, this applies in this situation. What this reader is not aware of is that Hebrew verbs can take on different forms and these forms are not identified in *Strong's Dictionary*. In Exodus 3:4 the Hebrew verb *ra'ah* is written וירא (*vai'yar*), which is the simple form of the verb and means "and he saw." But in Exodus 3:16 it is written as נראה (*nir'ah*), which is the passive form of the verb and means "and he was seen" or "and he appeared." According to the verb form of this Hebrew word in Exodus 3:16, the LORD is not the one "seeing," he is the one that "was seen."

All of the resources available for going into this depth of Hebrew study require the reader to have at least a basic knowledge of Hebrew. This excludes all those who wish to go deeper into the text, but don't know the basics of Hebrew. That is, until now. The author's Mechanical Translation is designed to provide the reader who has no background in Hebrew the ability to study the Hebrew language at this depth.

The following is the Mechanical Translation of the word "see" in Exodus 3:4:

and~he~will~SEE

Now the Mechanical Translation of the word "appear" in Exodus 3:16:

he~did~be~SEE

The word "be" in this translation indicates to the reader that this verb is in the passive form and we discover that the phrase "be seen" means to "appear." In this same way, whenever a verb is written in the causative form, the word "make" will be there; and whenever a verb is written in the reflexive form, the word "self" will be there. Now the reader has the ability to comprehend the Hebrew text without even knowing how to read Hebrew.

Ark

In the Ancient Hebrew mind, light is seen as order, because without light we would be lost in the chaos of darkness. The Hebrew word for light is אור (or) and a related word is ארון (aron). This word means a "box" and is also related to the idea of order, in the sense that items are placed within boxes as a way of bringing about order.

The "Ark of the Covenant" is a box used to place important items within it, including the stone tablets, Aaron's staff and the Manna, to keep them in "order."

Army

The Biblical and modern Hebrew word for "army" is צבא (tsava) and is derived from the verbal root צבא (Ts.B.A) meaning "to fight" or "wage war." The Israeli Defense Force (IDF) is the English translation of the Hebrew צבא ההגנה לישראל (tsava hahaganah l'Yisra'el), which literally means "Army for the defense of Israel." Usually written with its acronym צה"ל (acronym being when the apostrophe is placed before the last letter in a word), it indicates that the word is an acronym:

> Thus the heavens and the earth were finished,
> and all the <u>host</u> of them. (Genesis 2:1, KJV)

The word "host" in this passage is the Hebrew word tsava meaning "army."

Atonement

The Hebrew verb כפר (*K.P.R*) means "to cover over," but is often translated as "atonement." The word "atonement" is an abstract word, and in order to understand the true Hebrew meaning of a word, we must look to the concrete meaning. If an offense has been made, the one who has been offended can act as though the offense is covered over and unseen. We express this idea through the word "forgiveness." Atonement is an outward action that covers over the error.

Bare

The Hebrew word for "boy" is ילד (*yeled*) and the feminine form of this word is ילדה (*yal'dah*) meaning "girl." Both of these words come from the verbal root ילד (*Y.L.D*) meaning "to bring forth" and is usually used in the context of bearing children, such as in the passage below:

> Unto the woman he said, I will greatly multiply thy sorrow and thy conception; in sorrow thou shalt _bring forth_ (yalad) children; and thy desire shall be to thy husband, and he shall rule over thee. (Genesis 3:16, KJV)

This same verbal root is found in Genesis 20:17 and is usually translated in the same manner:

> So Abraham prayed unto God: and God healed Abimelech, and his wife, and his maidservants; and they _bare_ children. (KJV)

While the Hebrew word behind the word "bare" is the verbal root word ילד (*Y.L.D*), the translators added the word "children," which does not exist in the Hebrew text. Because of the translator's insertion of this word, the reader assumes Abimelech's punishment by God was that his women could not "bear children." However, there is another interpretation of this verse. First, note that the above passage states that God healed Abimelech as well as his wife and maidservants. If this affliction only affected the women from bearing children, why would Abimelech need healing? Also, note the following passage:

> But God came to Abimelech in a dream by night, and said to him, Behold, <u>thou art but a dead man</u>, for the woman which thou hast taken; for she is a man's wife. Genesis 20:3 (KJV)

Here God tells Abimelech, because of his sin, he is a dead man, and, evidently, the punishment is something that causes death, and the inability to bear children does not cause death. Now, let's look at verse 17 again but this time with a literal translation from the Hebrew text:

> And Abraham interceded to Elohiym and Elohiym healed Abimelech and his woman and his maid servants and they <u>brought forth</u>.

It is my opinion that the illness God gave to Abimelech and his people was constipation.

Battle

The Hebrew word for "a battle" is מלחמה (mil'hha'mah), which is derived from the verbal root לחם (L.Hh.M), meaning to "fight." Also derived from the verb לחם is the noun לחם (lehhem), which means "bread." Anyone who has made bread from scratch can understand the connection between "fighting" and "bread:" the bread dough must be kneaded, which we could say is a "fight" with the bread dough.

Before

> *The earth also was corrupt <u>before</u> God, and the earth was filled with violence.* (Genesis 6:11)

A very common Hebrew word found in the Bible is the word לפני (liph'ney), which is translated as "before" in this verse. If you look this up this word in *Strong's Dictionary*, #6440, it is identified as the Hebrew word פנים (paniym), which is a plural word that literally means "face." *Strong's* states that the plural noun פנים (paniym) is derived from the unused noun פנה (paneh). Let me note here that if a root word ends with the letter ה (H), then this letter is dropped when a suffix, such as the ים (iym) suffix, is added to the word. I believe that the plural form is used for a "face" because we have multiple faces; happy, sad, mad, confused, etc. Even though the word פנים (paniym) is plural, it is translated as the singular word "face." But notice that while *Strong's* identifies this word as פנים (paniym), in the Hebrew text it is actually written as לפני (liph'ney).

The word לפני (liph'ney) begins with the prefix ל (L), which means "to." Also notice that the letter ם (M) is dropped from the word פנים (paniym), which occurs whenever a plural noun is in the construct state. The literal translation of לפני (liph'ney) is "to the face of..." Let's take another look at the verse from above, but this time translating the word לפני (liph'ney) literally:

The land was corrupt to the face of the Elohiym and the earth was filled with violence. (Genesis 6:11)

The imagery of this verse in the context of the use of the word לפני (*liph'ney*) is that the corruption and violence on the earth is "visible" to *Elohiym* (God), it is "in front of" him, or "before" him. Because of this context, the Hebrew word לפני (*liph'ney*) is often translated as "in front of" or "before." But in the Mechanical Translation, which attempts to preserve the literal concreteness of the Hebrew text, I will usually translate this phrase literally, "to the face of."

Beginning

The word ראשית (*reshiyt*) comes from the root ראש (*rosh*), a noun meaning *head*, and may be used for the head of a man (Genesis 3:15) or an animal (Exodus 29:10), the summit of a mountain (Genesis 8:5) or it may be used for a person of importance, such as the leader of a family (Numbers 1:4) or tribe (Numbers 30:1).

The Hebrew language uses the same words for space and time (Interestingly, scientists today have determined that space and time are related). As an example, the Hebrew word קדם (*qedem*) can mean *east* (space) or *ancient* (time). The word *rosh* may also be used for the *head* of a time, such as the *beginning* of a month (Exodus 12:2).

The word *reshiyt* has a similar meaning, in that it may refer to the *head* of a time, such as the *beginning* of a year (Deuteronomy 11:12), but may also be used for someone or something of importance: the *head* or *summit* of a group. An example of this can be found in Exodus 23:19, where the word *reshiyt* is used for the *best* or *choicest* of their firstfruit offerings:

> The <u>first</u> of the firstfruits of thy land thou shalt bring into the house of the LORD thy God. Thou shalt not seethe a kid in his mother's milk. (Exodus 23:19, KJV)

The *origin* in Genesis 1:1 is not just the *beginning* of a time, but *summit* of time, the most important event in history.

Believe

> And he <u>believed</u> in the LORD; and he counted it to him for righteousness. (Genesis 15:6, KJV)

What does one mean when saying, "I believe in God"? The dictionary defines "believe" as "to accept as true or real." Does a belief in God simply mean knowing that God exists? The Hebrew behind this word has absolutely nothing to do with the English definition given above. Instead, it is a very concrete concept that can be experienced through the senses and not the mind.

The Hebrew word behind the translation "believe" is the verb אמן (*A.M.N*). Just a simple cursory look at the various ways this word has been translated indicates that there is much more to this word than just knowing that something exists. The King James Version uses the following translations for the verb אמן (*A.M.N*): "believe, assurance, faithful, sure, established, trust, verified, steadfast, continuance, nursing father, bring up, nurse, be nursed, surely, stand fast, and trusty."

The basic meaning behind the Hebrew word *aman* is "to support" as can be seen in the following passages:

And bring your younger brother to me and he will be a <u>support</u> (aman) for your words and you will not die and they did this. Genesis 42:20

And Naomi took the child and placed him in her bosom and she was for him for a <u>supporter</u> (aman - as a nurse). Ruth 4:16

And your house will be <u>supported</u> (aman) forever and your kingdom will be before you for an eternity, your throne will be firm for an eternity. 2 Samuel 7:16

My mercy will guard him forever and my covenant will <u>support</u> (aman) him. Psalm 89:28

And I will thrust him like a tent peg in a place of <u>support</u> (aman)... Isaiah 22:23

This last passage is an excellent illustration of the concrete understanding of this word. Firm ground is chosen as the site for setting up a tent, so when the tent pegs are driven into the soil, the firm ground will "support" the tent even in a strong wind. In this same way, Abram "supported God."

Now, let's look at Genesis 15:6 in its context:

And he brought him forth abroad, and said, Look now toward heaven, and tell the stars, if thou be able to number them: and he said unto him, So shall thy seed be. And he <u>believed</u> (aman) in the LORD; and he counted it to him for righteousness. (Genesis 15:5,6, KJV)

At first glance, and from a Greek perspective, it appears that the word "believe" is referring to Abram's knowledge that God will follow through with his promise to provide him many descendants, but as we shall see this is not what is meant by Abram's "belief."

God's promise to Abram, that he would have many descendants, was repeated to Abram's son Isaac:

> *And I will make your descendants numerous like the stars of heaven and I will give to your seed all these lands and all the nations of the land will be blessed through your seed because Abraham heard (shama) my voice and obeyed my charge and my commands and my decrees and my teachings.* Genesis 26:4,5

The verb שמע (shama) means "to hear." When the Bible speaks of "hearing" the voice of God, it means "pay attention to what is spoken and respond."

The word *shama* is a synonym of *aman* as can be seen in the following passage.

> *And Moses answered and he said, "They will not support (aman) me and they will not hear (shama) my voice..."* Exodus 4:1

Why did God promise to give Abram many descendants? Because Abram was obedient to the voice of God, as indicated in Genesis 26, and Abram supported God as indicated in Genesis 15.

Will you "support" God through your actions (a Hebraic perspective) or only through your mind (a Greek perspective)?

Bread

> With the sweat of your brow you will eat
> _bread (lehhem)_... Genesis 3:19

Bread dough is placed on a table and is kneaded by hitting it with the fists, rolling it back and forth, picking it up and turning it over, and... Kind of sounds like a fight, doesn't it? Actually, the Hebrew noun לחם (lehhem), meaning "bread," comes from the verbal root לחם (L.Hh.M), meaning to "fight."

> Come on, let us deal wisely with them; lest
> they multiply, and it come to pass, that, when
> there falleth out any war, they join also unto
> our enemies, and _fight_ (L.Hh.M) against us,
> and so get them up out of the land. (Exodus
> 1:10, KJV)

Could this be because we also have to fight the ground to bring up the crop, fight the grain to remove the husk from the seeds, fight the seeds to turn them into flour, and fight the dough to make the bread?

Buck

> Then the _dukes_ of Edom shall be amazed; the
> _mighty men_ of Moab, trembling shall take
> hold upon them; all the inhabitants of Canaan
> shall melt away. Exodus 15:15 (KJV)

In this verse are two related Hebrew words, אלוף (aluph) and איל (ayil).

The word איל (ayil) is translated as "mighty men" in the KJV, but is often translated in various ways including "buck" in

Genesis 15:9 and "posts" in Ezekiel 40:14. Hebrew nouns are descriptive of character, and to understand the character of the word איל (*ayil*), we need to look at its parent root אל (*el*). While this word is frequently translated as "God" or "god," it literally means "might," "mighty" or "mighty one" as can be seen in the following passage:

> Thy sons and thy daughters shall be given unto another people, and thine eyes shall look, and fail with longing for them all the day long: and there shall be no *might* in thine hand. (Deuteronomy 28:32, KJV)

Based on the context of the use of the word איל (*ayil*) in various passages and the meaning of its root, we can conclude that this word literally means "one that stands tall in might," like a buck, a post or a person of great authority.

The Hebrew word אלוף (*aluph*), translated as "duke" in the KJV, but also translated as "chief," "leader," and "prince" in other translations, is derived from the verbal root אלף (*A.L.Ph*), also derived from the parent root אל (*el*), meaning "to train through experience." Derived from אלף (*A.L.Ph*), is the word אלף (*eleph*), meaning an ox. An אלוף (*aluph*) is "one like an ox in strength and power."

Build

Hebrew words usually have more than one meaning. For instance, the Hebrew word אבן (*even*) means a "stone," such as you might find in a creek or field, but can also be a "weight" such as used with a balance scale, as it is made from a stone. This word can also be used for a "block" of hewn stone that is used to construct a building.

This Hebrew word is derived out of the parent root בן (*ben*). In the original Hebrew alphabet, this word was written as ⌐\⊃. The first picture on the right is a picture of a tent, our house. The second picture is a germinating seed, but can also mean to "continue," as a seed continues the next generation. When combined these letters mean "continue the house" and is the Hebrew word for a "son," the one who continues the line of the house.

From the parent root בן (*ben*) come several other roots, and the words derived out of them. These roots and words are closely related to the concept of "continuing the house."

בנן (*B-N-N*): *beniyn*–a building

אבן (*A-B-N*): *even*–a stone; *ovehn*–a stool (made from stone)

הבן (*H-B-N*): *hovehn*–ebony (a hardwood used in building)

בהן (*B-H-N*): *bohen*–thumb (called "the builder" as it is needed for building)

בנה (*B-N-H*): *banah*–to build; *beniyah*–a building; *mavenah*–structure

בון (*B-W-N*): *tevunah*–intelligence (needed to build)

בין (*B-Y-N*): *beyn*–understanding (needed to build)

לבן (*L-B-N*): *lavan*–a brick (as used like stone to build)

Cherubims

And thou shalt make two cherubims of gold, of beaten work shalt thou make them, in the two ends of the mercy seat. (Exodus 25:18, KJV)

There is a problem with the "*cherubims*;" it is a double plural. The Hebrew is כרובים (*keruvim*), which can be transliterated as *cherubim*. The "im" at the end of the word is the plural suffix and the singular form of this word is כרוב (keruv/cherub). Because "cherubim" is a plural noun, there is no need for the "s." Other translations, such as the Revised Standard Version and American Standard Version correctly transliterate this word as "cherubim." The Young's Literal Translation uses "cherubs," also a more correct way of transliterating this word.

Clean

The Hebrew verb טהר (T.H.R) literally means to clean or be clean as seen in Numbers 8:7:

> And wash their clothes and cleanse (taher) themselves.

Derived from this verb is the noun טהור (tahor) meaning "clean" and is often used in the context of "clean gold:"

> And you shall overlay [the ark] with pure (tahor) gold. Exodus 25:11

Clean gold has had all the impurities (dirtiness) removed from it. This same word is also used in the context of animals:

> To make a distinction between the unclean and the clean (tahor) and between the living creature that may be eaten and the living creature that may not be eaten. Leviticus 11:47

Many would consider this a "ritualistic" clean, but I believe that this is a literal application. Those animals which are not allowed to be eaten (the unclean) have within them some "impurity" in the same manner as impure gold does. For instance, pork, an "unclean" animal, is known to carry trichinosis, an impurity within the meat; and the meat of shellfish, also an "unclean" animal, can cause severe allergic reactions in some people.

God's laws were not just a set of rituals with no physical substance; they were actual procedures for the preservation of life (i.e., salvation) from injury or disease, just as it says in Proverbs 3:1, 2:

> "My son, do not forget my teaching (תורה Torah), but let your heart keep my commandments (מצות mitsvot), for length of days and years of life and abundant welfare (שלום shalom) will they give you."

Come

The verb בוא (bo) is a good example to demonstrate the vast difference between Hebrew and English. In the examples below are two different English words with opposite meanings:

> As for yourself, you shall <u>go</u> to your fathers in peace; you shall be buried in a good old age. (Genesis 15:15, RSV)
>
> Isaac said to them, "Why have you <u>come</u> to me, seeing that you hate me and have sent me away from you?" (Genesis 26:27, RSV)

The English verb "go" generally means "to move from a position nearby to a position far away," while the verb "come" means "to move from a far position to a position nearby." An example would be, "I will <u>go</u> to the store; then I will <u>come</u> home." The context of this phrase implies that I am making the statement from home about leaving home for the store and then returning home.

In the two verses above, the one Hebrew verb בוא (*bo*) is being translated into two different English words in order to translate the context of its use.

The verb בוא (*bo*) does not mean "come" or "go" in the sense of direction but to "enter a void in order to fill it" in the sense of purpose. Because there is no English word with this meaning, the words "go" and "come" are used instead, but unfortunately this erases the more Hebraic meaning behind the word.

Command

This Hebrew word is usually translated as a "command" or "commandment." By definition, a command is "To direct with authority; give orders to" and "To have control or authority over; rule: a general who commands an army." Is this the meaning of the Hebrew word *mitsvah*? When the *Torah* says *"And it will be righteousness for us, if we are careful to do all this commandment before the LORD our God, as he has commanded us"* (Deuteronomy 6:25, RSV), is it telling us that God our general is giving us an order to obey or is the Ancient Hebrew understanding something different?

Remembering that the Ancient Hebrews were concrete thinkers, we need to understand the meaning of this word based on the Ancient Hebrew perspective of thought. We, as Western Greco-Roman thinkers, are very comfortable using abstract words but not the Ancient Hebrews. Each word painted a picture of action and this is also true for the word *mitsvah*. We are going to look at other roots and words that are closely related to this word and its roots and all of them when combined will paint a very clear picture of action which is completely lost in the English translations of the Bible.

The parent root צי (*tsiy*) means a "nomad" or "ship" (as a nomad on the sea). From this parent root comes the word ציי (*tsiyiy*) meaning a "desert" and ציון (*tsion*) meaning a "sign."

The parent root צא (*tsa*) means "excrement" in the sense of "going out." From this parent root comes the child root יצא (*yatsa*) meaning "to go out." From this child root comes the word מוצא (*motsah*) meaning a "going out" or to "proceed."

The parent root צו (*tsav*) means "direction." From this parent comes the child root צוה (*tsavah*) meaning "to direct." From this child root comes the word מצוה (*mitsvah*) also meaning a "direction."

At first glance these three sets of roots do not appear to have anything in common; that is, not until we see these words through Hebrew eyes. The action painted by the parent root צי (*tsiy*) and its related words are the landmarks (signs such as mountains, ranges, wadis, rock outcroppings, etc.) of the desert followed by the nomad to the next encampment, pasture or water hole. The action painted by the parent root צא (*tsa*) and its related words is the migration of the nomad through the desert. The action painted by the parent root צו (*tsav*) and its related words including the word *mitsvah* is the directions taken by the nomad by following the landmarks through the desert.

Getting back to our word מצוה (*mitsvah*), we need to read this word as a "direction" one is to take in their migration. Our life is a journey through the desert, and in this life, we are given landmarks or signs which guide us in this journey. The *Torah*, the Bible, the words of God are these landmarks. When God says "honor your father and mother," he is giving us a landmark which gives us a direction to go. If we follow each of these landmarks we will not become lost in our journey and will arrive at the ultimate landmark: Zion. The word Zion is ציון (*tsion*) in Hebrew and is the very same word we looked at previously meaning a "sign" or "landmark."

Commandment

The word "command," as well as "commandment," is used to translate the Hebrew word מצוה (*mits'vah*), but "command" and "commandment" do not properly convey the meaning of this Hebrew word. The word "command" implies words of force or power, as a general commands his troops. The word *mits'vah* is better understood as a directive. To see the picture painted by this word, it is helpful to look at a related word, ציון (*tsiyon*, which is also the name Zion), meaning a desert or a landmark. The Ancient Hebrews were a nomadic people who traveled the deserts in search of green pastures for their flocks. A nomad used the various rivers, mountains, rock outcroppings, etc. as landmarks to give them their direction. The verbal root of *mits'vah* and *tsiyon* is צוה (*tsavah*) meaning "to direct one on a journey." The *mits'vah* of the Bible are not commands, or rules and regulations, they are directives or landmarks that we look for to guide us.

Congregations

The word "congregation" appears 331 times in the King James Bible, but this English word is used to translate three different Hebrew words; עדה (*eydah*), מועד (*mo'eyd*) and קהל (*qahal*).

> All the <u>congregation</u> (eydah) of Israel shall keep it. (Exodus 12:47, KJV)

The word עדה (*eydah*) is the feminine form of the noun עד (*eyd*) meaning "testimony" or "witness." An *eydah* is a group of persons or things that are gathered for carrying on a project or undertaking; a group with a common testimony:

> *And Aaron and his sons thou shalt bring unto the door of the tabernacle of the <u>congregation</u> (mo'eyd), and shalt wash them with water.* (Exodus 29:4, KJV)

The word מועד (*mo'eyd*) is derived out of the verbal root יעד (*Y.Ah.D*) meaning to "appoint," in the sense of arranging, fixing or setting in place. This root is also derived out of the noun עד (*eyd*) meaning "testimony" or "witness." The word מועד (*mo'eyd*) is an appointed place or time:

> *When the sin, which they have sinned against it, is known, then the <u>congregation</u> (qahal) shall offer a young bullock for the sin, and bring him before the tabernacle of the congregation.* (Leviticus 4:14, KJV)

The word קהל (*qahal*) is a large group gathered to one place, as a gathering of the flock of sheep to the shepherd. This noun is derived from the verbal root קהל (*Q.H.L*) meaning "to gather" or "round-up" a flock or group of people.

Copper

The Hebrew word *nehhoshet* is translated as copper one time (Ezra 8:27) in the King James Version. Copper is a pure mineral, meaning that it is not mixed with any other minerals. The King James Version translates this same word as "brass" one hundred and three times. Brass is an alloy (mixture) of copper and nickel (another pure mineral). Other translations translate *nehhoshet* as "brass" or "bronze." Bronze is an alloy of copper and tin (another pure mineral). It would appear that the translators are not certain of the meaning of the word *nehhoshet* as no consensus can be made on how to translate this word.

Jewish Hebrew dictionaries and Jewish translations of the Bible always translate this word as "copper." Why would Christian translations and dictionaries commonly translate *nehhoshet* as "brass" or "bronze," while Jewish dictionaries and translations use "copper?" Which is more accurate? At first glance, it may seem like an insignificant problem, but on further examination, it becomes evident that a proper translation is essential.

In Leviticus 19:19 we find three commands:

1. You shall not let your cattle breed with a different kind,
2. you shall not sow your field with two kinds of seed,
3. nor shall there come upon you a garment of cloth made of two kinds of stuff.

Throughout the *Torah,* God is demonstrating that mixtures are not appropriate. This would hold true especially for the items in the tabernacle. The altar was made of acacia wood and overlaid with *nehhoshet*. Is this *nehhoshet* brass, bronze or copper? Both brass and bronze are alloys, mixtures of pure minerals, while only copper is a pure mineral. Would God call for an alloy, a mixture of different "pure" metals such as brass or bronze in the tabernacle? It is unlikely.

Copper is the meaning of *nehhoshet,* so whenever you see the word "brass" or "bronze" in your English translation, make a mental note that this should be "copper."

Covenant

While the Hebrew word ברית (*beriyt*) means "covenant," the roots of the word and its cultural background are helpful in understanding its fuller meaning. This word comes from the root ברה (*barah*) meaning "to select the choicest meat." This meaning is also found in other nouns derived from this root. The word ברות (*berut*) means "meat" and ברי (*beriy*) means "fat" in the sense of choicest.

The word ברית (*beriyt*) is literally the choicest, fattest, animal that is slaughtered for the covenant ceremony:

> Now therefore come thou, let us <u>make a covenant</u>, I and thou; and let it be for a witness between me and thee. (Genesis 31:44, KJV)

The phrase "make a covenant" is found thirteen times in the Hebrew Bible where the word "make" is the Hebrew word כרת (*karat*) meaning "to cut." Literally, the phrase "make a covenant" means "cut the choice pieces of meat." When a covenant was made, the fattened animal was cut into two pieces and laid out on the ground; each party of the covenant then passed between the pieces. This symbolic act signified to both parties that if one of the parties failed to meet the agreement, then the other had the right to do to the other what they did to the animal:

> And I will give the men that have transgressed my covenant, which have not performed the words of the covenant which they had made before me, <u>when they cut the calf in twain, and passed between the parts</u> thereof, The princes of Judah, and the princes of Jerusalem, the eunuchs, and the priests, and <u>all the people of the land, which passed between the</u>

parts of the calf; I will even give them into the hand of their enemies, and into the hand of them that seek their life: and their dead bodies shall be for meat unto the fowls of the heaven, and to the beasts of the earth. (Jeremiah 34:18-20, KJV)

While the nation of Israel was encamped at Mount Sinai, God entered a covenant with them wherein Israel promised to obey the commands of God and God promised to protect and watch over Israel. Countless times over the years following the institution of this covenant, Israel failed to abide by the covenantal agreement. Just as the animal of the sacrifice was cut in two pieces, Israel was also cut in two because of their unfaithfulness to the covenant by being cut into two nations— Israel and Judah.

Crocodile

The Modern Hebrew word for a crocodile is תנין (*taniyn*). This word is also a Biblical Hebrew word and appears twenty-eight times in the Hebrew Bible, including the following verses:

When Pharaoh shall speak unto you, saying, Shew a miracle for you: then thou shalt say unto Aaron, Take thy rod, and cast it before Pharaoh, and it shall become a serpent (taniyn). (Exodus 7:9, KJV)

And Moses and Aaron went in unto Pharaoh, and they did so as the LORD had commanded: and Aaron cast down his rod before Pharaoh, and before his servants, and it became a serpent (taniyn). (Exodus 7:10, KJV)

Is it possible that Moses' staff turned into a crocodile instead of a serpent? Yes, I believe so. The usual Hebrew word for a serpent is נחש (*nahhash*) and this is the word used in these two verses:

> And he said, Cast it on the ground. And he cast it on the ground, and it became a _serpent_ (*nahhash*); and Moses fled from before it. (Exodus 4:3, KJV)

> Get thee unto Pharaoh in the morning; lo, he goeth out unto the water; and thou shalt stand by the river's brink against he come; and the rod which was turned to a _serpent_ (*nahhash*) shalt thou take in thine hand. (Exodus 7:15, KJV)

According to these verses, Moses' staff turned into a *taniyn* (7:9,10), but it is also called a *nahhash* (4:3, 7:15). I am of the opinion that the Hebrew word *nahhash* means "reptile," which could be a serpent or a crocodile. This leaves us with the word *taniyn*. In Genesis 1:21 the *taniyn*, translated as "whale" in the KJV, appears to live in the water, but in Psalm 91:13 the *taniyn*, translated as "dragon" in the KJV, appears to live on the land.

While there are some serpents that do swim in the water, they are predominately land animals. The crocodile, however, is at home in the water and on the land.

Daughter-in-law

The Hebrew verb כלל (*K.L.L*) means "to be complete." This verb is derived from the parent root כל (*kol*), which means "all," but in the sense of "everything that is needed to be complete."

Related to these roots is the word כלה (*kalah*), which is the Hebrew word for "daughter-in-law," but can also mean "bride," the woman who becomes the "daughter-in-law" of her husband's parents. Because this word is related to other words meaning "complete," we can assume that the Ancient Hebrews perspective of a "bride" is that she becomes "complete" upon marriage.

Day

In the ancient Hebrew pictographic alphabet, the letter י (*yud*) is a picture of an arm and hand (ﺢﻨ) and represents the idea of "working," "throwing" or "making." The letter ם (*mem*) is a picture of the ripples of water (ﷻ). When these two letters are combined they form the parent root word ים (*yam*), meaning *working water* and are the Hebrew word for "the sea," a large body of water, where the waves and storms are its work.

By placing the letter ו (*waw*) in between the two letters of the parent root, the child root יום (*yom*) is formed and means *day*. The Hebrew day ends when the sun sets in the west, the direction of the Mediterranean Sea. *Yom,* then, literally means, "The time of the setting sun over the sea."

The Hebrew word יום (*yom*) does not specifically mean a twenty-four hour period, but more generically, "a day that something occurs." Some examples would be the resting of the ark on "the seventeenth day of the month" (Genesis 8:4), "in that day YHWH made a covenant" (Genesis 15:18) and "until the day" (Genesis 19:37). This word can also refer to the light part of the day in contrast to night (see Genesis 1:5 and Exodus 13:21), but the related word יומם (*yomam*) specifically means "daytime," as can be seen in Job 5:14. This word can be used for a time, age or season, but that is only when this word is in the plural form, which is ימים (*yamim*), and, in my opinion, should simply be translated as "days," not time, age or season, as this can lead to incorrect interpretations of the text. The word היום (*hayom*) is the word יום (*yom*) with the prefix ה (*ha*) added and it literally means "the day," though sometimes this word means "today."

East

As I have pointed out many times previously, the Hebrew language and thought work very differently from our own Western language and thought. The Hebrew word meaning "ancient" is a good example. In the Hebrew mind, space and time are seen as being the same. Interestingly, modern science has come to the same conclusion and they call it the "space-time continuum." Both time and space have the present, such as the present place you are sitting and the present time you are at now. They both have distance, as a distant place or a distant time (as in the past or the future). For this reason the same Hebrew words are used for space and time. The Hebrew word קדם (*qedem*) can mean "east" (in space) or it can mean the "ancient past" (in time):

> He drove out the man; and at the _east_ (קדם) of the garden of Eden he placed the cherubim. (Genesis 3:24)

> I consider the days of old, I remember the years _long ago_ (קדם). (Psalm 77:5)

One of my favorite Hebrew words is עולם (*olam*) because of its unique ability to demonstrate how the Hebrew language works. While this word is frequently translated as "everlasting" or "eternal" (concepts which are foreign to Hebrew thought), it means a "distant time," either in the past or future, such as seen in the following verses:

> *I consider the days of old* (קדם)*, I remember the years long ago* (עולם)*.* (Psalm 77:5)

> *This is the sign of the covenant which I make between me and you and every living creature that is with you, for all <u>future</u>* (עולם) *generations.* (Genesis 9:12)

This same word can also mean a "distant place" as in the following passage:

> *Behold, these are the ungodly, who prosper in the <u>world</u>* (עולם)*; they increase in riches.* (Psalm 73:12)

The word עולם (*olam*) comes from the root עלם (*Ah.L.M*) meaning "to be hidden" and is often used in the sense of hiding in a place where one cannot be seen. Because Hebrew words for time are also used for space, we can say that *olam* literally means "a place hidden beyond the horizon" or "a time hidden beyond the distant time."

Eleven

The Biblical Hebrew word for "one," is אחד (*ehhad*):

> *And <u>one</u> kid of the goats for a sin offering...*
> Numbers 29:19 (KJV)

However, this word can also mean a "unit," a part of the whole:

> *And if they be married to <u>any</u> of the sons of the other tribes of the children of Israel...*
> Numbers 36:3 (KJV)

I have theorized that in the Ancient Hebrew language, there was another word to represent the ordinal number "one," and the word *ehhad* was solely used for a unit that exists within a unity. But over time, the original Hebrew word for "one" went into disuse, and the word *ehhad* was used for a unit as well as the ordinal number "one." This would not be a unique occurrence, as languages are constantly evolving, words are dropped and added, and definitions and usages change over time. However, there are some textual evidences to support this theory.

The number twelve is written in Hebrew as שני עשר (*sheney asar*), which can literally be translated as "two ten." We would then expect eleven to be written as עשר אחד (*ehhad asar*). While we do find this phrase in some verses, we also find עשתי אשר (*ashtey asar*), such as in the following verse:

> And on the third day _eleven_ bullocks...
> (*Numbers 29:20, KJV*)

The word עשתי (*ashtey*) is most likely the original Hebrew word for the ordinal number "one," but fell out of disuse, being replaced with the word אחד (*ehhad*).

Eternal

Hebrew words used for space are also used for time. The Hebrew word *qedem* means "east" but is also the same word for the "past." The Hebrew word *olam* literally means "beyond the horizon." When looking off in the far distance, it is difficult to make out any details, and what is beyond that horizon cannot be seen. This concept is the *olam*. The word *olam* is also used for the distant past or the distant future as a time that is difficult to know or perceive. This word is frequently translated as "eternity," meaning a continual span of time that never ends. In the Hebrew mind it is simply what is at or beyond the horizon, a very distant time. A common phrase in the Hebrew is *"l'olam va'ed,"* usually translated as "forever and ever," but in the Hebrew means "to the distant horizon and again," meaning "a very distant time and even further."

Eternity

When looking off into the far distance, it is difficult to make out any details, and what is beyond the horizon cannot be seen. This is the concept behind the Hebrew verb עלם *(Ah.L.M)*, meaning "to be beyond the horizon," "to be beyond view" or "to hide." The noun עולם *(olam)*, derived from this verb, means the "horizon" or "out of sight:"

> *Before the mountains were brought forth and you formed the land and the world, from* horizon *(olam) to* horizon *(olam) you are God. Psalm 90:2*

Hebrew words that are used for space, such as we see in the verse above, can also be used for time. In the verses below, the word עולם *(olam)* means "beyond the horizon of time" or "a long time" in the past or the future.

> *...Your fathers dwelt on the other side of the river a* long time ago *(olam)... Joshua 24:2*

> *I despise it, I will not live for a* long time *(olam) for my days are vanity. Job 7:16*

The word *olam* is frequently translated as "eternity" or "forever" with the mistaken understanding that it means a continual span of time that never ends—forever. However, in the Hebrew mind, this word simply means "beyond the horizon" or "a very distant time."

A common Hebrew phrase in the Bible is לעולם ועד (*l' olam va'ed*), which is translated as "for ever and ever" in the verse below:

> The LORD shall reign for ever and ever.
> (Exodus 15:18, KJV)

More literally, from a Hebraic perspective this phrase means "to the distant horizon and again." When this translation is applied to the above verse, it can mean, "YHWH will reign to the horizon and beyond" or "YHWH will reign for a distant time and beyond" or even both.

Face

The Hebrew word פנים (*paniym*) means "face," but with a deeper meaning than just the front part of the head. The first clue that there is more to this word than simply meaning "face" is that it is a plural word, as indicated by the suffix י‍ם (*iym*). In English, nouns denote inanimate objects and only if one adds a verb can the noun take on animation. Hebrew nouns, on the other hand, denote objects of action. The action behind *paniym* is the expression of emotion and personality in the face, and since we have an infinite number of "faces," the Hebrew word is plural. Our second clue that there is more to this word can be read in the following passage:

> And the LORD said unto Moses, depart, and go up hence, thou and the people which thou hast brought up out of the land of Egypt, unto the land which I sware unto Abraham, to Isaac, and to Jacob, saying, Unto thy seed will I give it: _And I will send an angel before thee_; and I will drive out the Canaanite, the Amorite, and the Hittite, and the Perizzite, the Hivite, and

the Jebusite: Unto a land flowing with milk and honey: for I will not go up in the midst of thee; for thou art a stiffnecked people: lest I consume thee in the way. (Exodus 33:1-3, KJV)

In these verses, we are told that YHWH refused to go with Israel to take them to the Promised Land, because they were stiffnecked and he would kill them. He would send an angel to go with them instead. A few verses later, we are given another description of this "angel."

And he said, My presence shall go with thee, and I will give thee rest. (Exodus 33:14, KJV)

The Hebrew word behind the word "presence" is *paniym,* the face, and is a description of the angel mentioned previously. The angel has the same personality as YHWH and therefore is the "face of YHWH."

Fear

The Hebrew word ירא *(yara)* is used in the two passages below:

And he said, I heard your voice in the garden and I feared because I was naked and I hid myself. Genesis 3:10

You will revere YHWH your Elohiym and you will serve him and in his name you will swear. Deuteronomy 6:13

Many would conclude from these two passages that this Hebrew word has two different meanings, "fear" and "reverence." This assumption is made with many Hebrew words, but this is caused by having an understanding of the

Hebrew vocabulary from a non-Hebraic perspective. Each Hebrew word has only one meaning but can have different applications. The literal concrete meaning of *yara* is a "flowing of the gut," which can be applied to "fear" or "reverence." Have you ever been so scared or been in the presence of something so amazing that you could feel it in your gut? This "feeling" is the meaning of this word. The Hebrews were a very emotional people, and in many cases their words are describing a "feeling," rather than an "action."

In the following verse the word "fear" is the noun יראה (*yirah*), which is derived from the verb *yara*:

> The _fear_ of the LORD is the beginning of wisdom: and the knowledge of the holy is understanding. (*Proverbs 9:10, KJV*)

The common understanding of this verse is if one is afraid of, or in great awe of, YHWH, he will have wisdom, but as we shall see, this is not consistent with its use in the Hebrew language. The Hebrew for "fear of the LORD" (as found in the verse above) is written with two nouns, יראת יהוה (*yirat YHWH*). When a noun precedes another noun, the first noun is in the construct state, meaning it is connected to the second noun—two words together forming one concept. An example of a construct noun can be found in the phrase מלכות אלהים (*malkut elohiym*), which means "kingdom of God." Notice the first noun, "kingdom," belongs to the second noun, "God."

Below is a complete list of construct phrases from the book of Genesis where the second word in the construct is "YHWH."

- The Voice of YHWH (Genesis 3:8)
- The Face of YHWH (Genesis 4:16)
- The Name of YHWH (Genesis 4:26)
- The Eyes of YHWH (Genesis 6:8)
- The Garden of YHWH (Genesis 13:10)

- The Word of YHWH (Genesis 15:1)
- The Angel of YHWH (Genesis 16:7)
- The Way of YHWH (Genesis 18:19)
- The Mount of YHWH (Genesis 22:14)

You will notice in every instance the first word in the construct (voice, face, etc.) belongs to the second word of the construct (YHWH). So, why do we think the word "fear" in the construct phrase "fear of YHWH" is "our" fear and not YHWH's? We know God cannot "fear," but as pointed out previously, the Hebrew verb *yara* literally means "to flow out of the gut." Now the question becomes, "What flows out of the gut of YHWH?"

Let's look at two other constructs, which will shed some light on what "the fear of YHWH" might be. The first is found in Psalm 1:2:

> But his delight is in <u>the law of the LORD</u>; and in
> his law doth he meditate day and night. (KJV)

The Hebrew for "the law of the LORD" is יהיה תורת (*torat YHWH*). The word תורת means "teachings" and is derived from the verb ירה (*yarah)* meaning "to throw" (in the sense of flowing) and is closely related to the verb *yara,* which we have previously examined above. Not only are they related in the sense that both are from the same parent root, יר (*yar)*, but they are also related by definition.

The second construct is found in Judges 3:10:

> And <u>the Spirit of the LORD</u> came upon him...
> (RSV)

In the construct יהוה רוח (*ru'ahh YHWH*) we find the word *ru'ahh,* meaning "wind" (another type of "flowing"), which can also mean the character of an individual.

What flows out of the gut of YHWH? His teachings and his character. Now, let's take another look at the beginning of Proverbs 9:10, but this time from a Hebrew perspective.

> *The flowings* (the teachings and the character)
> *of YHWH is the beginning of <u>wisdom.</u>*

Firmament

The Hebrew word translated as "firmament" is a very good example of how the Hebrew language works. English and all other modern languages are abstract-oriented. We commonly use words that have no connection to any physical activity or object. Hebrew, an ancient Eastern language, is very different, as all words are related to a physical action or object.

In many instances, it helps to look at all of the uses of a particular word and other words from the same root to get an idea of what that word really means. The word *raqiya* (translated as "firmament") comes from the root word *raqa*, which can be found in several passages including Isaiah 40:19:

> *"The idol! A workman casts it and a goldsmith overlays it with gold, and casts for it silver chains."*

The word "overlay" is the verb root *raqa* and is the process of hammering out a piece of gold or other metal into thin plates that are then applied to a carved or molten image.

Also, see Numbers 16:39:

> *So Eleazar the priest took the bronze censers, which those who were burned had offered; and they <u>were hammered out</u> as a covering for the altar.*

Here the phrase "were hammered out" is the verb root *raqa*. The gold was hammered into thin sheets, then laid over the surface of the altar.

The word *raqiya* is literally a "hammered out sheet." There are some scientists who have speculated that before the flood there was a thick sheet of water surrounding the earth high in the atmosphere. It is then possible that the "floodgates of heaven that were opened" at the beginning of the flood, was the collapse of this sheet of water. Interestingly, it is theorized that this sheet of water would have filtered out harmful sun rays and contributed to the longevity of life on earth before the Flood.

Firstborn

The firstborn of the father received a double portion of the inheritance as well as being the leader of his brothers. However, if a son other than the firstborn received this inheritance, he was called the "firstborn." Interestingly, this is a very common occurrence within the Biblical text, such as we see with Esau (the one born first) and Jacob (the one called the firstborn) and Manasseh (the one born first) and Ephraim (the one called the firstborn). This is an excellent example of how the Hebrew language uses words in both a literal and figurative sense.

Flesh

The Hebrew word בשר (*basar*) means "flesh," the skin or meat of animals or man; and when used in the phrase "all flesh," it means "all mankind." The verbal root of this word is בשר (*B.S.R*) and can be found in the following passage where it is translated as "proclaim the good news:"

The spirit of Adonai YHWH is upon me because YHWH has anointed me to <u>proclaim the good news</u> (בשר)... Isaiah 61:1

What does "flesh" have to do with "proclaiming good news?" Simple. When one proclaimed good news, such as the arrival of a new baby or visitors, or some other celebration, an animal was slaughtered and "flesh" was served.

Forgive

> *Arise, <u>lift up</u> the lad, and hold him in thy hand. For I will make him a great nation.* (Genesis 21:18)

The Hebrew word behind "lift up" is נשא (*nasa*) and means "to take hold of something and lift it up," either to move or remove it. This very same Hebrew word is also used in the following verse:

> *Consider mine affliction and my travail; And <u>forgive</u> all my sins.* (Psalm 25:18, ASV)

From a Hebraic perspective, the forgiveness of sins is the same as lifting them off and removing them, just as we see in Micah 7:19:

> *He will again have compassion upon us; he will tread our iniquities under foot; and thou wilt cast all their sins into the depths of the sea.* (ASV)

Another word translated as "forgive" is the Hebrew word סלח (*salahh*) and is used in the following verse, where the forgiveness of iniquity is being paralleled with the healing (or lifting up) of diseases:

> *Bless the LORD, O my soul, and forget not all*
> *his benefits, who <u>forgives</u> all your iniquity, who*
> *heals all your diseases.* (Psalm 103:2,3, RSV)

By investigating other words that are related to סלח (*salahh*) we can see that this word has a very similar meaning to נשא (*nasa*):

- סלד (*salad*) means "to leap up."
- סלע (*sala*) is a "cliff" (a wall that is lifted up).
- סלק (*salaq*) means "to ascend."

Fruit

The Modern Hebrew word for "fruit" is the word פרי (*periy*) and, as is the case with many Modern Hebrew words, has its origins in Biblical Hebrew:

> *And God said, Let the earth bring forth grass,*
> *the herb yielding seed, and the <u>fruit</u> tree*
> *yielding <u>fruit</u> after his kind, whose seed is in*
> *itself, upon the earth: and it was so.* (Genesis
> 1:11, KJV)

Fruits native to Israel use the same word found in Biblical Hebrew for Modern Hebrew. Below are a few examples:

- תפוח (*tapu'ahh*): Apple
- רימון (*rimon*): Pomegranate
- תאנה (*te'eynah*): Fig
- זית (*zayit*): Olive
- ענב (*eynav*): Grape

Fruits that are not native to Israel have no Biblical Hebrew origin, so Hebrew has adopted their names from other cultures. Below are a few Hebrew words for different fruits that you might recognize:

- בננה (pronounced *bananah*)
- קיווי (pronounced *qiwi*)
- מלון (pronounced *melon*)
- לימון (pronounced *limon*)
- אבוקדו (pronounced *avoqado*)

Etymology, the study of word origins, is a very interesting area of language study. Throughout our lifetime, we use thousands of words without stopping to ponder their origins or relationships to other words. Words can often be traced back through time and other languages to discover their origins and original meanings. Our purpose here is show a common relationship between Hebrew and English words and their meanings. This area of study is what has become called "Edenics."

All languages are based on a root system where a common set of letters can be found in different words of similar meaning. For example, the English words "FoLiage," " Flora" and "Flower" have a similar meaning and are derived from an ancient FL root which probably meant "plant."

The Hebrew word for "fruit" is פרי (*periy*) which is derived from the parent root פר (*PR*). Many of the English words for different types of fruit come from this PR Hebrew root including PeaR, aPRicot, PRune and PeRsimmon. Over time words evolve as they are transferred from one language or culture to another. One type of evolutionary change is the reversal of letters such as in the word gRaPe which is another fruit word from the PR root. Another type of evolutionary change is the exchange of one letter sound for a different similar sounding word. One common exchange of sounds is the R sound for the L sound such as we see in the fruit words apPLe and Plum, which have evolved from the PR root.

Another is the P to B or F giving us BeRry and the word FRuit, both evolved forms of the PR root.

The Hebrew word for "grain" is בר (BR - *bar*). In English, we have the words BaRley (a type of grain), BaRn (a place for storing grain) and BeeR (made from grains).

Function

Hebrew thought is more concerned with function, whereas our Greco-Roman thought is more concerned with appearance.

How would you describe a wooden pencil? You would probably describe it as "long and yellow with a pointed end." Notice that we like to use adjectives to describe objects. However, in Hebrew thought verbs are used much more commonly, and a pencil would be described as something you write with, a description of its function rather than its appearance.

When we read the Biblical text, we are constantly creating a mental image of what the text is describing. However, the original author is not describing an image of appearance—but an image of function.

> *And this is how you are to make it, the length of the vessel is three hundred cubits long, fifty cubits wide and thirty cubits high. (Genesis 6:15, RSV)*

Is this description telling us what the ark looked like? Not at all; it is describing the function by telling us this ark is very large and capable of transporting a very large load of animals.

Gate

> *And the two angels came to Sodom at even;*
> *and Lot sat in the gate of Sodom...* (Genesis
> 19:1, ASV)

Why did Lot sit "in the gate of Sodom?" In Ancient Near East the court was held at the gates of a city and those who "sat" in the gate were the judges. Lot was not just an ordinary citizen; he was in fact a judge. Because of this, the word "gate" is used as a euphemism for a "judge." A euphemism is the use of one word in place of another. A common euphemism in our English language is the word "dough" to mean "money:"

> *Lift up your heads, O ye gates; And be ye lifted*
> *up, ye everlasting doors: And the King of glory*
> *will come in.* (Psalm 24:7, ASV)

If we were to read this literally, we would ask, "How does a gate lift up its head?" However, knowing that a "gate" is a euphemism for a "judge," we can correctly interpret the author's use of a euphemism and know that the passage is speaking about judges and not a literal gate.

Generation

The Hebrew word דור (*dor*) is used 167 times in the Hebrew Bible and usually translated as "generation." While the Hebrew word דור (*dor*) and the English word "generation" are similar in meaning, it is important to understand the differences in order to have a clearer picture of the author's understanding of the word that may impact how a particular passage is understood.

A generation is the time from one birth to the birth of the next generation. While the word דור (*dor*) has this meaning, there are some differences between the Hebrew understanding of this word and our own. In our Greco-Roman culture we see time as a line with a beginning and an end, while the Eastern mind sees time as a continuous circle. While we may see a generation as a timeline with a beginning and an end, the Hebrews saw a generation as one circle with the next generation being a continuation of the circle. There is no beginning and no end.

The word דור (*dor*) is a child root derived from the parent root דר (*dar*), which in the ancient pictographic script was written as ℚ𝒱. The first letter is a picture of a tent door and has the meaning of an 'in and out' or 'back and forth' movement. The second letter is the head of a man meaning "man." When combined, these mean "the movement of man." A generation is the movement through the circle of one man, while the next generation is the movement of man through the following circle.

In the ancient Hebrew mind, a circle represents "order" and notice that the Hebrew word דור (*dor*) is found in the English word orDER. This circular order can also be seen in the creation/destruction of the world. In our Greco-Roman mind we see the creation as the beginning of a timeline and its destruction as the end of that timeline. But remember the ancient Hebrews saw time as a circle. This world was destroyed at the fall of man (a full circle). The world begins a-new with the new order of things and is destroyed again at the Flood, another circle. The world begins a-new and will be destroyed again (as prophesied by the prophets). Were there circles of time prior to Genesis 1:1 and will there be circles of time after the destruction to come?

Davar

I previously introduced the Biblical Hebrew word "dor" and the concept of "order." Now we will examine the Hebrew root דבר (*D.B.R*). Notice that the parent root דר (*dar*) is found within this three-letter root word.

The word דבר (*D.B.R*) is commonly found in the Biblical text and means to "speak," as in the phrase *vayiDaBeR YHWH el moshe l'mor* (and YHWH <u>spoke</u> to Moses saying). The ancient Hebrew understanding of "speaking," or a "speech" is an ordered arrangement of words, so the verb דבר (*D.B.R*) may better be translated as "order," as in "And YHWH gave orders to Moses, saying..." A commanding officer does not "speak" to his troops; instead, he formulates his action plans and determines the best means to have these plans carried out. Once all of this is determined, he gives his "orders," "an ordered arrangement of ideas."

Derived from this verb is the noun דבר (*davar*) and means a "word" or "an order." The plural form is דברים (*devariym*) and means "words" or "orders." The phrase, "Ten Commandments," does not actually appear in the Hebrew Bible; instead it is the Hebrew phrase עשרת הדברים (*aseret hadevariym*) and literally means "ten orders." The "Ten Commandments" are our orders (the troops) from God (the general). They are an ordered arrangement of ideas that, if followed, will bring about peace and harmony within the community.

Another noun derived from the root דבר (*D.B.R*) is the word דברה (*devorah*), which means "bee." A bee hive is a colony of insects that live in a perfectly ordered society. The word דברה () is also the personal name *Deborah*, which of course means "bee."

Another common word derived from the root דבר (D.B.R) is מדבר (mid'bar) meaning a "wilderness." In the ancient Hebrew mind, the wilderness, in contrast to the cities, is a place of order. Many people today live in the cities, a place of high crime and a place of hurrying, rushing and busying one's self with all the day-to-day tasks. The city can easily be seen as a place of chaos.

On the other hand, when we want to "get away from it all" and slow down and really rest, we go out to the "wilderness." We take walks out into the woods or sit by a lake and feel the peace in these places. These are places of order, where all of nature is in a perfect balance of harmony.

Seder

Continuing the Hebraic view of "order" we will examine the Hebrew root סדר (S.D.R), which again has the root דר (dar) within it. The verb סדר (S.D.R) is found in Job 10:22:

> A *land of darkness is like a darkness of death*
> *and without <u>order</u>, and the light is like darkness.*

This imagery is reminiscent of Genesis 1 where the heavens and the earth were in total darkness, a state of chaos. The creative power of God then "ordered" the world into a state of "order."

A Hebrew noun derived from this root is שדרה (sederah), which means a "row," an ordered arrangement, such as the boards of a fence or warriors of an army. Again, we see this work in the creation narrative where all of the plants, animals, water, sky, sun, moon, etc. are placed in their proper arrangement.

There are a couple of common Modern Hebrew words that are derived from the root סדר (S.D.R). The first is the Passover

Seder. A *Seder* is the meal served on Passover and literally means an "ordered arrangement." The entire Passover meal is like a symphony of many parts making one harmonious sound. The second word is the *Sidur*, which is usually translated as "prayer book," but is literally an "ordered arrangement" of prayers.

Eder

Continuing the Hebraic view of "order" we will examine the Hebrew verb עדר (*Ah.D.R*). Again, we see the parent root דר (*dar*), meaning "order," in this word.

In Isaiah 7:25 is the phrase "to be hoed," which is the Hebrew verb עדר (*Ah.D.R*) that means to "hoe," "rake" or "dig." The concept behind this word is the cultivating of a field, the removal of the weeds, so that a crop can grow. This action is seen as bringing the field into order. The noun מעדר (*m'ader*) is a tool, such as a hoe, rake or shovel that is used to hoe, rake or dig.

Removing what is unnecessary brings about order. In the case of a field, it is the removal of the weeds, briers and thorns. In the case of a battle, it is the removal of fear (see 1 Chronicles 12:33).

This concept of removing what is unnecessary in order to bring about order is also seen in the Flood account. The world was full of sin and to bring about order once again, the Flood came to "weed out" the bad and begin again with a new crop, Noah and his family.

Glory

> *And in the morning you shall see the glory of the LORD.* (Exodus 16:7, RSV)

What is the "glory" of YHWH? First, we must recognize that the "glory" is something that will be seen, as stated in the passage above. Secondly, the word "glory" is an abstract word, but because Hebrew uses concrete words, we must search to find its concrete meaning.

The Hebrew word translated as "glory" is כבוד (*kavod*) and, if we look at how this Hebrew word is paralleled with other words in poetical passages of the Bible, we can discover the original concrete meaning of this word. In Psalm 3:3 the *kavod* of *Elohiym* is paralleled with his shield, and in Job 29:20, Job's *kavod* is paralleled with his bow:

> Who is this king of the <u>kavod</u>, YHWH is strong
> and mighty, YHWH is mighty in battle? (Psalm
> 24:8)

In the above passage, *kavod* is paralleled with "strong and mighty in battle." The original concrete meaning of *kavod* is "battle armaments." This meaning of "armament" fits with the literal meaning of the root of *kavod*, which is "heavy," as armaments are the heavy weapons and defenses of battle. In Exodus 16:7, Israel will "see" the "<u>armament</u>" of YHWH, the one who has done battle for them with the Egyptians.

God

In order to understand the full Hebraic meaning of the Hebrew word אלהים (*elohiym*), we will need to look at the roots from which it is derived. The parent root אל (*el*) is a "strong leader." Derived from this parent root is the child root אלה (*alah*), meaning an "oath," or, more Hebraically, a binding yoke that binds the "strong leader" to another in an agreement. The word אלה (*alah*) is found in the following verse:

and they said, we surely see that YHWH existed with you and we said, please, an <u>oath</u> will exist between us and you and we will cut a covenant with you, (Genesis 26:28, RMT)

The word אלוה (*eloah*) is derived out of the child root אלה (*alah*) and refers to the "strong leader" that one is "bound" with:

"Behold, happy is the man whom <u>God</u> reproves; therefore, despise not the chastening of the Almighty. (Job 5:17, RSV)

The plural form of אלוה (*eloah*) is אלהים (*elohiym*) and means the "strong leaders that the people are bound to" and can be found in the following passages:

"You shall have no other <u>gods</u> before me." (Exodus 20:3, RSV)

"Then his master shall bring him unto the <u>judges</u>." (Exodus 21:6, KJV)

This plural word is also used for the Creator of the heavens and the earth and is the most common word translated as "God" in the Bible:

"In the beginning <u>God</u> created the heavens and the earth." (Genesis 1:1, NIV)

The God who created the heavens and the earth is not just a god, but the all-powerful God, mightier than any other god:

"For the LORD (יהוה) your <u>God</u> (אלהים), he is <u>God</u> (אלהים) of the <u>gods</u> (אלהים), and Lord of lords, a great <u>God</u> (אל)" (Deuteronomy 10:17, RSV)

Grace

Most theologians will define "grace" as "unmerited favor." But we must be careful not to interject a theological bias into the text. First, we need to understand what the English word "grace" means outside of theology. The dictionary provides two basic definitions for grace:

1. Elegance or beauty of form, manner, motion or action
2. Mercy; clemency; pardon

Because the Hebrew language is vastly different from English, we need to examine the Hebrew meaning of this word to see if one or both English definitions are appropriate definitions for the Hebrew word translated as "grace."

The Hebrew word translated as "grace" is חן (*hhen*) and is a two-letter parent root. In order to uncover the original meaning of this word, it is important to first examine each of the roots and words that are derived from this parent root.

From חן (*hhen*) comes the verbal root חנה (*Hh.N.H*), spelled exactly the same except with the addition of the letter ה (*h*) at the end. The following verse provides a good example of the meaning of this verb:

> And Isaac departed thence, and <u>pitched his tent</u> in the valley of Gerar, and dwelt there. (Genesis 26:17, KJV)

This verb means "to pitch a tent" or "to camp." The noun derived from this verb is מחנה (*mahhaneh*):

> And it came between the <u>camp</u> of the Egyptians and the <u>camp</u> of Israel; and it was a cloud and darkness to them, but it gave light by night to these: so that the one came not

near the other all the night. (Exodus 14:20, KJV)

When we think of a camp, we think of tents scattered about in a general area. However, the camps of the Ancient Hebrews were a little different and the tents were set up in a sort of circle and these tents served as a "wall" separating the inside of the camp from the outside. At this point it would be helpful to examine the pictographic Hebrew script that was used originally to write the word חן (*hhen*). The first letter is the letter *hhet*, which was written as ㅂ and is a picture of a wall, and means "separation," as the wall separates the inside from the outside. The second letter is the letter *nun*, which was written as ⤴ and is a picture of a sprouting seed with the meaning of "continue," as the seed continues a lineage to the next generation. When these two letters are combined they mean "the wall that continues." The tents in the picture above are a wall that continues around the camp.

A second verbal root derived from the parent root חן (*hhen*) is חנן (*Hh.N.N*), spelled exactly the same with the addition of the letter ן (*n*) at the end. This verb is often translated: "to be gracious" or "have mercy." However, these are abstract terms and do not help us understand the meaning of this verb from a Hebraic perspective, which always relates words to something concrete. One of the best tools for finding the more concrete meaning of a word is to look at how that word is paralleled with other words in poetical passages. In the following verses, the translation of the verb חנן (*Hh.N.N*) will be underlined and the word paralleled with it will be in bold:

> <u>Have mercy</u> upon me, O LORD; for I am weak: O LORD, **heal** me; for my bones are vexed. (Psalm 6:2, KJV)

> Hear, O LORD, and <u>have mercy</u> upon me: LORD, be thou my **helper**. (Psalm 30:10, KJV)

But thou, O LORD, be merciful unto me, and raise me up, that I may requite them. (Psalm 41:10, KJV)

Be merciful unto me, O God, be merciful unto me: for my soul trusteth in thee: yea, in the shadow of thy wings will I make my refuge, until these calamities be overpast. (Psalm 57:1, KJV)

O turn unto me, and have mercy upon me; give thy strength unto thy servant, and save the son of thine handmaid. (Psalm 86:16, KJV)

Through this process we find this Hebrew verb is paralleled with such ideas as "healing," "help," "being lifted up," "finding refuge," "strength and salvation" (literally rescue). From a concrete Hebraic perspective, חנן (*Hh.N.N*) means all of these, which can be summed up as "providing protection." Where does one run for protection? The camp, and now we see how חנה (*Hh.N.H*), "the camp," and חנן (*Hh.N.N*), "protection," are related. Now we need to see how these words are related to the parent root חן (*hhen*):

A gift is as a precious stone in the eyes of him that hath it... (Proverbs 17:8, KJV)

In this verse, the Hebrew word חן (*hhen*) is translated as "precious," something of beauty and value.

A gracious woman retaineth honour: and strong men retain riches. (Proverbs 11:16, KJV)

In this verse the "grace," or "beauty," of the woman is contrasted with the strength of a man.

> *Favour* is deceitful, and beauty is vain: but a
> woman that feareth the LORD, she shall be
> praised. (Proverbs 31:30)

Again, this Hebrew word is being paralleled with "beauty." This "beauty" is something that is precious and graceful, which is exactly how the Hebrews would have seen the "camp of protection," "a graceful and precious place."

Let us now return to our original definition of the English word "grace:"

1. Elegance or beauty of form, manner, motion or action

2. Mercy; clemency; pardon

While these definitions do apply to the Hebrew word חן (*hhen, KJV*), they do not completely convey the full emotion and spectrum of the Hebrew word. This is the problem with translating Hebrew into English. The English vocabulary is limited in how it can express the full meaning of a given Hebrew word.

Ground

> *And YHWH Elohiym formed the human of dust
> from the ground (adamah)...* (Genesis 2:7)

The Hebrew behind the word "ground" is אדמה (*adamah*) and is related to the Hebrew word אדם (*adam*), also found in the sentence above and translated as "human." Hebrew authors loved to use similar sounding words together, such as seen in the sentence above. Here is another example:

And he said, what did you do? The voice of the
blood (dam) of your brother is crying out to me
from the ground (adamah). (Genesis 4:10)

Gut

I delight to do thy will, O my God: yea, thy law
is within my heart. (Psalm 40:8, KJV)

The word translated "heart" in this verse is not the Hebrew word לב (*lev*), which means "heart," but מעה (*meyah*), which means "gut" or "abdomen." When King David wrote ותורתך מעי בתוך (*v'torat'kha betokh mey'ai* / your *Torah* is within my guts) he was expressing a very concrete perception of God's *Torah* (a Hebrew word meaning "teachings," not "law"). Have you ever been so excited about something that your guts moved or churned? David was so excited about God's *Torah* that it caused his guts to move. This is the feeling that Job had when he said "*My guts boiled*" (Job 30:27). Do our guts churn when we hear the teachings of God like David did?

We often use the expression, "I had a gut feeling," which refers to a thought that does not come from the mind, but from deep down in our subconscious, the gut. I am of the opinion that these "gut" feelings are sometimes God speaking to us, but our heart and mind (actually in Hebraic thought, the mind being in the heart, not the brain) are our own thoughts that cloud over what God is speaking.

Heal

The parent root רף (*raph*) is the root to several Biblical Hebrew words related to health and sickness. The original pictographs for this word are the ꗷ, representing "man," and ꕥ, representing the "mouth" with the meaning "open." Combined, the word ꕥꗷ means an "open man" and is exactly what happens when one is cut or wounded. A common ancient medicine was the use of a poultice placed on an open wound. Hyssop was most likely used as a poultice because of its antibacterial properties. The Hebrew verb רוף (*R.W.P*), derived from רף, means "to pulverize," which is what is done to plants when being made into a poultice. From רוף comes the noun רופה (*ruphah*) meaning "medicine." Another verb derived from רף is the verbal root רפא (*R.P.A*), meaning "to heal." This verb was first used when Avraham interceded on Avimelekh's behalf to heal him and his family from their illness (Genesis 20:17). When this verb is used in its participle form, it can mean "healing" or "healer" (a physician). One other verbal root derived from רף is רפה (*R.P.H*) meaning "weak" or "feeble," as when someone is sick.

Heart

When I began studying the Bible, I loved to do word studies. I would select a word and study its uses and contexts in as many verses as I could find them. Below is a sampling of verses from the King James Version that include the word "heart:"

> Genesis 6:5 *And GOD saw that the wickedness of man was great in the earth, and that every imagination of the thoughts of his <u>heart</u> was only evil continually.*

Exodus 7:3 *And I will harden Pharaoh's <u>heart</u>, and multiply my signs and my wonders in the land of Egypt.*

Exodus 23:9 *And a sojourner shalt thou not oppress: for ye know the <u>heart</u> of a sojourner, seeing ye were sojourners in the land of Egypt*

Proverbs 2:2 *So as to incline thine ear unto wisdom, And apply thy <u>heart</u> to understanding;*

Psalm 40:8 *I delight to do thy will, O my God; Yea, thy law is within my <u>heart</u>.*

Psalm 55:4 *My <u>heart</u> is sore pained within me: And the terrors of death are fallen upon me.*

However, I was soon to discover that there was a flaw in this type of word study. I purchased a Concordance, a book with a complete list of all the words in a particular translation, which would cross reference any word in the translation with *Strong's Dictionary*. This would give the Hebrew word behind the English translation, as well as a definition of that word.

With this tool I discovered that the English translation was not very consistent on how it translated Hebrew words. For instance, in the examples I gave above, the word "heart" is a translation of three different Hebrew words. The Hebrew word *Lev*, which is the Hebrew word for "heart," is translated as "heart" in the first, second, fourth and sixth verses above. The word *nephesh*, which is usually translated as "soul," is translated as "heart" in the third verse. *Me'ah*, which is literally the "intestines," is translated as "heart" in the fifth verse. Each of these Hebrew words has a specific meaning, but the translators chose to ignore this and just translate all three as "heart."

The use of the concordance also revealed that the Hebrew word *lev* (heart) was translated as other English words, as you can see in the verses below, also from the King James Version:

> *Genesis 31:20 And Jacob stole away <u>unawares</u> to Laban the Syrian, in that he told him not that he fled.* (A literal translation of the Hebrew is *"And Jacob stole the heart of Laban the Aramean because he did not tell him that he fled."*)

> Exodus 9:21 *And he that <u>regarded</u> not the word of Jehovah left his servants and his cattle in the field.*

> Numbers 16:28 *And Moses said, Hereby ye shall know that Jehovah hath sent me to do all these works; for I have not done them of mine own <u>mind</u>.*

> Job 36:5 *Behold, God is mighty, and despiseth not any: He is mighty in strength of <u>understanding</u>.*

> Psalm 83:5 *For they have consulted together with one <u>consent</u>; Against thee do they make a covenant:*

> Proverbs 19:8 *He that getteth <u>wisdom</u> loveth his own soul: He that keepeth understanding shall find good.*

All of this playing with words in the English translations did not settle well with me. How was a person to properly interpret the Bible if there was no consistency in how the Hebrew was translated? If one is given the proper translations and definitions, some interesting revelations appear:

Jeremiah 17:9 *The heart is deceitful above all
things, and it is exceedingly corrupt: who can
know it?*

Based on the above verse, I had previously thought that the
"heart" (in the sense of emotion) was deceitful, but the mind
was logical and trustworthy. After discovering that the heart
to the Hebrews was the mind, I realized that Jeremiah was
saying that the "mind" was deceitful. In another study, I
discovered that emotion, which we consider to be the heart, is
actually the kidneys to the Hebrews.

I should point out that this is not an isolated case by any
means; in fact, I have seen this same scenario played out time
after time with many different words and in all translations.
Anyone desiring to do a serious word study can never rely on
an English translation alone. At a minimum, a concordance
and dictionary are going to be essential.

Holy

Ye shall be *holy*: for I the LORD your God am
holy. (Leviticus 19:2, KJV)

The word "holy" is an abstract word used to translate the
Hebrew noun קדוש (*qadosh*). This noun is derived from the
root קדש (Q.D.Sh), which is commonly translated as
"sanctify." To say one is "sanctified" or is "holy" implies that
one is exceptionally pious and righteous. But as we shall see,
these words have a very different meaning. Also derived from
the root קדש (Q.D.Sh) and related to the noun קדוש (*qadosh*)
is the word קדש (*qadesh*), which is used in the following
passage:

No Israelite man or woman is to become a temple prostitute. (Deuteronomy 23:17, NIV)

We would never consider a "prostitute" as holy and yet the root of the Hebrew word קדש (*qadesh*) is often translated as "holy." To resolve this oddity, we can examine the following verse to determine the true meaning of the verb קדש (*Q.D.Sh*):

> *"Take the anointing oil and anoint the tabernacle and everything in it; consecrate it and all its furnishings, and it will be holy."* (Exodus 40:9, NIV)

Furniture is an inanimate object that cannot be holy, pious or righteous in themselves, but can be "set apart for a specific function," which is the true meaning of קדש (*Q.D.Sh*). These can be the furnishings of the Temple that are used for this purpose alone or a prostitute who is set apart from the rest of society for a specific purpose. The children of God are set apart from all others; they have the specific function of living for God and showing the world who God is.

Images

Compare these two translations of Genesis 31:34:

> *Now Rachel had taken the images, and put them in the camel's furniture, and sat upon them. And Laban searched all the tent, but found them not.* (KJV)

> *Now Rachel had taken the household gods and put them in the camel's saddle, and sat upon them. Laban felt all about the tent, but did not find them.* (RSV)

Why did the KJV translate the Hebrew word תרפים (*teraphim*) as "images," but the RSV translated it as "household gods?"

At the time the KJV was written, no one really knew what this Hebrew word meant, other than it was some kind of idol. Thanks to the advancements of archeology and linguistics, over the next few hundred years we learned a lot more about the Hebrew culture and language, and it was discovered that this Hebrew word was used for the family idol, the god that "protected" (the root of this word means "to heal") the family. Because of this, the later translations could be more precise in their translations.

Iniquity

> *And when the morning arose, then the angels hastened Lot, saying, Arise, take thy wife, and thy two daughters that are here, lest thou be consumed in the <u>iniquity</u> of the city.* (Genesis 19:15, ASV)

Our modern Greco-Roman languages commonly use abstract terms like "iniquity." But as Hebrew is a concrete language rarely using abstracts, we must understand the word "iniquity" from its Hebraic concrete meaning. The Hebrew word for "iniquity" is עוון (*ah-von*), which is derived from the verbal root עוה (*Ah.W.H*) This verbal root is found in the following passages:

> *He hath walled up my ways with hewn stone; he hath made my paths <u>crooked</u>.* (Lamentations 3:9, ASV)

Behold, the LORD will lay waste the earth and make it desolate, and he will <u>twist</u> its surface and scatter its inhabitants. (Isaiah 24:1, RSV)

Already we are beginning to see the "concrete" meaning in the Hebrew word that lies behind the English word "iniquity:" it is something "crooked" or "twisted." The first letter in this word is the letter ע (*ayin*). This single letter was originally two different letters, the ◉ (*ayin*) and the 𐤏 (*ghayin*), when Hebrew was written with a pictographic alphabet. The *ghayin* is a picture of a twisted cord and is clearly the original letter in this word.

As we have demonstrated, the verb עוה (*Ah.W.H*) means "to be crooked" or "to be twisted." Therefore the noun עוון (*ah-von*), derived from this verb, means "crookedness" or "twistedness." Let's return to our original passage and read this from a more concrete perspective:

> *And when the morning arose, then the angels hastened Lot, saying, Arise, take thy wife, and thy two daughters that are here, lest thou be consumed in the <u>twistedness</u> of the city.* (Genesis 19:15, ASV)

This same noun is also found in the following passage:

> *And Cain said unto the LORD, My <u>punishment</u> is greater than I can bear.* (Genesis 4:13, KJV)

Why the translators chose the word "punishment" for this word is a mystery because this translation implies that Cain was saddened by the punishment. The truth is, this word means "twistedness," and he was instead saddened by his "actions."

Jealous

> *For thou shalt worship no other god: for the
> LORD, whose name is Jealous, is a jealous God.*
> (Exodus 34:14, KJV)

From a Western perspective, the idea of one being named
"Jealous" seems odd, especially as a name for God. As a name
represents the character, this implies that God is by nature
jealous. Our cultural understanding of the word is a type of
anger felt over the suspected unfaithfulness of a spouse. As
we shall see in the discussions that follow, the Hebrew word
has a very different meaning.

Nest

The parent root קן (*qen*) is a nest:

> *"Like an eagle he wakes up his nest, over his
> chicks he hovers, he spreads his wings, he
> takes them, he carries them over his feathers."*
> Deuteronomy 32.11

The first letter of the parent root in the ancient script is ቀ, a
picture of the sun at the horizon where the light is gathered
during the sunrise or sunset. The second letter ؎ is a
sprouting seed, the beginning of new life that came from the
parent plant. Combined, these letters form the meaning, "A
gathering for the seeds." A bird goes about "gathering"
materials for building a nest for her "seeds" (eggs) of the next
generation.

Several words are derived from the parent root קן (*qen* -
nest), all related to the idea of building a nest:

Builder

The child root קנה (Q.N.H) is the construction of a nest by the parent bird:

> And he blessed him and he said, Blessed is Abram to God most high, _builder_ of heaven and earth. Genesis 14:19

Some translations translate the above verse as, "Creator of heaven and earth." The ancient Hebrews did not see God as an unknowable force that creates the universe for some unknown reason; rather, he is the bird that goes about gathering all the necessary materials for building a home for his children. Man was not created as an additional component to the creation; the earth was created as a home for man.

Guard

Another word derived from קן (qen) is קנא (Q.N.A). This is the word translated as "jealous" in our introductory passage. The Hebraic meaning of this word is the passion with which the parent guards over the chicks in the nest. While our Western mind may see the term a "jealous God" in his feelings and actions toward us, it is in fact his feelings and actions toward our enemies. The heathens and false gods are like predators invading the nest, and God fights them, protecting his children from their clutches.

Judges

> In the beginning _God_ created the heaven and the earth (Genesis 1:1, KJV)

> Then his master shall bring him unto the _judges._ (Exodus 21:6, KJV)

What do these two verses have in common? Simple. They both contain the Hebrew word "*Elohiym*." When studying the Bible, one of my greatest frustrations is the translator's complete lack of ability to translate words consistently. If you are reading a translation, you are being given the translator's "opinion" of what the Hebrew/Greek text is saying and not the original author's "conviction."

The Hebrew word translated 'God' in Genesis 1:1 is "*Elohiym*" and this same word is translated as "judges" in Exodus 21:6. The word *Elohiym* is a plural form (as indicated by the '*iym*' suffix) of the word *elo'ah*. Elo'ah means a judge, or one of power and authority. Therefore, *elohiym* means "judges," as we see in Exodus 21:6. So, why isn't *Elohiym* translated as "judges" in Genesis 1:1? First of all, it can't be. The verb translated as "created" is *bara* and identifies the subject of the verb (*Elohiym*) as a masculine singular: "he" (not they). So, *Elohiym* has to be understood as a proper name and a simple plural noun:

> And the LORD said unto Moses, See, I have made thee a _god_ to Pharaoh. (Exodus 7:1, KJV)

The Hebrew word translated as 'god' is again the word *Elohiym*. Did God "make" Moses "judges?" That really does not make sense in English, nor does it make sense in Hebrew. Again, we are looking at a translator's opinion. The word "made" is their translation of the Hebrew word *natan,* which more literally means "to give." The LORD (more on this word in another article) "gave" Moses *Elohiym* (someone, or something with a name meaning "judges"). As I mentioned, the meaning behind *Elohiym* is "power" and through the events of the plagues and Israel's wanderings through the wilderness, we see Moses manifest this "power."

From this, we can conclude that Moses is *Elohiym*, and he has been given the quality and character of the *Elohiym* that created the heavens and the earth. This, of course, goes contrary to our understanding of what God is; after all, isn't God the old man sitting on the throne of heaven? I think not. The word *Elohiym* is not a reference to a person, but a character trait.

Jungle

Many Modern Hebrew words are transliterations of European words. For instance, the Modern Hebrew word for "telephone" is טלפון, which is pronounced *telephone*. The Modern Hebrew word for a "jungle" is ג'ונגל, which is pronounced "*jungle*" (the letter ג is a "g" sound, but when followed by the apostrophe it takes on a "j" sound in Modern Hebrew). This Modern Hebrew word is a transliteration of the European word "jungle," which is found in English, Italian, German, Spanish, Polish and French.

According to Isaac Mozeson and his work in Edenics, the study of Semitic/Hebrew origin of words around the world, the word "jungle" comes from the Semitic/Hebrew word יער (*ya'ar*). At first glance there does not seem to be any connection between this Hebrew word יער and "jungle," until we examine the sound shifts that have occurred over time. When a word is transferred from one language to another, the sounds of letters are swapped for other letters of similar sound. For example, the Latin word for foot is "*ped*" (where we get our words pedestrian and pedal). The "p" is exchanged for the "f" (both sounds being made at the lips) and the "d" for "t" (both sounds being made at the roof of the mouth just behind the teeth) and the word "*ped*" becomes "fet" or "feet."

In the case of the word יער, the י (*y*) is exchanged for a "j," the ע (a guttural stop) for an "*ng*," and the ר (*r*) for an "l" and יער (*ya'ar*) becomes JuNGLe. The Ancient Hebrew יער traveled through many different other languages to become the European word "jungle," which was then transliterated back into Hebrew as ונגל'ג. Interestingly though, the Modern Hebrew word for a "forest" is the Ancient Hebrew word יער (ya'ar).

Kneeling

Each Hebrew verb may be written in specific ways to express varying nuances of a verb. These different verb "forms" are always related to the meaning of the original verb. Below are a few examples in their English translations to demonstrate this:

Simple	Passive	Causative	Intensive
Take	Be taken	Cause to take	Steal
Hear	Be heard	Cause to hear	Summon
Speak	Talk	Command	Promise
Know	Be known	Make known	Understand
Turn	Be turned	Make turn	Turn away
Cut	Be cut	Cause to cut	Hack
Sit	Be set down	Cause to sit	Set in place
Eat	Be eaten	Cause to eat	Devour
Die	Be dead	Kill	Destroy
Send	Be sent	Send away	Dismiss

And I will make of thee a great nation, and I will <u>bless</u> thee, and make thy name great; and thou shalt be a blessing. (Genesis 12:2, KJV)

The word "bless" in the above passage is the intensive form of the verb ברך (*B.R.K*). The **simple** form of this verb means "kneel down" as can be seen in the following passage:

And he made his camels to <u>kneel down</u>… (Genesis 24:11, KJV)

We can easily recognize that the English words "kneel" and "bless" have no relationship to each other, and therefore "bless" cannot be a valid translation for the Hebrew verb ברך (*B.R.K*). Instead, we need to define the intensive form of the verb ברך (*B.R.K*) as it relates to the idea of "kneeling."

The Passive form of this verb would be "be knelt down." The Causative form would be "cause to kneel down." The Intensive form would then have a meaning related to the idea of kneeling down. The intensive form of this verb is always used in the context of showing respect to someone else, as can be seen in Genesis 12:2 above.

Before we determine the intensive meaning of this verb, let's look at the word "gift." The Hebrew word is the noun ברכה (*berakah*), which is derived from the verb ברך (*B.R.K*). While the KJV often translates this noun as "blessing," the KJV also translates it as "present" as found in the following passage.

And when David came to Ziklag, he sent of the spoil unto the elders of Judah, even to his friends, saying, Behold a <u>present</u> for you of the spoil of the enemies of the LORD; (1 Samuel 30:26, KJV)

A *berakah* is a "present" or "gift." This noun is related to the verb ברך (*B.R.K*), meaning to "kneel," in the sense of presenting a gift to another on bended knee. This is a sign of "respect" and it is this word that I believe the intensive form of ברך (*B.R.K*) means, but with the fuller concrete meaning of "to kneel down before another in respect" (note that this does not have to mean a literal kneeling down, as the Hebrew often uses concrete terms in a figurative sense):

> *And I will make you a great nation, and I will*
> *<u>respect</u> you and I will make your name great*
> *and it will be a <u>gift</u>.* (Genesis 12:2)

Many people will say, "YHWH will never bow before a man, literally or figuratively." If we think of YHWH as a Supreme Ruler, sitting high upon a throne, then I would agree, YHWH could never kneel before another. However, this is not the YHWH I read about in the Bible. The YHWH that I read about walks among his people like a father does with his children, and when a child looks up at his father with a question or comment, wouldn't a father kneel down before his child and get eye to eye with him and talk with him? This is a father that shows respect to his children. Kneeling before another is not a sign of submission, but instead a sign of respect, which we could say is a blessing to his children.

Lampstand

> *And six branches shall come out of the sides of*
> *it; three branches of the <u>candlestick</u> out of the*
> *one side, and three branches of the <u>candlestick</u>*
> *out of the other side.* (Exodus 25:32, KJV)

The parent root of the Hebrew word מנורה (*menorah*), which is translated in the KJV as "candlestick," is נר (*ner*). In the

Ancient Pictographic script, this parent root is written as 𐤍𐤓. The first letter is the *nun* and is a picture of a sprouting seed. A seed is the beginning of new life that came from the parent plant. This cycle will continue for generation after generation. The second letter is the head of a man. The head is seen as the top of the body and can be the top or head of anything, such as the body (the head), time (the beginning), a landscape (mountaintop) or a rank (chief). When these two letters are combined they mean a "seed beginning."

The literal meaning of the word נר is to "bring forth light" as well as a "freshly plowed field" because plowing is seen as "the bringing forth of light in the soil," to the ancient Hebrew. In order for a seed to grow/begin, there must be water in the soil. When the ground is plowed, the moist soil from underneath surfaces and shines from the water in the soil, and is a sign that the life-giving water is present.

Land

The Hebrew word often translated as "earth" is ארץ (*erets*) is more frequently translated as "land," the more literal meaning of the word. The word *erets* may refer to land in general or a specific piece of land, or a region, such as in the "land of Israel."

This word comes from the root רץ (*rats*) meaning "fragment." When a clay pot is broken, it is not wasted. The broken fragments called "ostracon," are commonly used as a surface for writing letters, receipts, messages, etc.

Did the Ancients view the earth as "fragments" in the sense of regions, or did they have the knowledge that the land of the earth was divided up into fragments, known to us as tectonic plates?

Languages

Genesis 10 is the genealogy of No'ahh's sons and says that they were divided into their respective lands and tongues. However, Genesis 11:1 says that the whole earth was with one language and speech. How can they be speaking different languages in chapter 10 before the incident of the Tower of Babel in chapter 11?

One of the problems we encounter when we read the Bible is that we are not aware that the Ancient Hebrews wrote differently than we do. When we write an accounting of events, we always write the events in the order they occurred. However, the Ancient Hebrews did not. They were not as concerned about keeping events in chronological order, but rather they used what is called "block logic," meaning that events can be listed in order of their significance or relationship rather than by chronology. While the account of the genealogies of No'ahh are found "before" the events at Babel, they occurred both before "and after" the events at Babel. As an example, Genesis 10:2 lists the sons of Japheth born prior to the events at Babel. But, in verse 3 we have the sons of Gomer (the son of Japheth) who most likely were born after the events of Babel.

We know that Noahh's sons were born prior to Babel, because all of their names are of Semitic (Hebrew) origin. Yet, some of Noahh's grandchildren have names that are non-Semitic showing a change in the languages.

Law

The Hebrew word "Torah" is usually translated into the English word "Law." Because of this translation, there is a great misunderstanding of what "Torah" truly is. "TORAH IS NOT

LAW." When we use the word "law," we assume a certain meaning and concept of the word that is not present in the Hebrew Scriptures.

Let us start by looking at the etymology of the Hebrew word *Torah* so that we may better understand its true definition. The word *Torah* comes from the Hebrew root word ירה (*Y.R.H*), a verb that means "to flow or throw something." This can be a flowing of an arrow from an archer's bow, or the flowing of a finger to point out a direction. Nouns are derived from the verb by making one or two changes to the verb root. In this case the Y (*yud*) is replaced by an O (*vav*) and an M (*mem*) is added at the front of the word to form the noun "*Moreh.*" A *Moreh* is "one who does the flowing." This can be an archer who "flows" an arrow, or a teacher who "flows" his finger to point out the way a student is to go in the walk of life. Another noun is formed the same way except that a T (*tav*) is placed at the front of the word instead of an M and we have the word "*Torah.*" *Torah* is "what is flowed by the *Moreh.*" This can be the arrow from the archer or the teachings and instructions from the teacher.

A Hebraic definition of *Torah* is "a set of Instructions from a father to his children; violations of these instructions are disciplined in order to foster obedience and train his children." Notice how the word "*Torah*" is translated in the New International Version translation in the following passages:

> "Listen, my son, to your father's instruction and do not forsake your mother's <u>teaching</u> [Torah]." (Proverbs 1:8)

> "My son, do not forget my <u>teaching</u> [Torah], but keep my commands in your heart." (Proverbs 3:1)

The purpose of a parent's *Torah* is to teach and bring the children to maturity. If the *Torah* is violated out of disrespect or defiant disobedience, the child is punished. If the child desires to follow the instructions out of a loving obedience but falls short of the expectations, the child is commended for the effort and counseled on how to perform the instructions better the next time. Unlike *Torah*, law is a set of rules from a government and binding on a community. Violation of the rules requires punishment. With this type of law, there is no room for teaching: either the law was broken with the penalty of punishment or it was not broken. God, as our heavenly Father, gives his children his *Torah* in the same manner as parents give their *Torah* to their children, not in the manner a government does to its citizens:

> "Blessed is the man you discipline, O LORD, the man you teach from your Torah" (Psalms 94:12)

Another noun derived from this root is מורה (*moreh*), which is a teacher, one who points out the way. The *Torah* is the teaching of the teacher, or more literally, the way pointed out by the teacher, "the journey." When we translate Psalm 1:2 with this literal understanding of *Torah*, we read; "His delight is in the journey of YHWH, and in his journey, he meditates day and night." Also, in Psalm 119:1; "Happy are the mature ones of the trail, the ones walking in the journey of YHWH."

A nomadic journey is a circuit, traveling from pasture land to pasture land, watering hole to watering hole, year after year. Much of the Hebraic lifestyle is related to this circular journey. Even the feasts are a nomadic journey of a circuit: *Pesahh* (Passover), *Shavuot* (Pentecost), *Sukkot* (Tabernacles) and back to *Pesahh* again. The entire *Torah* is read through the year and when the end of Deuteronomy is reached, the scroll is rewound and the reading continues with Genesis 1:1.

As I mentioned, the verb *yarah* means "to point," but is also used in the context of pointing an arrow or shooting an arrow, as we see in 1 Samuel 20:20: "And I will shoot three arrows." The word *moreh*, which we found meant "teacher," is also used for an "archer," the one who points the arrow. From this perspective, *Torah* is the arrow. If the arrow goes off course it "misses the mark, or strays from the path." When we stray from the path, we also miss the mark. The Hebrew word for "missing the mark" is חטאה (*hhatah*) which is often translated as "sin." Interestingly, another word for "sin" is to "trespass," to leave the path:

> And I looked, and behold, you have <u>sinned</u> against YHWH your Elohiym, and you made for yourself a molten calf, you quickly turned away from the trail which YHWH directed you. (Deuteronomy 9:16)

Interpreting the Hebrew word *Torah* as law is about the same as interpreting the word "father" as "disciplinarian." While the father is a disciplinarian, it is a very narrow interpretation. The same is true for *Torah*; a part of *Torah* is law, but this is a very narrow interpretation of it.

Lie

A man's wife comes to him and asks "How do you like the new dress I just made?" He can see from her expression that she loves the dress and is proud of her work, but personally he does not like it. How does he answer her? Most of us would agree that he is in a 'catch' difficult situation. If he says "I don't like it," he will crush her, but if he says "I love it," he is lying and guilty of sinning. We have all been faced with such dilemmas and are often unsure on the correct course of action. Believe it or not, God himself was faced with the same dilemma as recorded in Genesis 18:12, 13:

> *So Sarah laughed to herself, saying, "After I have grown old, and my husband is old, shall I have pleasure?" The LORD said to Abraham, "Why did Sarah laugh, and say, `Shall I indeed bear a child, now that I am old?'*

First, notice that in this translation Sarah states that both she and her husband are "old" and from this translation, we do not see a problem. Sarah laughed because she admitted that she was "old." When God goes to Abraham, he asks him why Sarah laughed and said she was "old." However, the translator "fixed" the text to remove what appears to be a problem with the text. In verse 12 the phrase "grown old," in reference to Sarah, is the Hebrew word בלה (*balah*), which does not mean "old," but instead to "wither away." The word "old," in reference to Abraham in verses 12, as well as the word "old" in verse 13, is זקן (*zaqen*), the Hebrew word which means "old." Let's now read that verse correctly:

> *So Sarah laughed to herself, saying, "After I have <u>withered away</u>, and my husband is <u>old</u>, shall I have pleasure?" The LORD said to Abraham, "Why did Sarah laugh, and say, `Shall I indeed bear a child, now that I am <u>old</u>?'*

We now see that Sarah laughed because she admitted she was "withered away" and her husband was "old." When God goes to Abraham, he asks him why Sarah laughed and said "she" was "old." Sarah never said she was "old." Did God "lie"? It would appear so, but in Numbers 23:19 we read "God is not a man and he does not lie." God cannot lie, yet we see him lying in Genesis 18.

The problem is not with the text but with our view of a lie. The Hebrew word for a "lie" in Numbers 23:19 is כזב (*kazav*). By looking at another verse using this same word we will see that this word does not literally mean "lie:"

> You shall be like a watered garden, like a spring of water, whose waters never *fail*.
> Isaiah 58:11

The word "fail" is the same word כזב (*kazav*). The original meaning of *kazav* is "Vain words spoken to deceive, cause failure or disappoint; what does not function within its intended capacity" (Ancient Hebrew Lexicon of the Bible). A spring that does not flow is a "lying" spring, because it does not function properly. One who gives vain words is a "liar" and one who causes disappointment in another through his words is also a "liar." If God had said, "*Why did Sarah laugh, and say, 'Shall I indeed bear a child, when my husband is old?'*" then God might have instigated an argument between Sarah and Abraham. So, he said that Sarah was "old" and he ignored the fact that she said her husband was "old."

Light

In the beginning the heavens and the earth were in darkness and chaos, therefore, God's first act was to shed some light on the subject to bring about some order. The Hebrew word אור (*or*) means "light" and comes from the verbal root אור (*or*) meaning "to illuminate." The absence of light is darkness and the absence of order is chaos. The Hebraic idea of "light" encompasses both of these aspects, "light" and "order." If a solution to a problem escapes us we are in chaos, but when that solution is discovered we have been enlightened. This imagery can be found in Psalm 19:8 where the verbal root *or* is translated as "enlightening ."..The directions of YHWH are pure, *enlightening* the eyes."

Likeness

> *And God said, Let us make man in our image,*
> *after our likeness...* (Genesis 1:26, KJV)

The parent root of the word דמות (*demut*) is דם (*dam)* and means "blood." One descended from the "blood" of another often resembles the one from whom they descended. Derived from the parent root דם is the child root דמה (*damah*) meaning "to resemble." Derived from this child root is the word דמות (*demut*) and means "a resemblance" or "to be like something else in action or appearance," just as a son "resembles" his father.

Lord

In most cases, the Hebrew word אדון (*adon*) lies behind the English word "lord." It is used throughout the Bible and is used commonly in prayer, but the actual meaning of the word has been robbed of its cultural meaning.

Again, we begin our search for the Biblical meaning of אדון (*adon*) by looking at its parent root דן (*dan*). In the ancient pictographic script, this word would have appeared as ᚤ. The letter ᚡ (*d*) is a door meaning "to enter" and the letter ᚤ (*n*) is a seed meaning "perpetual life." When these letters are combined, we find the Hebraic definition, "the door of life" or "to enter a perpetual life."

One child root derived from this parent is דין (*diyn*), meaning to "judge." This word is used as a legal term, but not in the modern Western sense of seeking guilt or condemnation; rather it is seeking innocence or life from an Eastern Hebraic sense. We can see this search for innocence in Genesis 15:4, where God punishes the guilty in order to bring life to the descendants of Abraham who were unjustly treated as slaves:

> "But I will _punish_ the nation they [the descendants of Abraham] serve as slaves, and afterward they will come out with great possessions." (NIV)

In the next two passages, the word דין (_diyn_) is paralleled with "save," meaning "to deliver from a trouble or burden" and "compassion." Just as a deliverer saves one's life from an enemy, a judge also brings life:

> "God, in your name save me, and in your might _judge_ me." (Psalms 54:1)

> "For YHWH will _judge_ his people, and on his servants he will have compassion." (Psalms 135.14)

We have seen that the parent root דן (_dan_) means "to enter life" and the child root דין (_diyn_) is "to bring life to another." We now come to the child root אדון (_adon_ - lord) which means "one who brings life" or "one who opens the door to perpetual life," the judge or deliverer. In the ancient Hebraic culture each family was a kingdom unto itself: the head of the family, the patriarch, was the king. Within the hands of this king was the power to take or grant life, and for this reason, he was seen as the אדון (_adon_). After Jacob fled from his family, Esau became the head of the family. He was the אדון. When Jacob returned he was afraid for his life and approached Esau as a servant, hoping Esau would spare his life:

> *"And you are to say, it is an offering from your servant Jacob sent to my lord (אדון) Esau and he is coming after us."* (Genesis 32:18)

Moses is also called אדון, the deliverer and judge of Israel:

> *"And Joshua son of Nun, attendant of Moses from his youth, answered saying, My lord (אדון) Moses stop them."* (Numbers 11:28)

As Genesis 1:1 states: "In the beginning God created…" All life is granted by God, which makes him אדון over all creation:

> *"And the angel answered saying, These are the four spirits of heaven going out from the standing over the lord (אדון) of all the earth."* (Zechariah 6:5)

Love

In our modern Western culture, love is an abstract thought of emotion or how one feels toward another, but the Hebrew word אהב (*A.H.B*) goes much deeper than simple emotion.

The verbal root אהב (*A.H.B*) has several words related to it that can provide the concrete meaning of this word. The word הבהב (*havhav*) is a noun meaning "gift." The word יהב (*yahav*) is a verb meaning "to provide."

We do not choose our parents or siblings, but instead they are given to us as a gift from above, a privileged gift. Even in the Ancient Hebrew culture, one's wife was chosen for him. It is our responsibility to provide and protect those privileged gifts. As a verb, the Hebrew word אהב (*A.H.B*) means "to provide and protect what is given as a privileged gift." We are to love

God, neighbors, and family, not in an emotional sense, but in the sense of our actions.

Machine

The Biblical Hebrew word for a machine is חשבון (*hhishbon*):

> In Jerusalem he set up <u>machines</u>, invented by skilled workers, on the towers and the corners for shooting arrows and large stones. And his fame spread far, for he was marvelously helped until he became strong. (2 Chronicles 26:15, NRS)

This Hebrew word is derived from the verbal root חשב (*Hh.Sh.B*) meaning to "think," but is used in the Biblical text for devising, planning, inventing or counting, all being forms of "thinking." The noun form, חשב (*Hheyshev*), is a skillfully woven band:

> And the <u>skilfully woven band</u> upon it, to gird it on, shall be of the same workmanship and materials, of gold, blue and purple and scarlet stuff, and fine twined linen. (Exodus 28:8, RSV)

Each of these Biblical Hebrew words has been brought into Modern Hebrew, but with slightly different meanings. The verb חשב (*Hh.Sh.B*) has the same meaning as "thinking." However, the noun form חשב (*hheyshev*) is an "accountant," one who counts, and the noun חשבון (*hhishbon*) is an "account."

The Modern Hebrew word for a machine is now מכונה (*makonah*), a transliteration of the word "machine." A common "machine" is an automobile, which in Modern Hebrew is מכונית (*makoniyt*), a derivative of מכונה (*makonah*).

Man

The word *iysh* is derived from the root אנש (*anash*), meaning weak and frail. When the writer of the text wished to refer to "man" from the perspective of "humankind," in the sense of being related by blood, he chose the word *adam*, its roots being in the word דם (*dam*) meaning "blood." On the other hand, if he wished to refer to "man" and his mortality, then he chose *iysh*, its roots being in the word *anash* meaning weak and frail (mortal).

Just as the English word "woman" contains the word "man" within it, the Hebrew word for "woman," which is אישה (*iyshah*), also contains the Hebrew word for "man," which is איש (iysh). The reason for this is given in Genesis 2:23 where it states, *"Because she was taken out of man (iysh)."*

Manna

The following article is the result of a survey I had taken which asked the question: "What was the Hebrew name for the bread-like substance God gave Israel in the wilderness?"

It is a provable fact that translations of the Hebrew Bible relied more on the *Greek Septuagint* (a 2,000-year-old Greek translation of the Tanakh/Old Testament) than the Hebrew Bible itself, dramatically influencing how we read the Hebrew Bible. This is why we say Moses (*Greek Septuagint*) instead of Mosheh (Hebrew Bible), Aaron (*Greek Septuagint*) instead of Aharon (Hebrew Bible), Eve (*Greek Septuagint*) instead of Hhava (Hebrew Bible) and why we say "manna" (the focus of the survey I had taken) instead of its proper Hebrew pronunciation.

In Exodus 16:15 most translations read "...they said one to another, 'What is it?'" The King James reads," ...they said one to another, It is manna..." In the survey most people agreed that the Hebrew name of the bread-like substance God gave Israel in the wilderness was "Manna" with many adding that it means "What is it?" Some wrote that the Hebrew was "man na," identifying that it was two Hebrew words meaning "What [is] It?" So, what does the Hebrew of Exodus 16:15 actually say? It says "man Hu" which is the Hebrew words meaning "What is it?" Manna (or mannah or man Na) does not occur in this verse, nor does it occur in Exodus 16:31, which uses the Hebrew word "man" alone. If the word "manna" does not occur in the Hebrew Bible, where does it come from? The only place this word is found is in the *Greek Septuagint* where the Hebrew word "man" is written in Greek as "manna."

What I have found really amazing is that while there is a heavy Greek influence on Christian translations, this influence has also entered into Judaism, as well. Here is the Jewish Publications Societies (JPS, 1917) translation of Exodus 16:31," ...Israel called the name thereof Manna..." Why does a Jewish translation of the Hebrew Bible use the word "manna" as found in the *Greek Septuagint* for the Hebrew word "man?" What surprised me through the survey was that a large majority of the Jews who follow Judaism thought the Hebrew word for the bread-like substance was "manna."

Mark

The Modern Hebrew word for a "letter" (as in the letters of the alphabet) is אוֹת (*ot*), the plural form is אוֹתִיּוֹת / *otyot*). This word can be found in the following passage:

> Then the LORD said to him, "Not so! If any one slays Cain, vengeance shall be taken on him

*sevenfold." And the LORD put a mark on Cain,
lest any who came upon him should kill him.*
(Genesis 4:15, KJV)

Is it possible that the "mark," the אות, was an actual "letter"
of the Semitic alphabet? Let's take a look at another passage
that uses the word "mark:"

*And the LORD said unto him, Go through the
midst of the city, through the midst of
Jerusalem, and set a mark upon the foreheads
of the men that sigh and that cry for all the
abominations that be done in the midst
thereof.* (Ezekiel 9:4, KJV)

Again, we have YHWH placing a "mark" on a person, but this
time it is not the Hebrew word אות, but instead the word תו
(*tav*). This is another Hebrew word that means "mark," but it
is also the 22nd and last "letter" of the Hebrew alphabet, which
in Modern Hebrew is written as ת and as ✝ in ancient times. Is
it possible that the אות (mark) YHWH placed on Cain was the
letter ✝?

Mercy

The Hebrew word חסד (*hhesed*) is usually translated as
"mercy" or "kindness" or some similar definition.

The Hebrew language of the Bible is a very concrete language,
meaning that Hebrew words have a definition of something
that can be seen, heard, felt, tasted or touched. Examples of
concrete words would be: tree, river, sky, bowing, walking,
etc.

Words describing something that cannot be experienced by
the five senses are abstract words. Words such as kindness,

mercy, bless, hope, love, etc. are abstract words. Hebrew much prefers concrete words, but they can express abstract thought, yet those abstract words are rooted in a concrete meaning.

In the case of the word *hhesed*, the concrete meaning is to "bow the head" as a sign of respect to another. The abstract meaning derived from this concrete idea is to show "kindness." The noun חסידה (*hhasiydah*), which is derived from *hhesed*, is a "stork," which has a neck that is "bent down."

Messenger

What has always perplexed me is why the translators of the Bible see the need to translate one Hebrew word with two or more different English words when there is no grammatical or contextual need to do so. Note the different translations of the Hebrew word מלאך (*malak*) in the following passage:

> And Jacob went on his way, and the _angels_ of God met him. And when Jacob saw them, he said, This is God's host: and he called the name of that place Mahanaim. And Jacob sent _messengers_ before him to Esau his brother unto the land of Seir, the country of Edom. (Genesis 32:1-3,KJV)

According to the translation above, Jacob came upon a camp of angels and then sent messengers, presumably some of his own men, to his brother Esau. But according to the Hebrew text, these events should be interpreted differently, as the word "angels" and "messengers" are the very same Hebrew word, *malak*. Either Jacob came upon a camp of men who were messengers of God and sent them to his brother Esau, or he came upon a camp of angels, which he then sent to his brother Esau.

In the verse above, the first use of the word *malak,* translated as "angels" in the King James Version, is translated in the *Septuagint* with the Greek word *aggelos,* which is the origin of the English word "angel." The second use of the word *malak,* translated as "messengers" in the King James Version, is translated in the *Septuagint* with the Greek word *apostolos,* which is the origin of the English word "apostle." It is clear that the King James, as well as most modern translations, were using the *Septuagint* rather than the original Hebrew for their translation of the text.

Incidentally, another example of the translator's use of the *Septuagint* instead of the Hebrew can be found with the word *"manna,"* the bread from heaven. The Hebrew for this word is simply מן (*man*), but the *Septuagint* uses the Greek *manna.* Because of this, we call it *manna* from the Greek, rather than *man,* from the Hebrew. See "Manna" for more on this topic.

Why do the translators "trust" the Greek more than the Hebrew? Why use a Greek translation of the Hebrew to make an English translation when the original Hebrew is available? Because the translators and their readers were/are Greek thinkers more comfortable with the Greek than the Hebrew.

Now back to our verse. What is a *malak*? Literally, the word means "one who is sent by another to do his business." It is related to another Hebrew word, מלאכה (*melakah*), meaning business:

> *And on the seventh day Elohiym finished his* <u>*business*</u> *(melakah)...* Genesis 2:2

Are the *malak* (is this singular or plural) of God who perform God's business men or supernatural beings or both?

Technically speaking, anyone doing the business of God is a *malak*. This can include men:

> Then Haggai, the <u>messenger</u> (malak) of the LORD, spoke to the people with the LORD's message, "I am with you, says the LORD. (Haggai 1:13, RSV)

As well as God himself:

> ...The God before whom my fathers Abraham and Isaac walked, the God who has led me all my life long to this day, the <u>angel</u> (malak) who has redeemed me from all evil... (Genesis 48:15,16, RSV)

Messiah

The Hebrew word משיח (*mashiach/mah-shee-ahh*) is usually transliterated "Messiah." Let us first examine how this word is transliterated and translated. In the Hebrew Bible this word is usually translated as "anointed," but in Daniel it is transliterated as "Messiah:"

> If the priest that is <u>anointed</u> do sin according to the sin of the people; then let him bring for his sin, which he hath sinned, a young bullock without blemish unto the LORD for a sin offering. (Leviticus 4:3,KJV)

> Know therefore and understand, that from the going forth of the commandment to restore and to build Jerusalem unto the <u>Messiah</u> the Prince shall be seven weeks, and threescore and two weeks: the street shall be built again,

and the wall, even in troublous times. (Daniel 9:25,KJV)

The root word of *meshiyach* is the verb מָשַׁח (*M.Sh.Hh*) meaning "to smear" or "to anoint." In the ancient Hebrew culture, it was customary to pour oil on the head of one being given a position of authority. This practice was called "anointing." One of the most common misunderstandings is that there is only one *meshiyach*, but the Tanakh identifies several. The word is used 39 times and just a few of these are listed below:

> *If the anointed (mashiyahh) priest (kohen) sins bringing guilt to the people...* (Leviticus 4:3)

> *And he (David) said to his men, YHWH forbid me if I should do this thing to my lord (Saul) the anointed (mashiyahh) of YHWH.* (1 Samuel 24:6)

> *Do not touch my anointed (mashiyahh), my prophets do not harm.* (1 Chronicles 16:22)

I chose these passages for one reason: to demonstrate from a Hebraic perspective who is *mashiyahh*. The Priests, Kings and Prophets of Israel are the *mashiyahh* of Israel; they are the ones who are anointed as men of authority.

While the original meaning of the word *mashiyahh* was applied to one actually anointed with oil, it can also refer figuratively to anyone who holds an office of authority whether they were anointed or not. The Tanakh identifies Cyrus, the King of Persia as a *mashiyahh*:

> *Thus says YHWH to his anointed (mashiyahh) Cyrus (the King of Persia)...* (Isaiah 45:1)

Mezuzah

The modern Mezuzah is a piece of paper or parchment with Deuteronomy 6:4-9 and 11:13-21 written on it and placed in a box. This box is then attached to the doorpost of the house. This 'Mezuzah' is to fulfill the *Torah* requirement of Deuteronomy 6:6-9:

> And <u>these words,</u> which I command thee this day, shall be in thine heart: And thou shalt teach them diligently unto thy children, and shalt talk of them when thou sittest in thine house, and when thou walkest by the way, and when thou liest down, and when thou risest up. And thou shalt bind them for a sign upon thine hand, and they shall be as frontlets between thine eyes. And thou shalt <u>write them upon the posts of thy house,</u> and on thy gates.

The first question that needs to be answered is "What are 'these words' that are to be taught and written?" According to modern Judaism, it is Deuteronomy 6, as they are what are written on the Mezuzah. However, I contend that it is the commands given prior to Deuteronomy 6, the '10 commandments' found in Deuteronomy 5.

The second question is, "Is the modern Mezuzah the correct application of the command in Deuteronomy 6?" If you read the passage above literally, it says that you are to write "these words" on the "doorposts." The Hebrew word for a doorpost is "mezuzah" (literally, a mezuzah is 'not' the paper or the box which are today identified as a mezuzah). The command is not stating that a Mezuzah is to be placed on a doorpost but that "these words" are to be written on the doorpost (the mezuzah).

I am of the opinion that the Ancient Hebrews wrote the 10 commandments directly on the doorposts (mezuzah) of their homes.

Mighty

The Hebrew word אביר (*aviyr*) is identified in *Strong's Dictionary* with two different numbers, #46 and #47. In the Masoretic Hebrew text of the Bible, *Strong's* #46 is written as אֲבִיר (*aviyr*) and *Strong's* #47 is written as אַבִּיר (*abbiyr*). The *nikkudot* (the vowel pointings appearing as dots and dashes) were invented by the Masorites and were not part of the original Hebrew text. If we remove these *nikkudot*, we find that these two words are spelled identically – אביר (*ABYR*).

These *nikkudot* were added to aid in the pronunciation of Hebrew words, but I also think that some *nikkudot* were added to separate out words to give the impression they are two different words for reasons which will be apparent below.

The Hebrew word אביר (*aviyr/abbiyr*, *Strong's* #46/47) is translated in the KJV as "bull," "strong," "mighty," "stouthearted," "valiant," "angel" and "chiefest," but we must remember that, being a concrete language, the Hebrew language concentrates on the function or action of something rather than its appearance. This noun is not attempting to describe a specific entity, but an action that is common among different entities.

If you have ever watched an eagle soar and thought how majestic it is, you understand the meaning of the Hebrew word אביר (*aviyr/abbiyr*). The root of this word is the verb אבר (*A.B.R*) meaning "soar" and is used only once in the Hebrew Bible.

Is it by your wisdom that the hawk <u>soars</u>, and spreads his wings toward the south? (Job 39:26, RSV)

My translation of the noun אביר (*aviyr/abbiyr*) is "valiant" and defined as: "Possessing or acting with bravery or boldness. The mighty power of a bird in flight. Anything or anyone of great mental or physical strength."

The differences between *Strong's* #46 and #47 are the application of the use of this Hebrew word. Strong's #46, which is the word אֲבִיר (*aviyr*), is always used in the context of YHWH being the "valiant one of Israel/Jacob:"

> *...I am YHWH your rescuer and your redeemer, the <u>valiant one</u> of Jacob.* (Isaiah 49:26)

Strong's #47, which is the word אַבִּיר (*abbiyr*), is used for any other "valiant" one:

> *Then the heels (hoofs) of horses will strike from the galloping, the galloping of his <u>valiant</u> ones.* (Job 5:22)

Name

The Hebrew word נשמה (*neshemah*) is formed by adding the letter ה (*h*) to the adopted נשם (*nasham*) which comes from the parent root שם (*shem*). This word is used in Genesis 2:7 and means "breath:"

> *And the LORD God formed the man of dust from the ground and he blew in his nostrils the <u>breath</u> (נשמה) of life and the man became a living soul.*

While the Western mind simply sees "breath" as the exchange of air within the lungs, the ancient Hebrew mind understood the "breath" in an entirely different way, as can be seen in Job 32:8:

> The wind within man and the <u>breath</u> (נשמה) of the Almighty teach them.

Our Western understanding of the "breath" does not easily grasp the concept that a "breath" can teach. While our Western understanding can easily associate thoughts and emotions as the function of the "mind," the Easterner sees the same function in the "breath." The "breath" of both men and God has the ability to carry thought and emotion.

Skies

A related word that we will examine is the child root שמה (shamah) meaning "heaven," "sky" or "the place of the winds." It is always used in the plural form שמים (shamayim):

> In the beginning God created the <u>skies</u> (שמים) and the land. (Genesis 1:1)

The Hebrew mind sees נשמה (neshemah), "breath," and שמה (shamah), "heaven," as synonyms. The נשמה is the "breath/wind of a man," and the שמה is the "breath/wind of the skies." Just as we saw above where the נשמה can teach, so also the שמים (shamayim) can also speak:

> The <u>skies</u> (שמים) proclaim his righteousness, and all the people see his glory. (Psalms 97:6)

Dry Wind

The root word שמם (shamam) is formed by doubling the second letter of the parent root. By adding the letter ה (h) to the end, the word שממה (shememah) is formed. Both words mean, "desolate" and are used in the following passage:

> Many shepherds will ruin my vineyards, they will trample my fields, they will turn the fields of my delight into a desert of <u>desolation</u> (שממה). And it will be made into <u>desolation</u> (שממה), parched and <u>desolate</u> (שמם) before me, all the land will be <u>desolate</u> (שמם) because there is no man to care for it. (Jeremiah 12:10,11)

When the dry winds blow through the desert, any moisture in the ground or air is removed, causing the desert to become dry and parched: שמם (shamam) and שממה (shememah) are dry and desolate places formed by a dry wind.

Another child root ישם (yasham), with the same meaning as שמם (shamam), a dry desolating wind, can be seen in the following verse:

> All your resting places of the cities will become dry, and the high places will be <u>desolate</u> (ישם). (Ezekiel 6:6)

Shem

By gathering together all the words derived from the parent root שם (shem), and looking for the common thread that all have in common, we can discover the original Hebraic meaning of the parent root. Each of the words has the basic meaning of a "wind" within them. נשמה (neshemah) is the wind or breath of man, שמים (shamayim) is the wind of the skies, and שמם (shamam), שממה (shememah) and ישם (yasham) refer to the desolation caused by a dry wind. From this we can conclude that the ancient Hebraic meaning of שם is "breath."

The שם of a man is his breath, which in the Hebraic Eastern mind is the essence or character of the individual. The actions of the individual will always be related to his character. From this we understand that the שם, the breath, is the place of origin of all the actions of the individual. The following are a few passages that demonstrate this Hebraic understanding of שם:

> O God, in your _name_ (שם) save me; and in
> your strength rescue me. Psalms 54:1

A very common form of Hebrew poetry is called parallelism, where one idea is stated in two different ways. By studying these forms of poetry we can see into the Hebrew mind by observing how he paralleled one word with another. In the verse above, the phrase "in your name save me," is paralleled with the phrase "in your strength rescue me." In this passage we see that the Hebrews equated one's "name" with his "strength," an attribute of character.

> "O LORD, your _name_ (שם) is forever; O LORD,
> your fame is from generation to generation."
> Psalms 135:13

In this verse, שם is paralleled with "fame." The Hebrew word for "fame" is זכר (zakar) which literally means "remembrance." The "fame" of the LORD are his "actions" that will be remembered throughout the generations. Through the poetic imagery of this verse, we see that the psalmist equated the שם of the LORD with his actions.

> "I will declare your [the LORD's] _name_ (שם) to
> my brothers; within the assembly I will praise
> you." Psalms 22.22

In the passages just quoted, the phrase "I will declare your name" is parallel with "I will praise you," paralleling the שם (*shem*) of the LORD with "you," the LORD himself.

> *Your [David's] God will make the* <u>*name*</u> *(שם) of Solomon more beautiful than your* <u>*name*</u> *(שם) and his throne greater than your throne.* 1 Kings 1.47

The poetry of this passage parallels the name of Solomon with his throne, a difficult concept for a Western thinker to grasp. Let us remember that the throne is not to be thought of in terms of physical description, but in function. The function of the throne is "authority," a characteristic of the king. The שם of Solomon is his "authority."

Names and Titles

A common mistake in Biblical interpretation is to make a distinction between a name and a title. For example, "King David," is often understood as containing the "name" "David" (an identifier) and his "title" "King." The Hebrew word דוד (*david*) literally means "beloved" or "one who loves" and is descriptive of David's character. The Hebrew word מלך (*melek*) literally means "ruler" or "one who rules," also descriptive of David's character. As we can see, both of these words are descriptive of David's character. The Hebrews made no such distinction between a name and a title. The phrase "King David" is hebraically understood as "the one who *rules* is the one who *loves*," a very fitting title for the great benevolent king of Israel and the friend of God.

Neck

The Hebrew noun for the neck is עורף (*oreph*), which is derived out of the Hebrew verb ערף (*Ah.R.P*) meaning "to be necked," as in "breaking the neck."

Isaac Mozeson, the founder of the study of Edenics, has some very interesting things to say about this Hebrew word:

> If you think the GIRAFFE is a strange animal, check out its weird (given) etymology. French "giraffe" and Italian "giraffe" are said to be a corruption of Arabic "zirafah," even though the term is meaningless in Arabic and, in addition, a G from a Z corruption is unnatural... The Hebrew for the neck is OReF, more correctly pronounced by Sephardim as KHoReF or GHoReF. Now we've got the perfect sound and sense for GiRaFFe, since GHoReF means the scruff of the neck, with sCaRF and sCRuF being neck words whose initial S is non-historic.

A related *Gimel-Resh* term, GaRoN (throat, neck) gives us other long-necked animals, like the CRaNe, eGRet and HeRoN, along with neckwear like the GoRGeous GoRGet, the throaty GRoaN of a CRooNer and the GaRGling of a GouRmet GaRGoyle.

Obey

In the King James Version of the Bible the word "obey" appears 43 times. In all but two of these occurrences, the word "obey" is the the translation of the Hebrew verb שמע

(sh'ma). However, "obey" is a poor translation of this verb as can be demonstrated with these two verses:

> Now therefore, my son, <u>obey</u> my voice according to that which I command thee. (Genesis 27:8, KJV)

> And the LORD said, I have surely seen the affliction of my people which are in Egypt, and have <u>heard</u> their cry by reason of their taskmasters; for I know their sorrows; (Exodus 3:7, KJV)

Both of the underlined words are the Hebrew verb *sh'ma* and YHWH certainly did not "obey" the cry of the Israelites in Exodus 3:7. The literal meaning of *sh'ma* is "to hear" or "to listen," but also to respond to what one has heard.

In the case of Genesis 27:8 the son is told to "hear" and "respond" to his father's voice and we could interpret this to mean "hear" and "obey." In the case of Exodus 3:7 YHWH "heard" the cries of the Israelites and he "responded" to that cry by delivering them the Egyptians.

Offering

The most frequent Hebrew word translated as "offering" is מנחה (*minhhah*). Most likely this noun is derived from the root verb ינח (*Y.N.Hh*), which means "to deposit in place," especially for safekeeping or as a pledge. From this perspective, a *minhhah* (offering) is something that is "given as a pledge:"

> And in process of time it came to pass, that Cain brought of the fruit of the ground an <u>offering</u> unto the LORD. And Abel, he also

brought of the firstlings of his flock and of the
fat thereof. And the LORD had respect unto
Abel and to his <u>offering</u>: (Genesis 4:3, KJV)

Maybe the difference between Cain and Abel's offering wasn't the offering itself, but the pledge or action behind the offering.

Oil

In today's culture, oil symbolizes wealth. Nothing has changed over thousands of years. In the ancient cultures of the Near and Middle East, oil was a symbol of wealth. Also, oil was used in lamps for making light. Different types of oils, including olive oil, were used for medicinal purposes. Oil was poured on one who was taking the office of king or priest. Oil was used in offerings to *Elohiym*.

The Hebrew word for oil is שמן (*shemen*). The verb form is שמן (*Sh.M.N*) and means "to be fat." The parent root of this word is שם (*shem*), which is usually translated as "name" but more hebraically means "character." Isn't your character your wealth? Isn't the character of YHWH his wealth?

One

The Hebrew word אחד (*ehhad*) is derived from the parent root חד (*hhad*), which was written in the ancient pictographic script as 𐤇𐤄. The first letter in this word is 𐤇 (*hh*), representing a tent wall, such as that which divides the male from the female sides, and means "to separate or divide." The second letter, 𐤄 (*d*), represents a door or entrance, such as that which allows passage between the two sides of the tent, and means "to enter." Our parent root 𐤇𐤄 (*hhad*) has the pictographic meaning of "a wall with a door" or "a wall for entering." The Hebraic idea being expressed in this word is that one thing or one person serves more than one function. Just as the wall separates the two sides, the door in the wall unites them. This Hebraic imagery can be clearly seen in the following passage:

> *"And you son of man, the sons of your people are speaking about you next to the walls and in the doors of the houses; and one (חד) speaks at one (אחד) man and at his brother saying, "Please come and hear what the word of the one coming from the LORD is saying." And they come to you like they are coming of a people, and my people sit before you. And they listen to your words but they do not practice it; adoration is in their mouths but their hearts walk after their greed."* (Ezekiel 33:30,31)

In this passage we see the two opposite actions of the people. While they go to hear from the LORD, they practice evil in their hearts, "one" individual with two opposite manifestations. It is also interesting to note that Ezekiel shows that these people are speaking about him at the walls and doors, a direct connection to the word חד, whose pictographs are of a wall and a door.

Another word derived from the parent root חד (hhad), is חוד (hhud) and has the meaning of a riddle:

> *"Son of man, give a riddle (חוד - hhud) of a riddle (חידה - hhiydah, the feminine form of hhud); and give a parable of a parable to the house of Israel."* (Ezekiel 17:2)

From the Hebrew poetry of this verse we can see that the word חוד (hhud) is similar to a parable. A riddle or parable presents a story to an audience, using events and people familiar to the listeners. Then, the one giving the parable presents a twist that cannot be understood easily. Keeping in mind the pictographs of the word חד (hhad), this "twist" in the story is the wall that separates the listener from the meaning of the parable. When the speaker explains the parable, the door is opened and the listeners are united with the meaning.

The word אחד, keeping with our foundational meaning in the parent root, means those that are separated come together in unity. While this word is often translated as "one," where the actual Hebraism is lost, it is better translated as a "unity."

The Western mind sees "one" as a singular, void of any connection to something else. For instance, "one" man is an individual entity to himself, just as "one" tree is an entity to itself. To the ancient Hebrew Eastern mind, nothing is "one;" all things are dependent upon something else. A man is not "one," but a unity of body, mind and breath that is expressed in the Hebrew word נפש (nephesh). The man is also in unity with his wife and family, as well as with the larger community. Even a tree is a unity of roots, trunk, branches and leaves, which is also in unity with the surrounding landscape. "One" year is a unity of seasons. The first use of אחד (ehhad) is found in Genesis 1:5, where "evening" and "morning," two states of opposite function, are united to form "one" day:

> "And there was evening and there was morning, one day"

With all of this said, we do find the Hebrew word "ehhad" meaning "one" in the sense of individuality:

> And Elohiym said, The waters under the sky will be gathered to <u>one</u> (ehhad) place...
> (Genesis 1:9)

Oxen

> The _oxen_ likewise and the young asses that till
> the ground shall eat savory provender, which
> hath been winnowed with the shovel and with
> the fork. (Isaiah 30:24, ASV)

In the verse above is the Hebrew noun אלף (_eleph_) meaning
"oxen." Oxen are the largest of the Ancient Hebrews' livestock
and were most frequently used for plowing the fields, usually
in pairs. An older ox would be yoked to a younger one in order
for the older one to teach the younger through association.
This same noun is also found in Judges 6:15, where it is
translated as "family." In a family, the children learn from the
parents through association, in the same manner as do the
oxen.

The verbal root of this word is אלף (_A.L.Ph_) and means "learn,"
but more literally, "to learn through association," as can be
seen in the following verse:

> Make no friendship with a man that is given to
> anger; And with a wrathful man thou shalt not
> go: Lest thou _learn_ this way, and get a snare
> to thy soul. (Proverbs 22:25, ASV)

As oxen are "very large" animals, the word אלף (_eleph_) is also
used for a "thousand," a "very large" number. From this
aspect of the noun, a second verb is formed. Normally,
Hebrew nouns are derived out of verbs. However, on occasion
a verb is derived out of a noun, and this verb is called a
demonstrative verb. The demonstrative verb formed out of
אלף (_eleph_) is אלף (_A.L.Ph_) meaning to "give a thousand."

In summary, the Hebrew word אלף can be:

- A verb meaning to learn by association.

- A noun meaning oxen, a large beast, which learns through association.
- A noun meaning family, through the idea of association.
- A noun meaning a thousand, a large number.
- A verb meaning to give a thousand.

Pharaoh

The Hebrew word for "Pharaoh" is פַּרְעֹה, pronounced *par'oh*. However, if the letter פ (*pey*) follows a vowel, then it is pronounced as a spirant (*ph/f*) and this word would be pronounced *pha'roh*. But if it follows a consonant, then it is pronounced as a stop (p). Or if the word begins with the letter פ and is listed in a dictionary, and, therefore, does not follow a consonant or a vowel, then it is pronounced as a stop (p). Here are a couple examples from the Bible demonstrating the different pronunciations:

> Genesis 12:15 - אֶל פַּרְעֹה (*el par'oh* – To Pharaoh): Here the letter פ follows the consonant ל (*lamed*), so it is pronounced as a stop (*p*).

> Genesis 12:18 - וַיִּקְרָא פַרְעֹה (*wai'yiq'ra phar'oh* – And Pharoah called): Here the letter פ follows a vowel (*a*), so it is pronounced as a spirant (*ph/f*).

The Hebrew word פַּרְעֹה (*par'oh*) is a transliteration of the Egyptian word *pr-aA*, which means "great house." When the Hebrew Bible was translated into Greek, the Hebrew word פַּרְעֹה (*par'oh*) was transliterated as Φαραω (*pharaoh*) and is written with the letter Φ (phi) regardless of whether it follows a consonant or a vowel. The English word "Pharaoh" is a transliteration of the Greek form and not the Hebrew.

Pluck

The Hebrew verb meaning "to pluck" is זמר (*Z.M.R*) and is frequently used for "plucking" fruit (Strong's #2168) and "plucking" a music instrument (Strong's #2167):

> *Six years thou shalt sow thy field, and six years thou shalt <u>prune</u> thy vineyard, and gather in the fruit thereof.* (Leviticus 25:3, KJV)

> *Therefore I will give thanks unto thee, O LORD, among the heathen, and I will <u>sing praises</u> unto thy name.* (2 Samuel 22:50, KJV)

Many nouns are derived from this verb including:

זמר	ze'mer	Mountain Sheep	#2169
זמרה	zim'rah	Melody	#2172
מזמרה	maz'mey'rah	Pruning hook	#4211
זמיר	zamiyr	Plucking	#2158 & #2159
זמירה	z'mi'rah	Music	#2158
זמורה	z'mo'rah	Vine	#2156
זימרה	zim'rah	Choice fruit	#2173
זימרת	zim'rat	Music	#2176
מזמרה	m'zam'rah	Snuffer	#4212

מזמור	*miz'mor*	Melody	#4210

Power

The original pictographic form of the Hebrew word אל (*el*) is ∠ඊ. The first picture is the head of an ox, while the second is a shepherd staff.

The Ancient Hebrews were an agricultural people raising livestock such as oxen, sheep and goats. The strongest and most valuable of these was the ox. Because of its strength, it was used to pull large loads in wagons, as well as to plow the fields. The letter ඊ represents the concrete idea of "muscle" and "strength."

A shepherd always carried his staff. It was a sign of his authority and was used to lead the sheep by pushing or pulling them in the correct direction, as well as to fight off predators. Since the yoke is also a staff that is used to direct the oxen, the yoke is seen as a staff on the shoulders (see Isaiah 9:4). The letter ∠ represents the concrete view of a staff or yoke, as well as the idea of leadership and authority from the shepherd who leads his flock.

When the two letters are combined, the parent root ∠ඊ (*el*) is formed with the meaning of an "ox in the yoke" as well as a "strong authority." It was common to place two oxen in the yoke when pulling a plow. An older, more experienced ox was matched with a younger inexperienced one, so that the younger would learn the task of plowing from the older. This older "ox in the yoke" is the "strong leader" of the pair and was the ancient Hebrews' concrete understanding of "God."

God is the older ox who teaches his people, the young ox, how to work.

Besides the pictographic evidence for the meaning of the word ∠Ϧ (el), the historical record supports the idea that the original meaning of ∠Ϧ (el) is an ox. A Biblical example is found Exodus 32:

> And he [Aaron] took from their hands [the gold earrings] and formed an idol made into a small bull, and they said; 'Israel, this is your God who brought you up out of the land of Egypt'. And Aaron saw it and built an altar before it and Aaron called out saying 'tomorrow is a feast to the LORD. Exodus 32:4,5

In this passage, Israel formed an idol of the LORD in the image of a bull. Why did Israel choose a bull for its idol? Many ancient cultures worshiped a god in the form of a bull. The Egyptians name for their bull god was "Apis" and the Sumerians called him "Adad." The Canaanites, whose language was very similar to the Hebrews, worshipped ∠Ϧ (el), a bull god.

The word ∠Ϧ (el) is frequently translated as God, the "strong authority" of Israel, such as in the following passages:

> "Blessed be Abram by <u>God</u> Most High, Creator of heaven and earth." (Genesis 14:19, NIV)

> "For the LORD your God, is God of gods, and Lord of lords, the great <u>God</u>, mighty and awesome." (Deuteronomy 10:17, NIV)

When the reader of the Bible sees the English word "God" (beginning with the uppercase "G"), it is always applied to the

Creator of the heavens and the earth. The Hebrew word $\angle \triangleright$ (el) can refer to this same God, but as the concrete understanding of the word $\angle \triangleright$ (el) is a "strong and mighty one," this same Hebrew word can be applied to anyone or anything that functions with the same characteristics as seen in the examples below:

> "I [Laban] have the <u>power</u> to harm you" (Genesis 31.29, NIV)

> "When he rises up, the <u>mighty</u> are terrified." (Job 41:25, NIV)

> "The mountains were covered with its shade, the <u>mighty</u> cedars with its branches." (Psalms 80.10, NIV)

> "Your righteousness is like the <u>mighty</u> mountains." (Psalms 36:6, NIV)

> "Do not worship any other <u>god.</u>" (Exodus 34:14 NIV)

The imagery of the ox and the shepherd staff were common symbols of strength, leadership and authority in ancient times. Chiefs and kings commonly wore the horns of a bull on their head as a sign of their strength and carried a staff representing their authority over their flock, the kingdom. Both of these symbols have been carried through the centuries to the modern day, where kings and queens carry scepters and wear crowns. The Hebrew word "qeren," meaning "horn," is the origin of the word "crown."

Prayer

In our modern religious culture, prayer is a communication between man and God. While this definition could be applied to some passages of the Bible, such as in the verse below, it is not a Hebraic definition of the Hebrew verb פלל (*P.L.L*):

> *Now therefore restore the man his wife; for he is a prophet, and he shall <u>pray</u> for thee, and thou shalt live: and if thou restore her not, know thou that thou shalt surely die, thou, and all that are thine.* (Genesis 20:7, KJV)

When we examine the etymology of this word, we find that פלל (*P.L.L*) comes from the parent root פל (*pal*), meaning "fall." *Pal* is also the root of the Hebrew verb נפל (*N.P.L*), also meaning "fall." The verb פלל (*P.L.L*) literally means to "fall down to the ground in the presence of one in authority pleading a cause." This can be seen in Isaiah 45:14 where the Sabeans fell down and made supplication (the Hebrew word פלל) to Cyrus:

> *Thus saith the LORD, The labour of Egypt, and merchandise of Ethiopia and of the Sabeans, men of stature, shall come over unto thee, and they shall be thine: they shall come after thee; in chains they shall come over, and they shall fall down unto thee, they shall make <u>supplication</u> unto thee, saying, Surely God is in thee; and there is none else, there is no God.* (KJV)

Priest

While the priests of Israel were the religious leaders of the community, this is not the meaning of the word כוהן (kohen). The Hebrew word for the priests of other nations is כומר (komer - see 2 Kings 23:5), from a root meaning "burn," and may be in reference to the priests who burned children in the fires of Molech (2 Kings 23:10). The word kohen comes from the parent root כן (ken) meaning "a base," such as the base of a column. The koheniym (plural of kohen) were the structural support of the community. It was their responsibility to keep the community standing tall and straight. They were the administrators of the community.

Sabbath

The word שבת (shabbat) is always transliterated as "sabbath" and most assume it is simply a name for the day of the week and are unaware that this word has a meaning. It is derived from the verb שבת (Sh.B.T) meaning "to cease or stop." The noun shabbat is "a time of ceasing" and, as stated in this verse, the seventh day is a time for ceasing business:

> Six days you will serve and do your business.
> (Exodus 20:9)

This verse also states it is the "shabbat of YHWH Elohiym" in reference to Genesis 2:2:

> And Elohiym finished his business which he did on the seventh day and he <u>ceased</u> in the seventh day from all his business which he did.

The word "ceased" in this passage is the verb שבת (Sh.B.T) , the root of the word shabbat.

The parent root of the word *shabbat* is שב (*shav*), which is written in the ancient pictographic script as ⵑⵡ. The ⵡ is a picture of teeth, and represents the idea of pressing, as pressing on food with the teeth when chewing. The ⵑ is a picture of the nomadic tent. When combined, these mean to "press to the tent/house" or "return." This parent root is also the root of the word שבת (*shabbat*) with the letter t. The letter ת, which is attached to the parent root שב to form the word *shabbat*, is written in the pictographic script as ✝ and represents a sign or mark as well as a covenant:

> *Wherefore the children of Israel shall keep the* <u>sabbath</u>, *to observe the* <u>sabbath</u> *throughout their generations, for a perpetual* <u>covenant</u>. *It is a* <u>sign</u> *between me and the children of Israel for ever: for in six days Jehovah made heaven and earth, and on the seventh day he rested, and was refreshed.* (Exodus 31:16,17, ASV)

On the seventh day, Israel "returns (שב) to the covenant (ת)."

Salvation

Let's begin this study, as should be done with any serious word study, with the root for the word "salvation:"

> *For the LORD your God is he that goeth with you, to fight for you against your enemies, to* <u>save</u> *you.* (Deuteronomy 20:4, KJV)

The Hebrew word translated as "save" in the verse above is the verbal root ישע (Y.Sh.Ah) meaning "to rescue." The context of this word throughout the Tanakh (Old Testament) is to rescue someone from his enemy, trouble or an illness, as seen in the verse above. Another form of this verb is מושיע

(*moshi'ah*). This is the "*hiphil* participle" form of the verb. A *hiphil* verb changes the action of the verb into a causative and would literally be translated "to cause one to be rescued." On the other hand, a *hiphil* participle verb changes the action of the verb into active tense and would literally be translated as "causing one to be rescued." Also, it can be the one who performs the action of the verb, which would then be translated as "one causing another to be rescued." The word מושיע (*moshi'ah*) literally means "one causing another to be rescued," or simply, a "rescuer," but this word is usually translated as "deliverer" or "savior:"

> And when the children of Israel cried unto the LORD, the LORD raised up a <u>deliverer</u> (moshi'ah) to the children of Israel, who <u>delivered</u> (the verb Y-Sh-Ah) them, even Othniel the son of Kenaz, Caleb's younger brother. (Judges 3:9, KJV)

> The God of my rock; in him will I trust: he is my shield, and the horn of my salvation, my high tower, and my refuge, my <u>saviour</u> (moshi'ah); thou <u>savest</u> (the verb Y.Sh.Ah) me from violence. (2 Samuel 22:3, KJV)

The word ישועה (*yeshu'ah*) is a noun derived from the verbal root ישע (*Y.Sh.Ah*) and means "relief," in the sense of being rescued from an enemy, trouble or illness. The *King James Version* translates this word as "help," "deliverance," "health and welfare," but most frequently as "salvation."

> And he said, If the Syrians be too strong for me, then thou shalt <u>help</u> (yeshu'ah/relief) me: but if the children of Ammon be too strong for thee, then I will come and <u>help</u> (the verb Y.Sh.Ah/rescue) thee. (2 Samuel 10:11, KJV)

And it shall be said in that day, Lo, this is our God; we have waited for him, and he will <u>save</u> (the verb Y.Sh.Ah/rescue) us: this is the LORD; we have waited for him, we will be glad and rejoice in his <u>salvation</u> (yeshu'ah/relief). (Isaiah 25:9, KJV)

The name Joshua is written as יהושע (*yehoshu'ah*) and is the name/word יה (*yah,* a form of the name/word YHWH) and the word ישועה (*yeshu'ah*) meaning "rescue." The name then means, "Yah is rescue." The Aramaic form of the Hebrew name יהושע is ישוע (*yeshu'a* – see Ezra 2:2). While the name *Yehoshua* has been Romanized as Joshua, the name *Yeshua* has been Romanized as Joshua and Jesus.

Say

The second most common Hebrew word in the Bible, the first being the word את (*et*), is the verb אמר (*A.M.R*), meaning "to say," and is found 5,379 times in the Hebrew Bible:

And God <u>said</u>, Let there be light: and there was light. (Genesis 1:3, ASV)

This verbal root is a child root, where the letter א (*aleph*) has been added to the two-letter parent root, which would appear to be מר (*M.L*). However, the parent root מר, a root meaning "bitter," is not the parent root of אמר, מל (*M.L*); a parent root meaning "word" or "comment" is its root. Over time, words evolve and letters are often interchanged with other letters that are formed in the same region of the mouth. While there are countless examples of this in English, let's just look at the English words "pedal" (a device on a bicycle for the foot) and "pedestrian" (a person on foot). These two words come from the Greek word *"ped"* meaning "foot." The English word "foot" is an evolved form of the word *"ped"* through the exchange of the "p" with the "f" and the "d" with the "t." Therefore, the original spelling of the verb אמר was אמל.

While the parent root מל (*M.L*) is not found in the Biblical text, its feminine form, מלה (*milah*), is and it is used 38 times, most frequently in the book of Job:

> Thy <u>words</u> have upholden him that was falling, and thou hast made firm the feeble knees. (Job 4:4, ASV)

Scroll

Books, as we know them today, are a fairly recent invention. Before the invention of books, codices were used. Codices are similar to books, but are square or rectangular sheets of papyrus or animal skin, with hand written text stacked on top of each other and stitched on one side. They usually included a wooden cover and back. Prior to codices, scrolls were used. Scrolls are long sheets of papyrus or animal skin with hand written text, which are rolled up for storage. The Hebrew word for a scroll is ספר (*seypher*) and is also the Modern Hebrew word for "a book."

The word *seypher* comes from the verbal root ספר (*S.Ph.R*) meaning "to count:"

> He brought him outside and said, "Look toward heaven and count the stars, if you are able to <u>count</u> them." Then he said to him, "So shall your descendants be." (Genesis 15:5, NRS)

Hebrew verbs are able to express variations of the meaning of a verb by changing the mood and voice of the verb. The *qal* form (active voice and simple mood) of the verb ספר is to "count," but the *hiphil* form (active voice and causative mood) means to "give an account" (note the word "count" in the word "account") or to "tell:"

> Consider well her ramparts, go through her citadels; that you may <u>tell</u> the next generation (Psalm 48:13, RSV)

The participle form of the verb ספר is סופר (*sopher*) and can mean "counting," "telling" or "one who counts or tells," a scribe:

> And Sheva was <u>scribe</u>: and Zadok and Abiathar were the priests. (2 Samuel 20:25, KJV)

From this verb comes the noun ספר (*seypher*), a scroll, which is used for recording counts or accounts and is written by a סופר (*sopher*), the scribe. Another noun derived from the root is מספר (*mispar*) meaning a "number:"

> None shall cast her young or be barren in your land; I will fulfil the <u>number</u> of your days. (Exodus 23:26, RSV)

Another noun derived from this root is ספיר (*saphiyr*), meaning "sapphire" and is also the origin of the word "sapphire." The connection between the sapphire stone and the other words related to it, such as counting, scribe and numbers, may be that the sapphire is something that is counted.

Serpent

In Hebrew thought, the action or character of something is much more important than its actual appearance. In our culture, and forms of thought, it is either a serpent or it is not. But in Hebrew, the word *nahhash* (the word translated as serpent) is something that is serpent-like. This can be an actual serpent or something that acts like a serpent. Many times the authors of the Hebrew text do not make the distinction, as we would. Such is the case here. We are not told if it is an actual serpent or someone or something that acts like a serpent. Our Greek-thinking mind needs to know which it is, but the Hebrew thinking mind doesn't care. A good example of this is the Hebrew word *ayil*. This word literally means a "buck." But it is used in the Hebrew text for anything that is "buck-like," such as an "oak tree," "fence post," "or "a chief," all of which have the characteristics of being strong and authoritative.

There is one other piece to this puzzle that opens up another possibility for the identity of the serpent:

> In that day the LORD with his hard and great and strong sword will punish Leviathan the fleeing serpent (nahhash), Leviathan the twisting serpent (nahhash), and he will slay the dragon (tanin) that is in the sea. (Isaiah 27:1, RSV)

In this verse, Leviathon is called a *nahhash*. So, it is possible that the serpent in Genesis 3 is Leviathon.

Serve

The Hebrew word translated as "serve" is the Hebrew verb עבד (*Ah.B.D*). The participle form of this verb, meaning "serving," is pronounced *oved* and may possibly be the origin of the English word "obey," as the "servant" is one who "obeys" the master. This is more evident in the word "obedience," which begins with *"obed,"* very similar to the Hebrew word *oved*. The noun form of this verb is עבד (*eved*) and is usually translated as "servant." Derived from this noun is the name Obadiah (*ovad'yah* in Hebrew) meaning "servant of Yah" or, "the one who obeys Yah."

While the verb עבד (*Ah.B.D*) is most frequently translated as "serve," it more literally means "to perform labor" or "work on behalf of another." The first use of this verb is found in the following passage:

> *when no plant of the field was yet in the earth and no herb of the field had yet sprung up --*
> *for the LORD God had not caused it to rain upon the earth, and there was no man to <u>till</u> the ground* (Genesis 2:5, RSV)

In this passage the verb עבד (*Ah.B.D*) is translated as "till," but if we apply the full meaning of this word in this passage, it says, "and there was no man to work on behalf of the ground." According to Genesis 1:28 man is to "subdue" the land, but here we see that man is to "serve" the land. Man's relationship with the land is symbiotic. While the land serves man, man is also to serve the land.

Service

While the word מלאך (*malak*) is "one who does business for another" in the sense of an employee, the word עבד (*eved*) is "one who serves another" in the sense of a slave, and is derived from the verbal root עבד (*Ah.B.D*) meaning "to serve as a slave." We understand a slave to be one forced against his will to work for another, such as we see with Israel in Egypt:

So they made the people of Israel <u>serve</u> (eved) with rigor, And they made their lives bitter with hard <u>bondage</u> (avodah)... (Exodus 1:13,14 RSV)

The noun עבודה (*avodah*) is another noun derived from the verbal root עבד (*Ah.B.D*).

There is another type of slave, what we might call a bondservant, one who is forced to work for another to pay off a debt owed or one who chooses to place himself under the authority of another in exchange for something, such as we see with Jacob who offered himself as payment for Laban's daughter (Genesis 29:18). Another example follows:

And Moses, the <u>slave</u> (eved) of YHWH, died there in the land of Moab according to the word of YHWH. (Deuteronomy 34:5)

Moses was, in the truest sense of the word, a slave to YHWH. From his first encounter with YHWH at the burning bush until his death, he never walked away from God. Sure, he erred and made his mistakes, but he always served God in the best way he could. It is interesting to note that he is never called "a slave" until the time of his death, almost as if the only way he could prove his loyalty was to remain in the service of YHWH until his death. Moses' successor Joshua is also called "a slave of YHWH" but again, not until after his death (Joshua 24:29). Only one other individual is called "a slave of YHWH" in the Bible:

...A Psalm of David, the <u>slave</u> (eved) of YHWH... (Psalm 18:1)

Shalom

The word שלום (*shalom*) is used in Modern Hebrew as a greeting, similar to our use of "hello," or as a farewell, similar to our use of "good-bye." A common phrase in Modern Hebrew using this word is *mah shlom'kha* and literally means "What is your shalom?" and is used the same as the English phrase "How are you?" The phrase *mah shlom'kha* is used when speaking to a male, but when speaking to a female this would be *mah shlo'mekh*.

This word is usually translated as "peace," but this translation does not adequately define this Hebrew word.

The root of this word is the verbal root שלם (*Sh.L.M*) and, by looking at the context this word in the Biblical text, we can get a better understanding of its meaning:

> When one man's ox hurts another's, so that it dies, then they shall sell the live ox and divide the price of it; and the dead beast also they shall divide. Or if it is known that the ox has been accustomed to gore in the past, and its owner has not kept it in, he shall <u>pay</u> ox for ox, and the dead beast shall be his. (Exodus 21:35,36, RSV)

In this passage the word שלם (*Sh.L.M*) is used to express the idea of "replacing" or "restoring" one dead ox for a live one due to negligence. The verb שלם (*Sh.L.M*) literally means "to make whole." The noun *shalom* has the same basic meaning as can be seen in the following verse:

> They said, "Your servant our father is <u>well</u>, he is still alive." And they bowed their heads and made obeisance." (Genesis 43:28, RSV)

In this passage the word "well" implies "wholeness" of the person in health and prosperity.

The word *shalom* is not only used as a greeting in Modern Hebrew but in Biblical Hebrew as well:

> And he said, <u>Peace be to you</u>, fear not: your God, and the God of your father, hath given you treasure in your sacks: I had your money. And he brought Simeon out unto them. (Genesis 43:23)

The next time you greet someone with the word *shalom*, recognize that you are not just saying "peace" or "hello," you are wishing "complete wholeness" on that person.

Shaped

> In the beginning God <u>created</u> the heaven and the earth. (Geneisis 1:1, KJV)

The Hebrew word translated as "created" is the Hebrew verb ברא (*B.R.A*) and literally means "to shape." This verb is deried from the parent root בר (*B.R*), which was written as שׁ𐤁 in the ancient pictographic Hebrew script. The first letter (reading from right to left) is the picture of a tent floor plan and means "house" or "family." The second letter is the head of a man and means "head." When combined these two letters mean "family of heads" and is the Hebrew word for "grain." Grains consist of a head with a cluster of seeds, and grains consist in a variety of species including barley or wheat: families of heads.

The Hebrew root ברא (*B.R.A*) is a child root formed out of the parent by adding the letter א. This verb is often translated as "create," but because "create" is an abstract word and as the

Ancient Hebrew did not think in abstract terms, this word more concretely means "to shape." This is related to the idea of "fat," which we will come back to shortly, in the sense that when an animal is fattened, its shape changes: it is shaped.

The Hebrew word "*B.R*" literally means "grain," as previously mentioned, but its meaning can also be extended to mean "soap" or "clean." As will be shown in more detail later, grains are fed to livestock to make them fat. The fat of animals is used to make soap. Of course, the soap is used to make one clean. It is this word *B.R* that is also translated as "pure:"

> "He that hath clean hands, and a pure (B.R)
> heart. (Psalm 24:4)

The Hebrews understood a "pure heart" as a "clean heart." You must also understand that "guilt" was seen as "dirt." In order to remove the dirt from the heart, you must clean it. Hopefully, this example will cause you to begin viewing the Bible from a different perspective, the perspective of its original authors.

A common means of forming an additional noun out of a two-letter word is to double the word. The word ברבר (pronounced "*barbur*") is "a fowl," as seen in the following verse:

> Ten fat oxen, and twenty oxen out of the
> pastures, and an hundred sheep, beside harts,
> and roebucks, and fallowdeer, and fatted <u>fowl.</u>
> (1Kings 4:23, KJV)

Again, we can easily see the connection between the word "*B.R*" and the idea of being "fattened."

This word is also used in the Aramaic language to mean "field," as a place for growing grains, as well as "son," probably through the idea of offspring in connection with the seeds of the grain.

The Hebrew root ברה (*B.R.H*) is a child root formed out of the parent by adding the letter ה. This root has the meaning "eat," as seen in the following verse:

> And when all the people came to cause David to <u>eat</u> meat while it was yet day, David swore, saying, So do God to me, and more also, if I taste bread, or ought else, till the sun be down. (2 Samuel 3:35, KJV)

The noun בריה (*biyr'yah*) is formed by adding the letter י (*y*) to the child root and has the meaning of "meat," or "what is eaten." When meat was eaten by the Hebrews, it was the choicest and fattest of the stock. For this reason, the word *B.R.H* can also mean "choice" or "to choose:"

> And he stood and cried unto the armies of Israel, and said unto them, Why are ye come out to set your battle in array? Am not I a Philistine, and ye servants to Saul? <u>Choose</u> you a man for you, and let him come down to me. (1 Samuel 17:8, KJV)

Another word derived from the root ברה (*B.R.H*) is the word ברית (*b'riyt*). This word literally means "meat," but is always translated in most English translations as "covenant." In the times of the Ancient Hebrews a covenant was consummated by choosing a choice and fat animal from the herd or flock and sacrificing it. This may also be the meaning behind the English word "consummate," as in "to consume" a sacrifice. In most English Bibles is the phrase "make a covenant." The Hebrew word translated as "make" is the word "*karat*," which actually means "cut;" hence, "*karat beriyt*" is literally "cut the meat." The sacrifice was literally cut into two pieces and each party of the covenant would pass between the pieces. This signified the idea that if either party violated the covenant, the other party had the right to cut them into two pieces. This imagery of the cutting of pieces can be seen in Genesis 15. Interestingly, Israel, who did violate the covenant, was divided into two nations, Israel and Judah.

Shepherd

Throughout the Bible, God is compared to an ox, eagle, king, husband, as well as many other objects. Probably the most common imagery ascribed to God in the Bible is that of a shepherd:

> YHWH is my Shepherd. Psalms 23:1

The Hebrew word for a "shepherd" is רועה (ro'eh), which is the participle form of the verb רעה (R.Ah.H) and means "to feed." The parent root of these words is רע (ra), meaning "friend." The Shepherd is not a distant ruler or overseer, but a constant companion and friend to the flock. He spends more time with his flock traveling to watering holes and green pasture than he does with his own family. Our relationship with God is meant to be this type of relationship, where we become intimate friends with our guardian, protector and provider.

Sin

> When the sin, which they have sinned against
> it, is known, then the congregation shall offer
> a young bullock for the sin, and bring him
> before the tabernacle of the congregation.
> (Leviticus 4:14, KJV)

In this verse the word "sin" is the Hebrew noun חטאה (hhatah), and the word "sinned," is the verb חטא (Hh.Th.A), both from the root of חטאה (hhatah). Below is another verse that uses the verb form:

> Among all this people there were seven hundred chosen men lefthanded; every one could sling stones at a hair-breadth, and not _miss._ (Judges 20:16, ASV)

The word "miss" in this passage is the Hebrew verb חטא and literally means to "miss the mark," to miss what you are aiming at. YHWH gave his _Torah_ (teachings) to his people and _Torah_ was their mark, their target.

The noun חטאה (hhatah), derived from the verb חטא (Hh-Th-A) is "an error." When you shoot your arrow at the target and miss, you have made an error. When we aim to hit the target of God's teachings, but miss that target, we make an error.

From my understanding of the Bible, there are two types of sin, accidental and deliberate. I explain it this way: The Hebrews were a nomadic people and their language and lifestyle were wrapped around this culture. One of the aspects of a nomad is his constant journey from one watering hole to another and one pasture to another. If you are walking on a journey (literal or figurative) and find yourself "lost from the path," which is the Hebrew word רשע (rasha), you correct yourself and get back on the path. This was a "mistake" (accidentally missing the mark), but not deliberate. Once you are back on the right path, all is good. However, if you decide to leave the path and make your own way, you are again "lost from the path," but this time, being a deliberate act, it is an intentional mistake (missing the mark on purpose). In the Bible God gives his "directions" (usually translated as "commands") for the journey that his people are to be on. As long as they remain on that journey, they are _tsadiq_ (usually translated as "righteous," but literally meaning "on the correct path"), even if they accidentally leave the path, but return (this is the Hebrew verb *shuv*, usually translated as "repentance," but literally means "to return") back to the correct path.

Skies

The first thing to keep in mind is that in Ancient Hebrew thought there is no separation between the physical and non-physical; they are one and the same. An example of this is found in Psalm 24:4, where "clean hands" and "pure heart" is one and the same thing. A common form of Hebrew poetry, the "and" connects two phrases as one and the same thing. Clean hands are a sign of a pure heart and vice versa.

The heavens are the physical skies and the place of God, one and the same thing. It is Greco-Roman thinking that separates the two realms. We often see the "spirit" as spiritual and the "body" as physical, but in Hebrew thought they are one and the same thing. Without the spirit ("breath" in Hebrew), the body cannot survive and without the body the spirit cannot survive.

In Hebrew, the word שמים (*shamayim*) is always written in the plural form (identified by the "*yim*" suffix. You may see "heaven" or "heavens" in your Bible but they are both *shamayim*. Several Hebrew words are always written in the plural, including מים (*mayim*), meaning "water," and פנים (*paniym*) meaning "face." Personally, I prefer to translate the Hebrew word *shamayim* as "skies." This eliminates any confusion between heaven, heavens and sky.

From the perspective of an Ancient Hebrew who knew nothing of gas giants, such as the sun or stars, they saw the "heavens" as a "sheet" that covers the earth, just like the Hebrews' nomadic tent that covers the family. In fact, from the inside of a nomadic tent with pinpoint holes between the weaves, the cover looked just like the night sky, stars and all.

I believe the connection that the Hebrews made between God and his "host" is that they could see the "sheet" of the skies but they could not see beyond it, neither could they see or even speculate on what lay beyond that sheet. The Ancient Hebrew mindset did not concern itself with things they could not see, hear, feel, smell or touch. It is Greek thinking that delves into the philosophy of the unknown. The Hebrew word עולם (olam) is usually translated as "eternity" or "forever," but this word literally means "what is beyond the horizon" or "hidden." To the Hebrews, God is *olam*, not eternal but "unknown" or "hidden."

The Hebrew word for "heaven" is שמים (shamayim). There is some debate over the origins and meanings of this word, but there are a few common theories:

1. Derived from the unused root שמה (shamah) possibly meaning "lofty." The plural form of this word would be שמים (shamayim).

2. Derived from the root שמם (shamam) meaning "desolate", in the sense of a dry wind blowing over the land, drying it out. The plural form of this word would also be שמים (shamayim).

3. The word *shamayim* may be the Hebrew word מים (mayim), meaning "water," and the prefix ש (sh) meaning "like." Combined, the word שמים (shamayim) would mean "like water."

Aside from the debate over the origins of the word, it is clear that the word is commonly used in the Biblical text for "sky." It is frequently used in conjunction with the word ארץ (*erets*), meaning land (see Genesis 1:1, 2:1 and 14:19), representing the whole of creation and the domain of God.

In the New Testament this word was used as a euphemism (one word used in place of another) for God. This can be seen in some of the parables. The book of Luke (written for Gentiles) uses the phrase "Kingdom of God," whereas Matthew (written to Jews) uses "Kingdom of Heaven." In this context, "heaven" is meant to represent God, not a place.

Slave

The original pictograph for the word עבד (*eved*), meaning "servant" or "slave," is ⊘שׁﬞ. The ⊘ is a picture of an eye, meaning "to see" or "experience;" the שׁ is a picture of a house and the ד is a picture of a door. When these meanings for the three letters are combined, they define the word as "experience the house door." Now compare that with Exodus 21:6:

> Then his master shall bring him to God, and he shall bring him to the <u>door</u> or the doorpost; and his master shall bore his ear through with an awl; and he shall <u>serve</u> him for life.

Subdue

> And God blessed them, and God said to them, "Be fruitful and multiply, and fill the earth and <u>subdue</u> it; and have dominion over the fish of the sea and over the birds of the air and over every living thing that moves upon the earth." (Genesis 1:28, RSV)

The word subdue in Genesis 1:28 is the Hebrew verb "*kavash*" meaning "to subdue," but it is important to have the "full" picture of a Hebrew word, as "subdue" is very limited in its ability to fully describe the Hebrew. The noun form of this word is "*kevesh*" and means "a footstool," a place where one places the foot. The verb *kavash* literally means "to place your foot on the neck of your conquered enemy," signifying the submission of the enemy to his defeater. Figuratively, this verb means "to bring a people or nation into submission"/ (Numbers 32:29). The word can also mean "to bring into control" (Micah 7:19). Incidentally, this is the same word we use today, as in "put the *kabash* on it" meaning "to make an end of something" or to "subdue" it.

The Hebrew verb "*radah*," meaning "have dominion," is used in parallel with "*kavash*." Our normal understanding of "having dominion" over another is to rule over them, but this idea is found in the Hebrew verb *malak*. The Hebrew verb *radah* is related to other words that have the meanings of "descend," "go down," "wander" and "spread." This verb literally means "to rule by going down and walking among the subjects as an equal."

The use of the two Hebrew verbs "*kavash*" and "*radah*" imply that the man is to rule over the animals as his subjects, not as a dictator but as a benevolent leader. Man is also to walk among and have a relationship with his subjects, so that they can provide for man and that man can "learn" from them.

Sun

The Hebrew word שמש (*shemesh*) is "the sun," derived from the verb שמש (Sh.M.Sh), which appears only once in the Tanakh/Old Testament:

A fiery stream issued and came forth from before him: thousand thousands ministered unto him, and ten thousand times ten thousand stood before him: the judgment was set, and the books were opened. (Daniel 7:10, KJV)

While this is an Aramaic word, Hebrew and Aramaic are almost identical in their vocabulary. This word is also found in another verse that is often interpreted with difficulty because of its unclear use of the word:

But for you who fear my name the <u>sun</u> of righteousness shall rise, with healing in its wings. You shall go forth leaping like calves from the stall. (Malachi 4:2)

What or who is this "sun of righteousness?" It is very possible that "sun" is a poor translation for the noun שמש (*shemesh*). As the verb שמש (*Sh.M.Sh*) means to "attend," then the noun שמש (*shemesh*) could then mean an "attendant," and this word that is used for the "sun," as the "sun" is the attendant of the earth. If this is true, then the phrase in question should be translated as "attendant of righteousness."

Taniyn

In Exodus 7:10 Aaron casts Moses' staff down and it turns into a תנין (*tanniyn*). According to most English translations, the staff turned into a "serpent." However, in different Bible translations this Hebrew word is translated a variety of different ways including: "whales" (Genesis 1:21, KJV), "dragons" (Deuteronomy 32:33, KJV), "jackals" (Job 30:29, RSV) and "monsters" (Jeremiah 51:34, ASV).

What kind of animal did Moses' staff turn into? A serpent, whale, jackal or some kind of "monster?" According to several passages, the *tanniyn* lives in the sea and the rivers (Genesis 1:21, Psalm 74:13, Isaiah 27:1, Ezekiel 29:3, Ezekiel 32:2). There are also passages that show that the *tanniyn* lived on the land (Psalm 91:13, Isaiah 13:22, Isaiah 34:13, Isaiah 43:20, Jeremiah 51:37). The animal of the Near East that best fits with this type of creature is the crocodile, which in the Modern Hebrew language is a *tanniyn*.

However, according to a few passages, the *tanniyn* has venom (Deuteronomy 32:33) and breasts (Lamentations 4:3) and makes wailing sounds (Micah 1:8), which do not describe a crocodile or any other known creature. It is possible that different authors of the Bible called different creatures a *tanniyn*. One author may have called a crocodile a *tanniyn*, while another author may have called the jackal a *tanniyn*.

Tell

There are two common Hebrew verbs that are used to convey the idea that someone is about to speak. These are אמר (A.M.R), usually translated as "say" and דבר (D.B.R), usually translated as "speak." There is one other verb that is used in a similar way, but is not as common a verb as the other two:

> *And there came one that had escaped, and* <u>*told*</u> *Abram the Hebrew:* (Genesis 14:13, ASV)

The Hebrew verb behind the English "told," is the verb נגד (N.G.D), but this verb does not mean to "tell," but literally means "to be face to face."

Hebrew verbs can be written in different forms. The three most common are the *qal* (simple form), *niphil* (passive form)

338

and *hiphil* (causative form). As an example, the *qal* form of the verb ידע (*Y.D.Ah*) means to "know." The *niphil* form is the passive and means to "be known" or to "reveal." The *hiphil* is the causative form and means to "cause to be known" or to "declare." Notice that the meaning of each of these verbs is related to the idea of "knowing," but with slight nuances.

The verb נגד (*N.G.D*) is never written in the *qal* or *niphil* form, but only in the *hiphil* form, to "cause to be face to face." The *hiphil* form of this verb is always used in the context of "telling," in the sense of causing another to be face to face in order to "tell" them something.

Tent

The Hebrew word for a tent is אהל (*ohel*) and is derived from the parent root הל (*hal*) meaning "a distant shining light" or "a star" used to navigate by. After a hike through the woods where I lived, I made it back to my car, which was parked high over a large valley. Down in that valley, I could see a campfire about five miles away. It really amazed me how that small light could be so visible at such a distance. A nomad who had been out with his flock all day could use the campfire near the family tent as his guide for returning home.

Thunder

The Hebrew word קול (*qol*) means "voice," as can be seen in the following passage:

> And they heard the <u>voice</u> of the LORD God walking in the garden in the cool of the day... (Genesis 3:8, KJV)

While the KJV translates this word as "voice" in the passage, the RSV translates it as "sound," for the reason that the word קול can also mean "sound," as seen in the following passage:

> Then shalt thou cause the trumpet of the jubilee to _sound_ on the tenth day of the seventh month... (Leviticus 25:9, KJV)

The noise made by the trumpet is the "voice" of the trumpet.

When the word קול is written in the plural form (*qolot*), it means "thunder:"

> And Moses stretched forth his rod toward heaven: and the LORD sent _thunder_ and hail, and the fire ran along upon the ground; and the LORD rained hail upon the land of Egypt. (Exodus 9:23, KJV)

It is possible that the Hebrews believed that thunder was actually the "voice" of YHWH.

Tree

> Then I will give you rain in due season, and the land shall yield her increase, and the _trees_ of the field shall yield their fruit. (Leviticus 26:4, KJV)

The Hebrew word for a tree is עץ (*eyts*). In the passage above, the context clearly shows the word is used in a plural sense (trees). However, in the passage the word is written as עץ, the singular form. In Biblical Hebrew, the word עץ can mean a tree (singular) or trees (plural), while the plural form of this word, עצים (*eytsiym*), always means "wood," such as in the verse below:

> *Make yourself an ark of gopher <u>wood</u>; make rooms in the ark, and cover it inside and out with pitch…* (Genesis 6:14, RSV)

This allows for a different interpretation of the following passage:

> *And out of the ground made the LORD God to grow every tree that is pleasant to the sight, and good for food; the <u>tree of life</u> also in the midst of the garden, and the <u>tree of knowledge</u> of good and evil.* (Genesis 2:9, KJV)

Because the word עץ (*eyts*) can mean "tree" or "trees," the "tree of life" and the "tree of knowledge" can just as easily be translated as the "trees of life" and the "trees of knowledge."

The word עץ is a parent root (a two-letter root) from which a couple of other words are derived. The verb עצם (*Ah.Ts.M*) means "strong and mighty," as is a tree. Derived from this verb is the noun עצם (*etsem*), meaning "bones," the "strong tree" of the body. Also, the verb יעץ (*Y.Ah.Ts*) means "counsel," to give support to another just as the tree trunk supports the branches and leaves.

Truth

The Hebrew word for "truth" is אמת (*emet*) and is derived from the verbal root word אמן (*A.M.N*), a word often translated as "believe," but more literally meaning "support," as seen in the following verse:

> *I will drive him like a peg in a place of <u>support</u>…"* Isaiah 22:23

A belief in *Elohiym* is not a mental exercise of knowing that *Elohiym* exists, but rather is our responsibility to show him our support. The word *"emet"* has the similar meaning of firmness, something that is firmly set in place. Psalms 119:142 states that the *"Torah"* (the teachings of *Elohiym*) is *"emet"* (set firmly in place).

Unclean

The word טמא (*tamey*) means something that is "dirty" or "polluted," but usually is translated as "unclean." This can be a literal pollution, such as from eating something that can bring on a disease or illness, or it can be a moral pollution, such as sexual immorality, as we see in Genesis 34:2, where the word *"tamey"* is translated as "defiled:"

> And when Shechem the son of Hamor the
> Hivite, prince of the country, saw her, he took
> her, and lay with her, and <u>defiled</u> her. (KJV)

Interestingly, both the Hebrew word for clean, which is טהור (*tahor*) "clean, "and the Hebrew word טמא (*tamey*) "dirty," begin with the same letter, a *tet* (ט). The ancient pictographic picture for this letter is a picture of a basket - ⊗ and can mean "surrounding" or "contained." Do we surround ourselves with cleanness or dirtiness?

Underworld

The word *she'ol* is often understood as "hell," the place of the damned or the underworld. How did the Ancient Hebrews perceive *she'ol*? As I have said before, in order to better understand a word, it is essential to look at its root and other related words.

The verbal root שאל (Sh.A.L) is used almost 200 times and is usually translated as "asked," such as in Genesis 24:7:

> and I asked her and said...

Why do we ask questions? We are looking for information that is currently unknown to us. This word, "unknown," is the key to understanding the root שאל (Sh.A.L) and all the words derived from it.

The word שאלה (she'eylah) is a noun derived from שאל (Sh.A.L) and is found in Job where it is translated as a request:

> O that I might have my request, and that God would grant my desire" (Job 6:8, RSV)

A request is "to ask for something that is not possessed." As it is not possessed, it is an unknown. How many times have we asked for something that we knew we needed, but when we received it,we found out it was not what we thought it would be. In other words, we thought we knew what we were missing, but it turned out that what we were requesting was an unknown.

The word שאול (she'ol), also derived from שאל (Sh.A.L), was understood to be the place where one goes when they die. The question is, "Did they understand this to be simply the grave one is buried in or another place one goes after one dies?" This is a difficult question to answer, as the Hebrew Bible never really defines she'ol. There is evidence, however, that they understood it to be more than just the grave. First, the word qever is the Hebrew word meaning "grave "and, therefore, it is possible that she'ol was understood as something other than the grave. Second, most scriptures using the word she'ol imply a place other than the grave:

All his sons and all his daughters rose up to comfort him; but he refused to be comforted, and said, "No, I shall go down to Sheol to my son, mourning." Thus, his father wept for him (Genesis 37:35, RSV).

In this account Jacob believed his son Joseph had been eaten by a wild beast. As Joseph's body could not possibly be in a grave, Jacob knew that he would be with him somewhere: *she'ol.*

The Ancient Hebrews did not know where or even what *she'ol* was. To them it was an unknown place, hence, the use of a word related to שאל (*Sh.A.L*), and meaning "unknown." It should also be noted that the Ancient Hebrews never speculated on something unknown; it was simply not known and left at that. It is only the Greek mind that desires to know the unknown. Our Greco-Roman western mindset needs to know where and what *she'ol* is.

Unicorn

God brought them out of Egypt; he hath as it were the strength of an <u>unicorn</u>. (Numbers 23:22, KJV)

The Hebrew word ראם (r'em) is an unknown animal, but the King James Version translates this as "unicorn." Did the translators of the King James Version believe that unicorns existed? Actually, yes, they did.

The word "unicorn" is derived from two Latin words. The first is "uni," meaning "one," and the second is "corn," meaning "horn." A unicorn is a "one-horned animal" and is most likely the rhinoceros.

Walk

> *You shall walk after the LORD your God and fear him, and keep his commandments and obey his voice, and you shall serve him and cleave to him.* (Deuteronomy 13:4, RSV)

The Hebrew verb הלך (*H.L.K*) literally means to "walk," as can be seen in the following passage:

> *And Abner and his men <u>walked</u> all that night through the plain...* (2 Samuel 2:29, KJV)

This word is also used frequently in a figurative sense as can be seen in the following passage:

> *And if thou wilt <u>walk</u> in my ways, to keep my statutes and my commandments, as thy father David did walk, then I will lengthen thy days.* (1 Kings 3:14, KJV)

In this passage, YHWH is asking Solomon to "walk" in the footsteps of his father David, who walked in the footsteps of YHWH. A son "walks" in the footsteps of his father, a student "walks" in the footsteps of his teacher and a people "walk" in the footsteps of their ancestors. In our English language, we call this "culture." Many of your thoughts and actions are a result of "walking" in the footsteps of your parents, family, neighbors and community. In the case of Israel, their culture was patterned after YHWH's teachings, but the other nations' cultures were patterned after other gods:

> *And you shall not <u>walk</u> in the customs of the nation which I am casting out before you; for they did all these things, and therefore I abhorred them.* (Leviticus 20:23, RSV)

The Hebrew language always uses concrete concepts to express abstract thought. While we may use an abstract word like "culture," the Hebrew language used a much more concrete word, such as "walking," to express the same idea. Israel was commanded to walk in YHWH's footsteps (follow YHWH's customs) and not walk in the footsteps of other gods (follow the customs of other nations).

West

While the Hebrew word ים (yam) means "sea," it is also used for the direction "West," as the great sea, the Mediterranean, is "west" of Israel. The Ancient Hebrews related the four compass points to their geography in relation to the land of Israel. The word for East is קדם (qedem) and is from a root meaning to "meet," for the rising sun is "met" each morning in the east. The word for South is נגב (negev), a word meaning "desert region," and refers to the desert region in the south of Israel. Finally, the word for North is צפון (tsaphon), which comes from a Hebrew root literally meaning "hidden," probably alluding to the idea that the northern regions were unknown to them.

Wilderness

We have previously examined the Hebrew root word דבר (davar) meaning "to speak," but more concretely understood as an "ordered" arrangement of words. We also found that the feminine form of this word is דברה (devorah) and means "bee," an insect that lives in a perfectly "ordered" society.

Another common word derived from the root davar is מדבר (mid'bar) meaning a "wilderness." In the ancient Hebrew mind, the wilderness, in contrast to the cities, was a place of order. Many people today live in cities, a place of hurrying, rushing and busying ourselves with all the day-to-day tasks and high crime. The city can easily be seen as a place of chaos.

On the other hand, when we want to "get away from it all" and slow down and really rest, we go out to the "wilderness" to camp. We take walks out into the woods or sit by a lake and feel the peace in these places. These are places of order where all of nature is in a perfect balance of harmony.

The word דבר (*davar*) may better be translated "order" as in the phrase, "And YHWH gave orders to Moses saying." A commanding officer does not speak to his troops; he has formulated his action plans and has determined the best means to have these plans carried out. Once all of this is determined, he gives his "orders" to his troops. These orders are "an ordered arrangement."

The phrase, "Ten Commandments," does not actually appear in the Hebrew Bible. Instead, it is *aseret hadevariym* and is literally translated as "ten orders." The "Ten Commandments" are our orders from God (the general). They are an ordered arrangement of ideas that if followed will bring about peace and harmony.

Words

The Hebrew word דבר (*davar*) demonstrates an interesting aspect of Hebrew thought. This Hebrew word is frequently translated as "word," such as we can see in Genesis 44:2 where it says, "according to the word that Joseph had spoken." But this word is also frequently translated as "thing," such as we can see in Numbers 18:7, where it says, "all the things of the altar." In the Hebrew mind, "words" are "things," and have just as much substance as any other "thing." This helps us with understanding a few things in the Bible. When Jacob stole his brother's birthright in Genesis 27, he took the "words" from his father Isaac that were meant for his brother. When his brother Esau came for his blessing, his father said that he had already given it to Jacob. I often wondered why Isaac couldn't just tell Jacob that the blessing he gave him didn't count, as he stole it, and then just give it to Esau. But in the Hebrew mind, words cannot be taken back, as they have already been spoken. It is the same as if Isaac had given Jacob something physical, for instance, a glass of water. Once Jacob drank from the glass, it could not be taken back. We should keep this in mind when we speak. Your words have an effect on others, just as we see in Proverbs 12:18; "A rash speaker is like piercings of a sword, and the tongue of the wise is healing."

Worship

Webster's Dictionary defines "worship" as:

> 1. The reverent love and devotion accorded a deity, an idol, or a sacred object.
> 2. The ceremonies, prayers, or other religious forms by which this love is expressed.

As I have stated many times, but is worth repeating, when we read the Bible we must define our words from a Hebraic perspective and not from an English one. Unfortunately, when we see the word "worship" in the Bible, we automatically assume the above definition, causing our misinterpretation of the Biblical text.

If I ask the average believer, "Is it okay to worship a man?" the answer would be, "Absolutely not, we are only to worship God." Below are a few verses that use the word "worship" and support this view:

And the man bowed down his head, and <u>worshipped</u> the LORD. (Genesis 24:26)

So Samuel turned again after Saul; and Saul <u>worshipped</u> the LORD. (1 Samuel 15:31)

Give unto the LORD the glory due unto his name; <u>worship</u> the LORD in the beauty of holiness. (Psalm 29:2)

The first question we must ask is, "What is the Hebrew word behind the English word 'worship' and what does it mean?" In each of the verses above, the Hebrew word behind the English word "worship" is שחה (*Sh.Hh.H*). This Hebrew word appears 172 times in the Biblical text, but is only translated as "worship" 99 times in the KJV. Below are some other translations of this same Hebrew word:

Let people serve thee, and nations <u>bow down</u> to thee (Genesis 27:29)

In this passage other nations will bow down to the descendants of Jacob:

And Moses went out to meet his father in law, and did <u>obeisance</u>, and kissed him; and they asked each other of [their] welfare; and they came into the tent. (Exodus 18:7)

In this passage Moses bowed down to his father-in-law:

So king Solomon sent, and they brought [Adonijah] down from the altar. And he came and <u>bowed</u> himself to king Solomon: and Solomon said unto him, Go to thine house. (1 Kings 1:53)

In this passage Adonijah was found righteous when he bowed down to Solomon.

Whenever the Hebrew word שחה (*Sh.Hh.H*) is used as an action toward God, the translators translate this word as "worship." However, when this same Hebrew word is used as an action toward another man, the translators translate this word as "obeisance" or "bow down." As you can see, the translators are preventing the reader from viewing the text in its proper Hebraic context.

The concept of "worship," as defined by Webster's dictionary is not Hebraic in any way and is not found in the Bible. While there is nothing wrong with "worship" in the sense that we normally understand this word, we should recognize that it is not a Biblical concept. If the Hebraic meaning of "worship" is to bow down before another, whether God or man, as we have seen from the texts, then the answer to our question above is, "Yes, it is acceptable to worship other men." While this sentence may sound blasphemous due to our doctrinal view of "worship," we can do one of two things. We can remove the word "worship" from our vocabulary and replace it with "bow down," or we can use the word "worship," but recognize that it does not mean what we have always assumed it to mean.

www.ingramcontent.com/pod-product-compliance
Lightning Source LLC
Chambersburg PA
CBHW060241100426
42742CB00011B/1598